ANARCHISM: LEFT, RIGHT, AND GREEN

ULRIKE HEIDER

TRANSLATED BY DANNY LEWIS AND ULRIKE BODE

CITY LIGHTS BOOKS · SAN FRANCISCO

ANARCHISM: LEFT, RIGHT, AND GREEN
© 1994 by Ulrike Heider
Translation © 1994 by City Lights Books
Published under the title: *Die Narren der Freiheit: Anarchisten in den USA heute,* by Karin Kramer Verlag, Berlin, 1992.

All Rights Reserved

Cover design by Carin Berger

Library of Congress Cataloging-in-Publication Data

Heider, Ulrike, 1947–
    [Narren der Freiheit. English]
    Anarchism: Left, Right, & Green / by Ulrike Heider; translated from the German by Danny Lewis and Ulrike Bode.
        p.   cm.
    ISBN 0872862895; $12.95
    1. Anarchism. I. Title.
HXB33.H385 1994
335'.83–dc20
                                                                94-162
                                                                CIP

City Lights Books are available to bookstores through our primary distributor: Subterranean Company. P.O. Box 160, 265 S. 5th St., Monroe, OR 97456. 503-847-5274. Toll-free orders 800-274-7826. FAX 503-847-6018. Our books are also available through library jobbers and regional distributors. For personal orders and catalogs, please write to City Lights Books, 261 Columbus Avenue, San Francisco CA 94133.

CITY LIGHTS BOOKS are edited by Lawrence Ferlinghetti and Nancy J. Peters and published at the City Lights Bookstore, 261 Columbus Avenue, San Francisco, CA 94133.

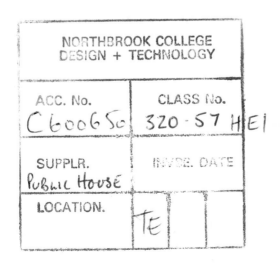

ACKNOWLEDGMENTS

As a newcomer to New York I could not have written this book without the support of numerous friends who talked with me about American anarchism and politics, who encouraged and inspired me, who helped me understand a foreign culture, learn the language, organize my everyday life, get access to libraries, and meet other people.

I would like to thank Paul Avrich, Paul Buhle, Eric Foner, Bill Koehnlein, Larry Gross, Bernd Metz, Lisa Henderson, Marie-Carol Poore, Claire Picher, Steve Rabinowitz, Ken Shaken, Jim Steakley, Julia Swales, Scott Tucker, Cristina Warchol, Bill Weinberg, Alice Wexler, Eddi Willies, and the people of Tamiment Library. I thank my agents Frances Goldin and Sydell Kramer, my publisher and editor Nancy J. Peters, and my translator Danny Lewis. Special thanks go to Ulrike Bode for revising the translation and helping to edit the text for American readers.

I would also like to thank Janet Biehl, Murray Bookchin, Noam Chomsky, Esther Dolgoff, Sam Dolgoff, Samuel Edward Konkin III, Jim Peron, Sharon Presley, George Resch, Murray Rothbard, David Thereaux, and Anne Wortham, who took time to give me interviews and to provide me with valuable information. Without them this book would never have come into being.

TABLE OF CONTENTS

INTRODUCTION

The so-called communist regimes in Eastern Europe have collapsed. The authoritarian ideology—allegedly Marxian—used by the Stalinist rulers and their successors as an excuse to abandon democracy and civil rights is discredited. Capitalism, as the seemingly victorious system and philosophy, is celebrating an increasingly global reach. Social concerns are viewed with suspicion, the welfare state equated with totalitarianism, and freedom is confused with the freedom of the marketplace. Those who are still looking for a leftist perspective have little to hold on to. It is logical, then, that anarchism, whose leftist tradition since the 19th century has been considered an alternative to both capitalism and authoritarian communism, is making a comeback.

There are many perceptions of anarchism, and not only from a left perspective. To some it is the domain of the ugly little man with the big round bomb; to others, it evokes Emma Goldman and Alexander Berkman, the Haymarket martyrs and Sacco and Vanzetti. Today those who regard themselves as anarchists include radical ecologists, animal rights activists, neopagans, and bohemians as well as labor-oriented anarchists. There are also laissez-faire libertarians who call themselves anarcho-capitalists. Derived from the Greek word *anarchia,* no rule, anarchism in its broadest sense is a stateless society of any kind.

Since its inception, anarchism has brought to mind the Roman god Janus whose two faces are turned in opposite directions: one of them, resembling the social-revolutionary forefathers Bakunin and Kropotkin, turns its eyes toward a stateless democratic socialism, collective self-administration, and mutual aid. The other, inheriting its features from Max Stirner, the philosopher of unlimited personal freedom, looks to the brutal chaos of the war of each against all, waged in the arena of the unfettered free market.

One reason for the confusion about anarchism and the broad range of its meanings is its bipolar source in the 19th century. The literature generally does not pay attention to this fact; instead, it attempts, in most cases, to fold everything called anarchism into one concept. Differences between social and individualist anarchism and all the varieties in between are overlooked, and parallels are stressed at any price. This book focuses on the differences between the traditional two main tendencies of anarchism.

1

Michael Bakunin (1814–1876), influenced by early socialist utopian[1] thinkers, was a socialist who warned against centralist and hierarchical organization, bureaucracy, and state dictatorship, as opposed to grassroots democracy and international labor organizations. While Bakunin and his followers were realistic down-to-earth unionists, the Russian revolutionary Alexander Kropotkin (1842–1921) and his successors developed the more utopian vision of "communist anarchism," stressing the local commune and people's good will instead of unions and economic conditions. At the turn of the century Kropotkin's successors abandoned the labor movement and attempted to realize the ideal society, in isolated colonies. The focus on lifestyle reform and spirituality depoliticized many. Some became agrarian or folk romantics who developed eccentric futurist visions or prefascist blood-and-soil ideologies. Others rediscovered 18th-century tyrannicide, resorting to terrorists' "propaganda of the deed," where revolutionary violence becomes an end in itself.

During the 1910s and 1920s leftist anarchists developed "anarcho-syndicalism," combining the ideas of Bakunin, Kropotkin, and early 20th-century syndicalism. In the anarcho-syndicalist blueprint for democratic socialism, society is held together by a network of unions, which are organized from the bottom up with democratically elected councils as representatives and, at the top, an economic council instead of a state. One country's unions are connected with the revolutionary unions in other countries—internationalism, instead of socialism in one country alone, is the first principle. During the Spanish revolution, when social-revolutionary anarchism was at its prime, the two tendencies of anarcho-syndicalism mirrored the gap between unionist Bakuninism and communalist utopian Kropotkinism. In the US Emma Goldman and Alexander Berkman, initially proponents of the propaganda of the deed, became anarcho-syndicalists. Anarcho-syndicalism strongly influenced the American Jewish labor movement and the IWW (Industrial Workers of the World) and was one reason for the latter's brutal persecution during and after World War I. Anarcho-sydicalism was revived in the antiauthoritarian movements of the late 1960s in France, Italy, Germany, England, and the US.

The first part of this book summarizes anarcho-syndicalist theory and history and highlights the ideas of the late Wobbly and veteran activist Sam Dolgoff. It also focuses on Noam Chomsky, the famous linguist and social critic, and his interpretation of anarcho-syndicalism.

With the disintegration of the New Left and the rise of ecological awareness, Kropotkin's communal ideas were rediscovered as a means of developing eco-anarchism, especially in the US. Murray Bookchin, whose works I analyze in the second part of this book, belongs to the avant-garde of eco-anarchist

---

1. I use the term utopia in its Marxian sense as a blueprint for a future society which is perfect but not attainable in reality.

philosophers. He combines the ecologist tenet of a natural equilibrium with elements of early socialism and communalism. He refers to nature as a "source of ethical meaning" and derives human spirit, ethics, and rationality from it. He distances himself from anarcho-syndicalism whose basis—unionism and the class struggle—he believes is outdated. In his own concept, called municipalism, Bookchin seeks to revive the New England tradition of public town meetings. The "community as a whole," he says, not the workers or their unions, should decide about community affairs.

While social anarchists seek to abolish the state as the source of private property, the individualists want to eliminate it because they see it as an obstacle to private property. Max Stirner (1806–1856), the founding father of individual anarchism, equates personal identity and freedom with property. The individual's unlimited freedom, guaranteed by the common value of egoism, realizes itself in the anarchy of the war of each against all. American individualism, whose most important representatives are Josiah Warren (founder of the colony Modern Times) and Benjamin Tucker, is another source of procapitalist anarchism. Both combined utopian-socialist ideas of social harmony and a far-reaching personal individualism with an antimonopolist and antigovernment free market ideology.

Today individualist anarchists in the US call themselves anarcho-capitalists or libertarians; some though not all, are organized in the Libertarian Party. Many of them, like their intellectual leader, Murray Rothbard, whose theory I trace to its origins and analyze in the third part of this book, are former Ayn Randians who turned antistatist in the late 1960s. Like Rand (who was far from being an anarchist), the anarcho-capitalists are followers of the Austrian School of Economics; its most famous theorist was Ludwig von Mises and its youngest leading intellectual is Milton Friedman, adviser to Margaret Thatcher and Ronald Reagan. The libertarians radicalize Mises's antisocial free market ideology to its extreme culmination in the abolition of government. They intend to privatize the entire public sector including the police, the judiciary, the army, public transportation, education, and welfare. The only bond that holds together this dystopia of competition and survival of the fittest is natural law reduced to property law. Society is not responsible for the well-being and survival of human beings who do not own property. The legal code is rooted in retribution and includes the death penalty and corporal punishment.

Opposed as I am to anarcho-capitalism and somewhat skeptical about eco-anarchism, I think it is anarcho-syndicalism in the Bakuninist tradition we can learn from most today. In light of the political collapse of the Eastern Bloc, Bakunin's visionary warnings against bureaucracy, technocracy, and centralized hierarchical state communism are very timely. Given the alarming increase in class differences throughout the world the anarcho-syndicalist focus on class struggle is everything but outdated. The concept of creating a democratic socialism and planning the economy through independent unions and their councils could probably not be put into practice in exactly the same way as attempted by the Spanish anarchists, but I believe nonetheless that it could serve as a guideline for a strategy to end exploitation and social injustice by organizing labor and production for the benefit of people worldwide. With the brief exception of the Spanish anarchists, those newly in power after a successful revolution have never given those who work control over the means of production, neither in the USSR nor in China, Cuba, or elsewhere. Furthermore, workers' control, another axiom of anarcho-syndicalism, has never been pursued seriously by the Left when it was is power. With the current globalization of capital, on the one hand, and the worldwide regression into destructive nationalisms and ethnic conflicts within nations, on the other, I think nothing is more urgent than an international approach.

Many contemporary anarchists regard anarcho-syndicalism, with its focus on labor, as a 19th-century anachronism. Concentrating on ecology, gender relationships and the cultural revolution, they are attracted to early socialist utopianism with its harmonious vision of playful and pleasant work in lush gardens where the new human being can develop a noble personality. As much as I agree with the cultural revolutionary message of early socialism and with the idea of anticipating the future society in our present activism, I also think that we must deal with labor, class realities, and the global economy. Work still must be done, although with a wiser use of technology it could be organized more efficiently and equitably. The conditions of labor are changing dramatically, but exploitation continues and increases. Workers in the Third World drudge for minimal wages in insane conditions; in Europe and the United States immigrant labor remains outrageously exploited; and the dismantling of social welfare programs is fostering greater poverty and more extreme class divisions.

I analyze the social-Darwinist philosophy of anarcho-capitalism because it is the extreme opposite of anarcho-syndicalism, and of leftist anarchism in general. It is a radical version of unfettered capitalism, one that shows most clearly what capitalism was, what it still is, and to what it leads. At this time, economic conditions have enabled capitalists to rapidly redevelop laissez-faire economics. Ideologues have wasted no time in generating theories to justify and support this state of affairs. Murray Rothbard's "anarchist" extension of Ludwig von Mises's theory, though (negatively) utopian in the assumption that a market society would function without a government, is part and parcel of the current drive to reproduce 19th-century capitalism with all its misery and cruelty.

The social means and strategic ends of leftist anarchism and anarcho-capitalism are as different from one another as day and night. Nevertheless there were and are leftist anarchists turning themselves into anarcho-capitalists and vice versa. There also was and is occasional cooperation among left and right anarchist organizations.

From Stirner's time artist bohemians and leftist anarchists have been attracted by individual anarchism's opposition to bourgeois morality and its far-reaching guarantee of personal freedom, especially in regard to sex and drugs. At the end of the 19th century the Irish-German poet John Henry Mackay shifted from Kropotkinism to terrorism and after that became an ardent admirer of Max Stirner. Eventually he developed his own version of a free-market-anarchism, in the style of Manchester capitalism, which is comparable to current anarcho-capitalism. Held in high esteem by intellectuals of his time, he was a friend of both Benjamin Tucker and Emma Goldman. The famous leftist anarchist martyr of the Munich council republic (1919-1921), Gustav Landauer, employed as minister of economy the expert on "free money," Silvio Gesell, whose theory of "shrinking money" was social-Darwinist, to say the least. Three decades later most of the exiled veterans of the Spanish Revolution, demoralized by the betrayal of the communists, lost their faith in socialism and began to espouse procapitalist, liberal views. The same is true for some anarchists of my generation: recently I spoke to a leftist anarchist of the 1960s, who has "nothing against capitalism" and views the Libertarian Party as "something leftist." Most anarchists have tried and still try to close their eyes to their comrades' shifting from left-libertarian to liberal or right-libertarian positions. I believe that this was and is a big mistake—it is time to deal with this destructive tendency by tracing the theoretical rationalizations that result in such shifts, instead of allowing a drift into liberal, watered-down anarchism, or fostering laissez-faire economics. One reason I chose Sam Dolgoff to exemplify anarcho-syndicalist theory and practice is that he was one of the few activists willing to critique procapitalist colleagues.

Laissez-faire ideologists are not the only ones who have tried (and still try) to appropriate anarchism by integrating both its name and its followers into their own political camp. There are also various populists and blood-and-soil ideologists about whom leftist anarchists should be wary. In Europe they can be found in green and ecological groups, as well as in neofascist parties and organizations. As much as I believe that awareness of the ecological crisis and the need for a policy of immediate action should form part of any leftist and anarchist thinking and practice, I believe that an ecological approach to social problems cannot be trusted unconditionally.

A brief glance at Germany, the country with the largest ecology movement in the world, may serve to shed further light on this matter: The German Green Party was founded as an alliance of conservative ecological groups (some of them rooted in the fascist past), single-issue groups, and New Left ecologists. Until the mid-1980s, conservative and quasi-fascist ecologists tried to infiltrate the Green Party, which had developed a progressive stance. Numerous scandals shook the party: it was revealed that several elderly members had belonged to the NSDAP (the Nazi party) or at times had been brownshirts,[2] and young

---

2. The populist wing of the Nazis which was ousted in 1934.

Greens were bewildered and at times sheepishly tolerant of these people. Right-wing ecologists eventually changed their strategy by joining parties and organizations of the New Right or, in the recent past, the newly founded traditional fascist party REP (the Republicans).

Typical for right radical ecological thinking is a naturalistic view of society. Neo-Nazis and so-called national revolutionaries in the tradition of the brown-shirts insist that the ecological crisis has caused the loss of a natural equilibrium and the diminishing of a human vibrancy rooted in nature. An allegedly natural inequality of humans and peoples follows from that, as do hierarchies that are considered part of nature. Right-wing ecologists say that man's alienation from homeland, people, and national culture has caused the ecological crisis. And immigration—labeled "foreign infiltration"—is viewed as an ecological problem of an "unnaturally overpopulated" country. Racist slogans derive from such language, as does nationalism, the latter often camouflaged as localism or "the search for identity." National-revolutionaries also try to attract Greens and anarchists with their conservative critique of capitalism, which is portrayed as an evil breeding ground for leveling egalitarianism, materialism, and economic growth.

Some have asked me why I don't present (leftist) anarchism in a positive way, emphasizing the best of its legacy and its most hopeful present activities in order to answer the ever-present question: What is to be done? I chose the critical approach because I think any theory on which we base our political activism needs permanent questioning. Without this corrective, a political philosophy might end as a distortion of itself. We only need to look at Old Left Marxism to see how what was once a truly humane philosophy eventually served to legitimize a most inhumane social reality. Why, we must ask, did major segments of the declining New Left not learn from that? Why did its activists blindly accept the authoritarian Stalinist/Leninist forms of organization, thus reproducing its totalitarianism in miniature? The warnings came from several quarters: from the anarchists, from Rosa Luxemburg and her non-Leninist Marxism (influenced by anarchism), and from the Frankfurt School and its Critical Theory. Why did only a few try to take advantage of this antiauthoritarian leftist legacy? In any case, the remnants of the left must do better now—be it ecological or anarchist theory, we ought to think it over, measure it by its own claims, and scrutinize it again and again.

I am aware of the problems in criticizing anarchism: In the old feud between communists and leftist anarchists the latter traditionally have been the victims and losers, ever since they were expelled from the First International. They were persecuted by the Bolsheviks after the Russian Revolution, and communists helped to destroy the anarchist revolution during the Spanish Civil War. The theoretical parallel to these events was the arrogance and intolerance of dogmatic communists, who indiscriminately disqualified any kind of anarchism as backward, or potentially fascist. Demagogically they used to blur the difference between individualist, terrorist, and social-revolutionary anarchism. In doing so they confirmed the distorted bourgeois images of anarchism and, at the same time, contributed both to the typical oversensitivity of anarchists to any critique and to an exaggerated tolerance towards right-wing anarchists. I think that careful analysis and fraternal critique by anarchists or their sympathizers is the only way to break the vicious cycle of unjust condemnation and blind tolerance.

I am influenced by the method of critique of ideologies as it was first developed in Marx's *The German Ideology,* in which he revealed the false consciousness of his contemporaries and explained it out of the objective historical situation. The Leninist left never understood this method, while such Marxists as Rosa Luxemburg and Karl Korsch used it as a point of departure. In the late 1920s Max Horkheimer, Theodor W. Adorno, Leo Löwenthal and Herbert Marcuse, founders of the Frankfurt School, directed their critique at the "false consciousness" of people who, like major parts of the modern working class, think and act irrationally and contrary to their own interests. They showed how the agents of the modern ruling class manipulate the people by creating a stultifying, seductive mass culture in order to produce this "false consciousness." Critical Theory aimed at bringing forth "critical consciousness," an emancipatory state of mind that would enable the oppressed to realize their own liberatory potential. Furthermore its goal was relentless scrutiny, to get to the roots of problems, to stick to the truth in the face of dogmatism, be it Marxist dogmatism or Critical Theory itself. Like Marx's, the Frankfurt School's critique was defamed in Germany as "the Jewish method," reflective of the allegedly negative, critical, and materialistic spirit of the Jews in contrast to the idealism and connectedness to nature of the Germans.

My intention is not to represent all currents of American anarchism, but rather to explore the difference between anarchism's two opposing main tendencies, in general, and to shed light on one of its most important new forms. I hope this will help clarify not only anarcho-syndicalism, eco-anarchism, and anarcho-capitalism, but various other forms as well. I did not select the representatives of the three types of anarchism for their influence, name, or fame, but because in each case their thinking seems to be particularly typical of the theory for which it stands. During my research I spoke extensively with anarchist theorists and activists. Because the encounters with Sam Dolgoff, Noam Chomsky, Murray Bookchin, Murray Rothbard, and others were personally very stimulating, I wanted to share these experiences; hence several chapters are more narrative than analytical. The book was first published in Germany with Karin Kramer Verlag in 1992. I have revised it for the English edition and have updated the chapter "Social Ecology and Deep Ecology," as well as some other details.

What is anarchism? Which principles, theories, and social models are subsumed under this common denominator? Which of them are reactionary, which progressive? Are the social revolutionary and individualist anarchists correct to accuse each other of false labeling? One thing is clear: The Janus face of anarchism has managed to confuse those who ask such questions for too long.

1   ANARCHO-SYNDICALISM

Sam Dolgoff—Encounter with the "Last Anarchist"

Sam Dolgoff, who died in November, 1990, at the age of eighty-eight, was often jokingly referred to by friends as "the last anarchist." He could proudly look back on six decades of anarcho-syndicalist, antifascist political activity as an official of the antiauthoritarian union IWW (Industrial Workers of the World). He was always a contentious figure, feared by many for his love of controversy, his sharp-tongued openness, and his often merciless criticism—especially in the US, where these qualities are never popular.

I met him and his wife Esther in New York while conducting research on the Russian-American anarchist Emma Goldman. On the telephone, Esther said she doubted that they had much to tell me about Goldman, but she promised faithfully that everything they told me would be the truth. Esther and Sam lived in a housing project for senior citizens on East Broadway, a neighborhood shared by Orthodox Jews and Chinese. Embracing me, Esther greeted me as her "young comrade." The eighty-three-year-old white-haired anarchist was wearing a brightly colored housedress and the black and red badge of the CNT (Confederación National de Trabajo), the Spanish anarchist union, on her collar. Her spontaneous friendliness, unconventional appearance, and profound humanity made all the elegant old ladies of the Upper East Side, whose appearance had fascinated me, pale in comparison. The apartment was furnished in a sober, modern style and bore witness to a craftsman's talent for improvisation. The furniture was of the type one might find on the street on a lucky day.

While Esther talked about Emma Goldman and showed me some books and photographs, Sam demonstratively turned his back on us. He, too, was an imposing figure, robust for his age, beaming with the militant rebelliousness of an unbroken revolutionary. He was barefoot and wore a checkered shirt and trousers with suspenders. His deep, sonorous voice betrayed his past as a professional speaker. Esther, waving my most recent book under his nose, finally managed to convince him to put on his hearing aid. He asked me with a dark expression on his face about a recent metal workers' strike in West Germany. I was embarrassed to admit that I knew absolutely nothing about it. Next he wanted to know what I thought of Daniel Cohn-Bendit, the spokesman for the German Green Party in Frankfurt and a former leader of the student revolt in Paris in May, 1968. I reluctantly confessed that I did not have much in common politically with Cohn-Bendit. Sam's face brightened with satisfaction. Neither did he; in his opinion "Danny the Red" had not been an anarchist for quite some time now, having long since deserted to liberalism. The ice was broken, and we became friends.

Born in 1902 in Russia, Dolgoff spent his childhood and teenage years in the Jewish immigrant slums of New York's Lower East Side. At the age of seven he got a job as a messenger boy to contribute to his family's meager income. After completing primary school he learned the painter's trade, working first in various factories and later as a migrant worker. The "bitter life of a wage slave" and his "rebellious temperament"[3] soon brought him into the labor movement. He assisted soap box speakers, hung up posters, and passed out flyers. At the age of seventeen he joined the Young Socialists, though not for long because, as he put it, by 1924 the Socialist Party and its unions had abandoned all internationalist and revolutionary principles. As an abrasive critic of social democratic reformism and of its attendant "electoral swindle,"[4] the young rebel was brought before a tribunal and expelled from the party.

> The judge came up to me. And he said: you did all right, but the truth is, the reason we can't get along is because you are not a socialist. You are an anarchist. So I said: give me the address of where the anarchists are. So they gave me the address. And I came to the anarchists.[5]

What he found there was a mixed group of bohemian eccentrics, Tolstoyan pacifists, and extreme individualists who were "against everything," including some who believed in nihilist terrorism—in short, all the anarchist varieties Dolgoff considers bourgeois. He never tired of poking fun at all kinds of life-style reformers and other eccentrics. One of them tried to convince him that Emma Goldman was revolutionary only during her menstrual period; another patiently explained to him that parents should only procreate when naked and bare-headed in the sunlight, for children conceived at night were stupid.

> They had nothing to say about what was going on in the world. They didn't have anything that would make ordinary people, workers, understand what they are going to do about unemployment and misery and so on. So I started to complain. They said, you know, you are all right, but you are a syndicalist, you are an IWW. So I said: what is their address? So since that time I became an anarcho-syndicalist.[6]

---

3.   Sam Dolgoff, *Fragments: A Memoir*. Cambridge, MA: Refract Publications, 1986, p. 5.
4.   Ibid., p. 8.
5.   Sam Dolgoff, interview with the author, 1988.
6.   Ibid.

Sam taught himself five languages. In his book *Bakunin and Anarchy* he translated passages by the classic theorist of anarchism from Spanish, French, and Russian into English. He told me proudly that when he and Esther traveled to Spain after Franco's death he saw his Bakunin book in the windows of many leftist bookstores. Dolgoff read several newspapers each day from all over the world, and no one was better informed politically. When I asked him about Gorbachev, Sam called him a son-of-a-bitch who wanted to restore capitalism and compared his economic reforms with Lenin's "New Economic Policy" (NEP) of 1921, which attempted to revive the Russian economy by allowing a limited number of private enterprises. Critics from the left, such as Alexandra Kollontai, Anton Pannekoek, other left communists, council communists,[7] as well as the anarchists all condemned this reversion to the market economy and the consequent loss of power for the workers' and peasants' councils and the unions. Dolgoff felt that Gorbachev, even more than Lenin, was seeking salvation in capitalism; the only difference was that Gorbachev was trying to reduce the power of the Communist Party rather than to increase it, as Lenin did. In any case, he said, *glasnost* would bring no good, and the standard of living would sink. He added dryly: "I think the prime minister should be no other than Murray Rothbard."[8]

On the subject of Emma Goldman, Dolgoff erupted into an aggressive outburst. After criticizing Goldman's earlier susceptibility to Nietsche and individualist anarchism and praising her later anarcho-syndicalist sympathies, he became agitated about the "Emma Goldman cult," for which, he felt, she herself was partially responsible. Esther did her best to calm him down. She emphasized Goldman's valuable contributions to sexual politics, feminism, abortion, and birth control. Sam raised his voice, Esther countered. They had both forgotten my microphone and were fighting yet another battle in the endless feud between the labor and the women's movements: the question whether sexual education and abortion rights are social-revolutionary matters or whether they are secondary, perhaps merely bourgeois, issues. The revolutionary veteran interrupted his wife again and again. When he finally fell silent she explained to me:

> The thing is that they do not realize what the life of the women was like. Even their clothes. They had to wear these awful corsets that pulled so hard that the women could not breathe. And then sex. You can't get along without sex, there would be no life. What did they make out of it, something very ugly, something that could not be discussed. But who got the brunt of it? The women. But the fact remains, these are important things that Sam thinks that are not important. All these little things, they seem like nothing. But if it is truly details of rebellion, it is important.[9]

---

7.   Council communism is libertarian socialism organized through councils elected by the grassroots in
 ·   the tradition of Rosa Luxemburg.
8.   Ibid.
9.   Esther Dolgoff, interview with the author, 1987.

Esther grew up in a Jewish family in Cleveland, where her father was a bricklayer. She got a degree in nursing and later received an M.A. in English. She, too, was a member of an anarcho-syndicalist organization and was active in the IWW. With her tolerant nature and her almost religious belief in Kropotkin's principle of mutual aid, she was the antithesis of her companion's pessimistic, critical character, a man always ready to spar. Even on her deathbed she hardly ever mentioned herself, but worried about the nurses' low wages and introduced her visitors to one another. She died in November, 1989.

When I visited Sam after Esther's death, he was contemplating the consequences of electronic technology: unemployment on a hitherto unknown scale might render the proletarian weapons of strike and boycott ineffective, thus perhaps leaving the underprivileged no other means of pressure than mass uprisings.

> And these young people will have to stop playing around with ecology and with zips and yips and greens and blues and stop that nonsense and get down to these things. If I was younger I would write a book. I have a subject for you: on the changing nature of the working force and the task of the proletariat and the new forms of struggle that will have to take place. I can't do it, because I am an *alter Kacker*.[10]

In a dramatic declaration of allegiance to Bakunin's *Spirit of Revolt*, he cursed all reformists and moderates:

> But he who has no confidence in the creative capacity of the masses and in their capability to revolt doesn't belong in the revolutionary movement. He should go to a monastery and get on his knees and start praying. Because he is no revolutionist. He is a son of a bitch.[11]

As a farewell he sang *"la bandiera rossa triumferà."*[12]

After Sam's death in the fall of 1990 his son Anatoli told me about his father's last political opinions as he had expressed them during the following conversation in a Latino restaurant in Brooklyn:

Anatoli: What do you think about the political situation?

Sam: Bloody bastard [George Bush]. He wants the war. He won't stop until he has one. He wants blood, blood. It's all about blood and oil and power.

Anatoli (as devil's advocate): Hussein is a dictator and a vicious tyrant.

Sam: So what? Granted, but is he any worse than the Syrians, the Saudis, Kuwaitis, Iranians? There is nothing that distinguishes him from the friends of the Americans. In fact he was a friend of the US.

Anatoli: Bush called Hussein Hitler.

Sam: He gets out of Kuwait. The oil starts to flow and all will be forgiven, and we will make friends with Hitler again.[13]

---

10.   Sam Dolgoff, interview with the author, 1988.
11.   Ibid.
12.   Song of the Spanish Revolution.
13.   Reported to me by Anatoli Dolgoff in 1992.

The Ancestors and Classics of Anarcho-Syndicalism

Michael Bakunin

Michael Bakunin is not only the principal theoretical source for Dolgoff and the anarcho-syndicalists, he is also the inventor of social-revolutionary anarchism in general. At the center of his teachings is the concept of liberty:

> Without political equality there is no real political liberty, but political equality will be possible only when there is social and economical equality.[14]

Since Bakunin's day the ideal of liberty has been badly abused by many of its fans. Whether degraded by liberals to mean freedom of trade or freedom for the fittest, or sacrificed by alleged communists on the altar of a forced collectivism termed "the common good," liberty has been the banner under which inequality, injustice, and dictatorship have all been practiced. Neither the bourgeoisie nor the socialists kept their promises of liberty, while Bakunin's followers rarely had an opportunity to translate their version of it into practice. They became history's eternal losers. Hounded and butchered by their opponents on both the right and left, all that remained to them were a certain moral triumph, a clean conscience, and their vision of a free and equal society.

Bakunin, born of Russian nobility, began his political career as a Panslavic populist. During the Revolution of 1848 he was arrested in Dresden, Germany, and spent twelve years in various West European and czarist Siberian prisons, until he managed a daring escape via Japan and America to Europe. After 1864 he became an anarchist and internationalist and joined the First International, from which he was expelled in 1872, along with the entire antistatist fraction of the labor movement. This was the first climax in the fraternal feud between anarchists and communists in which Marx, with many, often vindictive diatribes, played a role. Bakunin, for his part, blamed Marx for everything and everyone he disagreed with—Marx's associate Friedrich Engels, the Jacobin socialist Ferdinand Lassalle, and the German Social Democrats—thus rendering his "critique of Marxism," all too readily embraced by anarchists, both visionary and off the mark. Yet his nightmarish prophecies about the "people's state" with its bureaucracy, ruling experts, and technocrats, have all come true. It must be said, however, that the people's state was originally a social democratic concept criticized by Marx as much as by Bakunin.

One point on which Bakunin did, in fact, differ from Marx was in his demand that a revolution must be both social and cultural. In his view the creators of a better, future society must anticipate its structures in the given society.

> We must demand that the International, embryo of the society of the future, must be the true image of our principles of freedom and federation and must cast out any principle tending towards authority and dictatorship.[15]

---

14. Sam Dolgoff, ed., *Bakunin on Anarchism.* Montreal: Black Rose, 1980, p. 87.
15. Michael Bakunin, *Staatlichkeit und Anarchie.* Berlin: Karin Kramer Verlag, 1972, p. xxxii, translated by Danny Lewis.

Bakunin derived these "principles of liberty and federation" from the visions of the early socialists and from the practices of certain labor organizations of his day. From the early socialist Pierre Joseph Proudhon he adopted the concepts of federalism and of workers' association; from the French and Swiss labor movements he took the idea of the revolutionary labor union. Whereas Proudhon envisioned his workers' cooperatives as being united through a kind of loyal competition, Bakunin incorporated syndicalism into workers' self-administration. Ruling councils elected by workers in each factory were to join together in a huge economic union which would be charged with organizing the economy for the common good. The commune, which in Proudhon's system is envisioned as a largely autarkic entity, is in Bakunin's concept integrated into the larger society. The individual cooperatives are organized into a commune and the communes, in turn, band together with other communes. Bakunin, the social revolutionary, considers individual cooperatives and isolated utopian socialist projects, for instance, New Ikaria as reformist lightning rods. Such ideas, he writes, are "all fine, very magnanimous and noble," but in the long run a mere drop in the ocean. "Deliverance" can be attained only through "struggle and revolt."[16]

Bakunin's concepts of individualism and federalism result in the right to political and cultural autonomy for all regions and nations. National and separatist independence movements are positive forces only when they origi-nate with the people and not with a privileged class. Bakunin was one of the very first socialists to predict the uprisings in Third World countries. He speaks of "800 million sleepy and enslaved people in the Orient" which would "one day awaken and begin to move."[17]

Although he had come to reject Panslavist ideology, Bakunin nonetheless incorporated a few of its components into his theory of anarchism. In Bakunin's vision, the Slavic peasants resemble the noble savage who, unperverted by bourgeois civilization and in possession of infallible tribal instincts, is the ideal subject of the revolution. Similarly, he praises the "passionate" Italian Lumpenproletariat, playing it out against the German proletariat which has become "bourgeois." These are problematic notions, despite the grain of truth that these characterizations may hold. Even if one is inclined to agree with Bakunin's description of the Germans as "statists and bureaucrats by nature,"[18] when he goes on, in good old Russian tradition, to combine hatred of the Germans with anti-Semitism, we can no longer close our eyes to his racism. Fortunately Bakunin's psychological theories of national character never gained ground in the anarchist movement—unlike his anti-intellectualism, which has

16.   Michael Bakunin, *Statism and Anarchy*. Marshall Shatz, ed., Cambridge: Cambridge University Press, 1990, pp. 213-14.
17.   Quoted in Daniel Guérin, *Anarchismus*. Frankfurt: Suhrkamp Verlag, 1967, pp. 70-71, translated by Danny Lewis.
18.   Michael Bakunin, *Statism and Anarchy*. Op.cit., p. 34

become a chronic problem for many of his followers, who still agree that "for the preservation of a people's liberty, strength, and passion, ignorance is preferable to bourgeois civilization."[19]

Putschism and a spontaneous-romantic vitalism are other facets of his problematic legacies. In rapturous tones he describes an unchaining of evil passions in a revolution which "destroys everything that opposes the broad flow of popular life."[20] Bakunin's recurrent weakness for secret conspirational societies whose members become the driving force of the revolution still finds imitators today. He abandoned these notions, widespread in czarist Russia, only to take them up again under the influence of the young Russian Netchaev who dreamed of a revolution of revenge and destruction led by an avant-garde serving the people. Netchaev created the ideal of the totally committed revolutionary who possesses neither a private life nor feelings and traditional morals, and for whom the end justifies any and all means. Bakunin later fell out with Netchaev and once again abandoned such ideas.

Although Bakunin never completely freed himself from Slavic populism and Jacobin revolutionary theory, modern anarcho-syndicalism traces most of its main principles to him. Moreover, in this age of global relapse into nationalism, Bakunin's plea for internationalism cannot be quoted often enough:

> The revolution cannot be confined to a single country: it is obliged under pain of annihilation to spread, if not to the whole world, at least to a considerable number of civilized countries. In fact, no country today can be self-sufficient; international links and transactions are necessary for production and cannot be cut off. If a revolutionary country is blockaded by neighboring states the Revolution, remaining isolated, would be doomed.[21]

Peter Kropotkin

After Bakunin's death, social-revolutionary anarchism drifted away from the labor movement for a while, developing the utopia of "communist anarchism" which placed more emphasis on the commune and local autonomy than on the unions. While Peter Kropotkin, the classic proponent of this doctrine, never lost touch with the labor movement, many of his fellow believers became elitist individualists, reclusive eccentrics, and visionary founders of anarchist colonies. In Germany the movement had, by the turn of the century, become almost completely apolitical and individualistic, picking up mystical, folk-romantic, even prefascist characteristics. By the 1880s the early socialist idea of founding colonies as models of the future society also was accompanied by confidence in "the propaganda of the deed." Enrico Malatesta's (1855–1932) famous and often ridiculed mini-insurrection in an Italian mountain village is an example of the putschism of impatient revolutionaries. The revival of the

---

19.   Ibid., p. 27.
20.   Ibid., p. 133.
21.   James Guillaume, quoted in Sam Dolgoff, *Bakunin on Anarchism*. Montreal: Black Rose, 1972, p. 378.

bourgeois idea of tyrannicide was the next step in the development of the "philosophy of dynamite" developed by such assassins as Ravachol, who blindly blasted their way towards their goals. Typical for this period of escapism was the combination of utopianism and terrorism advocated by the former German social democrat Johann Most (1846–1906) who brought anarchism to the US in the early 1880s.

One of Kropotkin's invaluable contributions to social philosophy is his unfaltering criticism of social Darwinism, the inhumane theory of the survival of the fittest and of competition as the natural principle of life. Kropotkin counters this principle with the idea of "mutual aid," which he illustrates in his book of the same title with numerous examples of animals spontaneously helping each other. One of the most famous is his moving story of a blind pelican who is lovingly fed by his fellow pelicans instead of being left to die. Humans, too, says Kropotkin, have a natural inclination for solidarity and socially responsible conduct.

> There is, in mankind, a nucleus of social habits—an inheritance from the past, not yet duly appreciated—which is not maintained by coercion and is superior to coercion. Upon it all the progress of mankind is based. . . .[22]

A valuable document of his times, Kropotkin's autobiography *Memoirs of a Revolutionist* depicts his development from a page at the czar's court to a populist revolutionary and political prisoner, and finally to a social revolutionary in exile. Kropotkin's love of the common people was first inspired by his father's servants with whom the young prince grew up. One of the events that influenced him the most was the emancipation of the serfs by Czar Alexander II, which, in the end, thanks to generous compensation from the government, benefited the landowners far more than the serfs themselves. Kropotkin performed his first act of service to the people as a student by compiling statistics on the situation of the serfs. He later joined the nihilists, educated young Russians of wealthy and aristocratic background who had decided to "join the common people." The moral radicalism, material modesty, honesty, willingness for sacrifice, and courage of these professional revolutionaries deeply influenced the great idealist Kropotkin.

"Communist anarchism" is a composite of bourgeois-revolutionary, early socialist, liberalist, and social revolutionary elements. For Kropotkin, the term "communist" stands for the principle "to each according to his needs, from each according to his ability," rather than the demand that the laborer receive the full fruits of his labor. Evolution is just as important as revolution: society, writes Kropotkin, is moving towards communism of its own accord, as is visible in efforts to preserve and reintroduce archaic communist principles. Like the Russian Narodniks and Bakunin, he considered the *mir,* the commonly-owned pasture of the Russian peasants, the starting point for social change. Two other

---

22.   Peter Kropotkin, *Memoirs of a Revolutionist.* New York: Dover Publications, 1971, p. 401.

precursors of communism are the "voluntary contract," and the "voluntary agreement." Thus, trade and exchange associations independent of the state, the international postal association, the railroad association, scientific societies, and various other private initiatives anticipate free society. As does bourgeois tradition, Kropotkin sees the Greek *polis* and the European Renaissance as the models of true democracy, and praises the honest merchant of the Middle Ages with his "mercantile ethos." Under the nostalgic glow of the utopian lamp, the guilds seem like social associations of mutual aid, and the free cities like oases of democracy in the desert of feudalism. Since Kropotkin's day, many an anarchist has fallen victim to nostalgia's siren song.

Kropotkin's belief in evolution ends when it comes to exploitation. Evolution, he writes, is hindered by "the propertied classes," so that it "must now break its bonds by violence and realize itself in a revolution."[23] He considers the French Revolution of 1789 a positive model of a revolution, a negative example being the incomplete liberation of the Russian serfs. Kropotkin insists on the expropriation of capitalists and large landowners whom he sees not so much as representatives of their class, but rather as individual tyrants and evil-doers. At the revolution's ground zero (which Kropotkin imagined would most likely occur in Paris) the people will awake to its inherent reason, goodness, and a practical sense for organization. Groups of "well-intentioned citizens" will form spontaneously and rush to help the former. They will draw up statistics on expropriated dwellings and on the available food supply, and will distribute everything according to the egalitarian principle of the village community. There will be negotiations with the industrial workers, who are supplied with food and manufacture the tools for farming the land. For Kropotkin there seems to be no need to study the laws of the market and capital, since both will become obsolete at the time of the revolution, along with money, the division of labor, and social classes. Men, women, and children will instead farm in the parks and gardens of Paris and in the fields of nearby villages, producing "prosperity for all." The "renewal of health and joy" begins as a "festival,"[24] a celebration, which, under closer scrutiny, turns out to be a national one.

> Agriculture will have to be carried out on intelligent lines by men and women. . . . Of course . . . they will also produce those things which they formerly used to order from foreign parts. And let us not forget that for the inhabitants of a revolted territory, "foreign parts" may include all districts that have not joined in the revolutionary movement. . . . The revolted city will be compelled to do without these "foreigners."[25]

The question as to why the Parisian farm and industrial workers do not immediately forge alliances with the foreign proletariat is easily answered: they possess neither unions nor international contacts. It seems that the good genie

---

23.   Peter Kropotkin, *The Conquest of Bread*. New York: New York University Press, 1972, p. 55.
24.   Ibid., p. 104.
25.   Ibid., pp. 207–8.

of the people only has local powers. Autarchy alone guarantees revolution's success. This includes an agriculture of "versatile functions," which, thanks to scientific progress, will be easy to organize. Kropotkin prophesies solar energy, sees the wind as a giant vacuum cleaner, and speaks in glowing terms of greenhouse vegetables in a highly technological future world. Mixing agrarian romanticism and belief in technology, he presents his utopia as a paradisiacal farming culture devoid of toil and drudgery. Small artisans and small industry will be located in the villages, thus ending the division of labor. Large industry will be almost nonexistent. How this future society is to be organized is barely explained. Technology, good will, and reason seem to be sufficient guarantees for human cooperation.

As trapped as he was in his bourgeois and early socialist utopian vision on some points, he was well ahead of his times in other matters. Thus, as a sympathizer of the women's movement he says:

> Let us fully understand that a revolution, intoxicated with the beautiful words, Liberty, Equality, Solidarity, would not be a revolution if it maintained slavery at home. Half of humanity subjected to the slavery to the hearth would still have to rebel against the other half.[26]

Alexander Berkman

At the beginning of the 20th century the social revolutionary anarchists rejoined the labor movement. Anarcho-syndicalism came into being, drawing from the writings of Bakunin and Kropotkin and from revolutionary syndicalism. Syndicalism as a combination of anticapitalist and antistatist ideas was advocated by the CGT (Confédération Générale du Travail), founded in 1902 in France. Concentrating chiefly on the labor/capital contradiction, syndicalism did not have a vision for a socialist future, the main focus of anarchism. In Spain, where the labor movement had been strongly Bakuninist since the middle of the 19th century, the famous anarcho-syndicalist union CNT was founded in 1910. This union, which in its early days was limited to local concerns, had by the 1930s adopted organizational forms more suitable to modern industrial society.

Alexander Berkman (1870–1936), who lived for the most part in the shadow of his famous companion Emma Goldman, formulated the principles of anarcho-syndicalism in his brochure *The ABC of Anarchism,* published in 1929. The son of well-to-do Russian-Jewish parents, he first became interested in politics as a secret admirer of the nihilists who, after several unsuccessful attempts, assassinated Czar Alexander II in 1881. Berkman emigrated to the US, where he thought that liberty and democracy had already been realized. After experiencing first-hand the poverty and misery of working-class immigrants, and influenced by Johann Most, Berkman decided to commit tyrannicide. In 1892 when the steel magnate Frick ordered his private police force to shoot

---

26.   Ibid., p. 144.

striking workers, Berkman decided to execute him in the name of the people. He missed the mark, the capitalist tyrant survived, and Berkman, rather than dying as a young hero, spent fourteen terrible years in prison. Before the US entered World War I, Berkman and Goldman organized impressive mass antiwar meetings. As a result, both were deported to the USSR in 1919, at the time of the communist revolution. The Bolsheviks initially welcomed the world-famous revolutionaries with open arms and offered Berkman an important post in the Red Army. The former terrorist, however, chose to organize a chain of public restaurants to benefit the people of Moscow. The persecution of anarchists which began soon thereafter put an abrupt end to his and Goldman's cooperation with Lenin and his comrades.

What is particularly striking in *ABC of Anarchism* is its astonishing duality. While the principles of anarchism are presented in a visionary, idealistic way, questions of practice and organization are dealt with soberly and realistically. Berkman, a believer in both tyrannicide and anarcho-syndicalism, almost seems to embody two different authors representing different centuries.

For the idealist Berkman, history is the struggle between philosophies: ideas are the basis of the condition of the world. "The divine rights of the king, slavery and serfdom," exposed and discredited by "advanced thinkers,"[27] had been abolished. The problem is mainly a moral one, one of belief. Hence it is necessary to destroy the belief in the indispensability of government and private property.

> For that an ideal is needed, an ideal which appeals not only to the stomach but even more to the heart and imagination, which rouses our dormant longing for what is fine and beautiful, for the spiritual and cultural values of life.[28]

This "ideal" is anarchism. Like a *deus ex machina* it will lead to the abolition of the moral and physical bonds of authority, to "mental emancipation," a "new humanity," and a "new race."[29] The guarantee for its success lies in the innate goodness of human nature. Here, the social revolution begins to develop religious features and tyrannicide becomes a noble deed, the self-sacrifice of martyrs, who, like Christ, die for humanity. As an idealistic early socialist Berkman supported local and national autarchy as the only antidote to the colonial exploitation of undeveloped countries. For Berkman (as for Kropotkin) the goals of the world revolution and autarkic "anarchism in one country" appear to exist side by side.

Berkman's presentation changes drastically when he speaks from his own experience on revolutionary organization. In these passages industrial capitalism and the proletariat's international cooperation are the prerequisites for the modern social revolution. The nebulous "ideal" of "anarchy" takes on the

---

27.   Alexander Berkman, *The ABC of Anarchism*. London: Freedom Press, 1992, p. 36.
28.   Ibid., p. 72.
29.   Ibid., p. 28.

concrete form of council communism: wicked tyrants and good common people become different social classes with their respective interests, and the people's innate goodness becomes the proletariat's class consciousness. Berkman shares Bakunin's expanded concept of the proletariat, which includes the peasants and the "intellectual proletarian," though his main focus is on the urban industrial proletariat, with which the author was most involved in both the US and the USSR. The most important principle is the "emancipation of the workers . . . by the workers themselves."[30] Berkman's vision of social revolution, too, is a realistic one. He criticizes his earlier notion of the healing purgatory of passion unleashed. Instead he sees the general strike as the final means of effecting the systematically planned revolution. The workers' and peasants' organizations unite, and each branch also sets up its own "industrial council." Immediately after the revolution the liberated workers, peasants, and intellectuals do not experience instant harmony and eternal happiness, but rather are faced with "hard work and severe self-discipline,"[31] for as producers they must engage in the difficult task of assuming control of production. Like the later anarchists in Spain, Berkman makes a case for revolutionary experimentation in organizational forms and economics. Unlike the communist anarchists, however, he does not believe that the principle of "to each according to his needs" could be realized immediately; equal pay (or rationing) would be more realistic instead.

Unlike other anarchists (most of them anticommunist), Berkman criticized authoritarian communism, above all its Leninist variety. His close association with so many of these "fraternal" enemies prevented him from demonizing Marxism as a whole, whose final goals he declared to be his own:

> The greatest teachers of socialism—Karl Marx and Friedrich Engels—had taught . . . that anarchism would come from socialism. They said that we must first have socialism, but that after socialism there will be anarchism, and that it would be a freer and more beautiful condition of society to live in than socialism.[32]

After fleeing the Bolsheviks Berkman and Goldman were more or less politically homeless: for Western leftist intellectuals (almost all of whom had become blind followers of Lenin and Stalin) the two critics of Bolshevism, with their embarrassing revelations, seemed anticommunist, while in the eyes of ardent anticommunists they still embodied social revolution. Berkman, poverty-stricken and ill, committed suicide in France. Goldman was fortunate enough to experience firsthand the Spanish Revolution.

Rudolf Rocker

Rudolf Rocker is considered the most important classic author of anarcho-syndicalism. He was born in Mainz, Germany, in 1873, joined the labor

---

30.   Ibid., p. 44.
31.   Ibid., p. 74.
32.   Ibid., p. 1.

movement while he was an apprentice in a bookshop, and soon became one of the first leftist critics of German social democracy. Around the turn of the century he moved to Paris, and in 1908 to London. There he became an influential and well-liked activist in the Jewish anarchist movement and edited their magazine. Though not Jewish himself, he spoke and wrote perfect Yiddish. After World War I Rocker played an important part in establishing the German anarcho-syndicalist organization FAUD (Föderalistische Arbeiterunion Deutschlands) and later in founding the anarchist international IWA (International Workmen's Association). He fled from the Nazis to the US and died in New York in 1958. His autobiography is, like that of Kropotkin, a rich historical document and fascinating reading.

In his "declaration of principles," which he wrote in 1919 for the future FAUD, Rocker explains that capitalist society developed out of the emergence of private property and class differences. As the central institution of economic monopoly and power, the state has become the major obstacle to all progress. This view contradicts still popular anarchist dogmas, according to which the state is the source and cause of both class differences and private property.

Rocker's criticism of the social democrats and communists targets primarily centralism and state socialism. He traces these principles back to the petty-bourgeois Jacobin philosophy of the French Revolution, and explains that these notions were so popular in German social democracy because of its fixation with the authoritarian brand of socialism promulgated by labor leader Ferdinand Lassalle (1825–1864). "Unity of action," Rocker says, is a euphemism for centralism, and is, in reality, simply the "unity of a marionette play." He points to the sad example set by the social democrats' parliamentary vote in support of the war in 1914: as long as the party's central authority was opposed to the war, thousands of antiwar rallies were organized, but when the party changed its mind, "the defense of the fatherland became one's patriotic duty, and the same masses who had protested against the war a week earlier were now all for it."[33] The dictatorship of the proletariat in its Leninist form is also seen by Rocker as part of the Jacobin-Lassallean legacy. His own definition of the dictatorship of the proletariat is almost identical to that of the Marxist Rosa Luxemburg, who supported the idea of council communism:

> If dictatorship of the proletariat only means the assumption of the power of the state by one party ... then we are absolutely opposed to this so-called proletarian dictatorship ... If it means only the expression of the will of the proletariat at the moment of its victory to dictate to the propertied classes the end of their privileges, and the transferral of the administration of all social functions of life into the hands of working people, then we not only have nothing against this sort of dictatorship, but it is what we are striving for with all our might.[34]

---

33.   Rudolf Rocker, quoted in F. Barwich, *Arbeiterselbstverwaltung, Räte, Syndikalismus.* Berlin: Karin Kramer Verlag, 1973, p. 25, translated by Danny Lewis.
34.   Ibid., pp. 27–28.

For Rocker, unions, not the party, are the "spearhead of the labor movement."[35] Unions are "the seed of the future socialist economy and the basic school of socialism in general."[36] The strategies of the anarcho-syndicalist union comprise antimilitarist propaganda, economic boycotts, armed resistance, and, as the trigger of revolution, the general strike. Thereafter the workers need only use the organs of their own decentralized union to get production going again. Locally they are organized in "*Arbeiterbörsen*" (workers' exchanges: early socialist term for trade unions), which are the "central focus of local and union activity"[37] and are consolidated nationally into a federation of workers' exchanges. Unions are organized according to professions in industry-wide federations. The workers' exchanges are responsible for the distribution of consumer goods and local administration, while the industrial associations are in charge of production.

Rocker was a sharp critic of bourgeois and fascist nationalism, which he refers to as the "religion of the modern state." He considers the "education towards national unity" advocated by the nationalists as the means for preserving the "domination of the propertied classes."[38] As a passionate opponent of racism, which arises from nationalism, Rocker warns against applying "the characteristics of the individual indiscriminately to classes, nations, or races."[39] He mentions with disgust the "emotional outpourings of German racial theorists" on the "inferiority and dull spirit" of the peoples without "Nordic blood."[40] Anarcho-syndicalists, he writes in his declaration of principles, accept merely regional differences between groups of people, though they insist on all peoples' right to satisfy "their special cultural needs" with the "approval and solidarity"[41] of other groups. Rocker equally rejected the patriotism of the social democrats and Leninists, as well as the idea of socialism in one country. All problems created for the working classes by international capitalism, Rocker writes, can be solved only "through parallel efforts and methods of the workers in all existing states."[42] Social democrats, he says, have long since abandoned Marx's principle of the modern proletarian without a country and the recognition of the historical relevance of class contradictions and economic conditions, adopting nationalism instead. Not even the bloody experiences of World War I could bring them to abandon their sense of patriotic duty to defend the fatherland. During the struggle of the Ruhr workers in the 1920s, the interests of the German workers were once again sacrificed on the altar of the alleged national interests of big business. And the German Communist Party, the social

35.   Rudolf Rocker, *Anarcho-syndicalism*. London: Secker and Warburg, 1938, p. 88.
36.   Ibid., p. 89.
37.   Ibid., p. 11.
38.   Rudolf Rocker, quoted in F. Barwich, op. cit., p. 13.
39.   Rudolf Rocker, *Aufsatzsammlung*. Bd. I, Frankfurt, 1980, p. 146, translated by Danny Lewis.
40 .   Ibid., p. 148.
41.   Rudolf Rocker, quoted in F. Barwich, op. cit., p. 13.
42.   Rudolf Rocker, *Aufsatzsammlung*. Op. cit. p. 157.

democrats' "problem child," had even tried to outdo them in "cranking out nationalist gibberish."[43]

Rocker was outraged at the communists' glorification of Schlageter, the hero of the Ruhr struggle, by Communist Party functionary Radek as well as by Ruth Fischer's tactical propaganda slogan "hang the Jewish capitalists."[44] Rocker's position on the nationalist movements of oppressed peoples is just as uncompromising. Nationalism of any kind is "in its very essence reactionary" even if it is applying "so-called revolutionary means."[45] The same applies to the labor movements of rich countries, which sought and seek their salvation exclusively in the economic prosperity of their own (colonialist or imperialist) country at the price of exploiting foreign workers.

Even though Rocker's critique of nationalism during the 1920s and 1930s deals mostly with the question of class, he does at times use the "organic" arguments of early socialism: then, society and the people are "natural," and state and nation are "artificial." The *Bund* (medieval form of association) is a natural form of organization, and the decentralized society of the early Middle Ages is (in the tradition of Kropotkin) viewed as the paradise lost. It was the "uniform national state" that led to the "victory of uniformity over the rich variety of folklife of the people,"[46] Rocker wrote in an essay from the 1920s.

Unlike the communists, in the early 1930s Rocker called for an alliance of the left against the Nazis. At the same time, he increased his criticism of the Soviet Union and the German Communist Party almost to the point of a dangerous inversion of cause and effect, thus anticipating Ernst Nolte's popular position in the modern-day "historians' debate."[47] According to Rocker, "the victory of Bolshevism over the Russian revolution" was "the beginning of the fascist counter-revolution in Europe."[48] Later, in American exile, Rocker supported the Allies in World War II as the only possibility for stopping the Nazis' murderous deeds. In that point he was in agreement with most anarchists in the US, although some were opposed to the war on antimilitarist principle.

A life of struggle and commitment to the social revolution did not prevent Rocker from falling into the bourgeois anticommunist trap brought forth by the Cold War. Embittered by the crimes committed against anarchists by communists and by the sellout of communism's internationalist principles in the Hitler-Stalin Pact, many anarchist veterans made their peace

---

43.   Ibid., p. 127.
44.   Ibid., p. 198.
45.   Ibid., p. 139.
46.   Ibid., p. 138. Here Rocker uses the word *völkisch*, a term typical for prefascist and fascist authors meaning the people as an organic community or entity.
47.   The German historian Ernst Nolte holds that the Holocaust was caused by the "Bolshevist terror." When he and other German revisionist historians were challanged in 1986 by sociologist Jürgen Habermas's critique, the resulting discusssion became known as the "Historikerstreit," the historians' debate.
48.   Ibid., p. 195.

with capitalism. The liberalist elements of anarchism provided the bridge for those anarchists who had grown weary of a seemingly eternal war on two fronts. Rocker began to equate the Soviets' "red imperialism" with the Nazi regime. In his articles written during the 1950s, fascism is no longer an issue, while Soviet-style communism is portrayed as the "great and immediate danger."[49] He, who once had condemned sacrificing the class struggle in the interest of forging a temporary alliance between leftist forces to oppose fascism, was now proposing "a decisive cooperation between people of good will of all classes,"[50] and at the same time extolling the virtues of the American Revolution and American individualism. He even praised the astounding economic growth of contemporary American society which he credited to the country's federal structure. As if that were not enough, the former social revolutionary seemed to discover an "inner relatedness"[51] between war and revolution and between revolution and reaction. In the end he unhesitatingly rehabilitates everything against which he had struggled for most of his life:

> The belief that capitalism was the real cause of the system of imperialist domination and thus made war into a permanent social condition is merely a Marxist myth.[52]

Private property, social classes, and exploitation are no longer at issue, only the national, centralist organization of capitalism—caused by socialism. The "blind trust in the state propagated by most socialist schools of thought" has caused capitalism to take on forms "which were originally foreign to it."[53] Sauce for capitalists is sauce for anarchists.

Isaak Puente and Diego Abad Santillan

Spanish anarcho-syndicalism was the product of a cross between peasant communalism (as derived from commune) and the urban syndicalist labor movement. Especially in the underdeveloped province of Andalusia, old forms of communal land ownership similar to the Russian *mir* had survived. Bakunin's followers had agitated to turn the nostalgic provincial and particularist consciousness of the *mir* into the utopian ideology of village communism, whose declared goal was the autarkic "free commune." From 1931 there were numerous rural uprisings of this sort. The revolutionary self-administered cooperatives that sprang up all over Spain after the outbreak of the civil war also owed much of their energy to this brand of communalism. These cooperatives' remarkable attempts to put the principle "to each according to his needs, from each according to his abilities" into practice were driven by an anticapitalism comprising both progressive and conservative elements.

---

49.   Rudolf Rocker, *Aufsatzsammlung*. Bd. 2, Frankfurt: 1980, p. 7, translated by Danny Lewis.
50.   Ibid., p. 28.
51.   Ibid., p. 112.
52.   Ibid., p. 5.
53.   Ibid., p. 7.

Syndicalism, on the other hand, operating primarily in Catalonia, grew out of the industrial proletariat's future-oriented consciousness of reality and found its expression in a well-organized union movement. The theorists of Spanish anarchism reflected the traditional contradictions of its basis, subscribing either to Kropotkin's autonomous agricultural communalism or to Bakunin's proletarian integrationist internationalism. At the CNT congress in 1936 in Zaragossa, representatives of both wings of the movement presented their programs.

The country doctor Isaak Puente presented a concept for direct village democracy. According to this plan, the citizens of the community would assemble in a town meeting to elect a governing council from among the representatives of various technical committees; money would be abolished immediately after the revolution; the labor output of all active workers would be measured in daily units and credited to a "producer card," which would be cashed in for goods; all other members of the community would use a "consumer card" distributed by the commune. Though Puente retained internationalism as the guiding principle, his vision of autonomy and autarchy was even more extreme and backward-looking than Kropotkin's. He hoped that

> with time the new society will set up each commune with all the agricultural and industrial means necessary to make it autonomous, according to the biological principle that that person—in this case the respective commune—is freest who needs the least from others.[54]

In addition, Puente stressed the importance of cultural revolution and life-style changes. He demanded the right for nudists to establish autonomous communes. In a naive and amusing passage on the topic of family and sexuality, he recommended a change of scenery for his comrades suffering from love or jealousy. His suggestion, in the third year of Nazi rule in Germany, however, to expand sex education by instruction in eugenics, "human selection," appears less comical from today's perspective.

Diego Abad Santillan, a journalist, presented the opposing syndicalist view. He had translated the anarchist classics, including Rudolf Rocker, and was the publisher of various anarchist periodicals. He was one of the co-founders of the FAI (Federatión Anarquista Iberia) and in 1936 was appointed minister of economics for the Catalan government. After the fascist victory he fled to Argentina, where he wrote a book entitled *Why We Lost the Revolution.* Lack of organizational coordination, too few weapons, and the communist betrayal were in his view the main causes of defeat. Santillan's sketch of anarcho-syndicalism emphasized the main concepts of council communism, labor unions, and cooperation. The "free commune" is defined as a social project enabling all groups to lend expression to their revolutionary experiments. No one would be forced to accept a particular form of revolution. On the economic

---

54.   Isaak Puente, in *Ökonomie und Revolution.* Berlin: 1975, p. 150, translated by Danny Lewis.

level, however, he continued, the essential element is the federated commune anchored in an economic network linking all revolutionary countries. Communalism is "a relic of old legal concepts of the property of the commune."[55] A locally limited economic revolution, he warned, would only create collective poverty and a lack of goods.

> Above all we must be clear about the fact that we are no longer rocking the cradle of a small utopian world.[56] ... Each one of us should reap the benefits of all that which intelligence and work have brought forth. ... Even the most insignificant village is connected to the global national economy by a thousand bonds.[57]

Like Rocker, Santillan pleads for grassroots economic planning and for an economic council as the highest institution. Money, he said, has to be retained temporarily to allow for foreign trade and international financial relations. The functions of the bourgeois chamber of commerce are to be taken over by a council for credit and commerce.

Revolutionary realism, however, could not win out over a captivating arcadian vision. The CNT decided to adopt Puente's utopian variant of anarcho-syndicalism. Santillan himself later succumbed, as Sam Dolgoff told me, to another antipolitical temptation of anarchists, bourgeois liberalism.

The Last Anarchist

Nothing and no one was ever able to entice Sam Dolgoff away from his social-revolutionary credo and a deep-seated hatred of capitalism.

His definition of anarcho-syndicalism corresponds to Rocker's from the 1920s. Concerning Spanish anarchism, he assumes a middle position between Santillan and Puente, attempting to bridge the gulf between the two views. He cites both Santillan's warnings against provincial patriotism and Puente's praise of the free commune. Dolgoff, too, swings between critical pragmatism oriented toward immediate concerns and utopian idealist free-spiritedness. His interpretation of Bakunin is the expression of the first of the twin spirits in his soul. He points to the relevance of Bakunin's critique of authoritarian socialism and technocracy, and stresses social revolution, syndicalism, and workers' control. He goes to great lengths to defend his idol Bakunin against false interpretations, for example, in reference to the organic notion of the "natural society" adopted from Proudhon.

> It must be stressed, however, that Bakunin did not think a society necessarily good because it was "natural"—it could be either good or bad, depending on the material, intellectual, and ethical level of its members. ... When public opinion is poisoned by ignorance and prejudice, it can be even more tyrannical than the most despotic state.[58]

---

55.   Diego Abad Santillan, op. cit., p. 120.
56.   Ibid., p. 111.
57.   Ibid., p. 119.
58.   Sam Dolgoff, *Bakunin on Anarchy*. Montreal: Black Rose, 1972, pp. 6–7.

At the same time Dolgoff rescues Bakunin from agrarian-romantic anarchists. Dolgoff says that Bakunin did not idealize peasants; he realized that they were "ignorant, superstitious, and conservative,"[59] but he was convinced that the revolutionary industrial workers would be able to enlist the peasants in the struggle on their side if they could only overcome their own arrogant attitude. Hence, Dolgoff attempts to rescue Bakunin not only from the worshippers of nature and rural anarchists, but also from the conspirators and terrorists. Bakunin's conspirational concept and his temporary attraction to Blanqui's putschism, Dolgoff writes, belong to his pre-anarchist period, and *The Catechism of the Revolutionary* has been proven to be Netchaev's and not Bakunin's work. However, Dolgoff, the born iconoclast nay-sayer, does not shy away from criticizing the master himself. He just barely manages to smooth over the idea of the masses' revolutionary "instincts" by citing a passage in which Bakunin mutes his spontaneist viewpoint. Dolgoff mercilessly criticizes Bakunin's embarrassing racist remarks; his praise of Bakunin is always tempered by his rejection of Bakunin's anti-Semitism. Regarding Bakunin's national prejudices he says

> he did overstress the importance of "temperament" in revolution, asserting, for example that Latin and Slavic peoples were libertarian by nature—incapable of forming a strong state of their own, the Slavs' statism was, so to speak, imported from Germany. Yet we see that Russia and Spain are today notably totalitarian states. And in Italy, where Fascism first took hold, Mussolini was deposed only when he and his ally Hitler faced certain defeat.[60]

Dolgoff's strength, his ability for sharp-sighted political and ideological critique, finds its expression most clearly in his autobiography *Fragments: A Memoir*. In this book he never tires of distancing himself from the advocates of "ox cart anarchism," who oppose syndicalism and industrial production with "simplistic conceptions" of returning to the "primitive social life of a by-gone age."[61] The tension between romantic and pragmatic anarchism, however, was characteristic of Dolgoff even in his personal life. This opponent of escapist philosophies himself lived with Esther and their two sons in a community for alternative education and life-style, the Stelton colony in New Jersey from 1933 to 1942, where communists, anarchists, vegetarians, and other nonconformists lived in peace and harmony, united by their determination to protect their children from authoritarian and bigoted influences. Over the years the colony became increasingly individualist and life-style reformist, and so Dolgoff now has little positive to say about the colony. Anarchists, he writes, must respect the unrestricted individual freedom of their fellow human beings. But "the antics of food faddists, back-to-nature faddists, nudists, etc." only produce a "distorted conception of anarchism."[62]

---

59. Ibid., p. 17.
60. Ibid., p. 15.
61. Sam Dolgoff, *Fragments: A Memoir*. Cambridge, MA: Refract Publications, 1986, p. 14.
62. Ibid., p. 63.

Embittered, he tells how the Stelton school's principals viewed any influence on the child as authoritarian indoctrination and supported instead a kind of antipolitical anarchism of creativity. The children learned handicrafts, dancing, singing, and meditation instead of reading and writing. Politics were taboo. In speaking of attempts "to establish little 'heavens on earth' in the midst of universal corruption, exploitation, chaos and violence" Dolgoff concluded:

The Stelton Modern School Colony and all other colonies are essentially self-isolationist forms of escapism. I came to realize more and more that freedom will be attained not in isolation, but only in association with the rest of humanity.[63]

Dolgoff's political activities were extensive. While earning money as a house painter, he worked within the IWW and in various anarcho-syndicalist groups as a speaker, organizer, author of articles, and newspaper editor. A photograph taken in 1937 shows him as the speaker in honor of the 50th anniversary of the Haymarket tragedy, standing in front of the memorial for the executed martyrs. The enormous rally, at which Lucy Parsons, the elderly widow of one of the martyrs, spoke, was sponsored by the Chicago Free Society Group. This anarchist group was associated with the IWW and organized events with Goldman, Rocker, and other prominent anarchists; it also supported the Spanish anarchists. The Vanguard Group, to which some of the politically-minded Stelton residents belonged, also actively supported the Spanish Revolution, and as member of that group Dolgoff joined the ULO (United Libertarian Organizations), an antifascist league set up as an alternative to the communist organizations. He was one of the publishers of the ULO magazine *Spanish Revolution* and spoke at many meetings, which were often disrupted by communists. He also worked closely with the popular and influential Italian anarchist Carlo Tresca (1879–1943) to fight against American fascist groups, especially the notorious Silver Shirts.

Dolgoff viewed World War II as a necessary evil for destroying Nazi rule. "The very existence of what was left of civilization," he writes, was dependent on the victory over the "fascist barbarian hordes." It was, however, he continues, the responsibility of the left to make sure that no one profited from the war and that "social justice must simultaneously accompany the defeat of fascism."[64] Dolgoff is puzzled how liberal academics like George Woodcock or anarchist purists like Marcus Graham, the publisher of the individualist magazine *MAN,* could be so relentless in their opposition to the war. Didn't they care who won? Was the mass murder of six million Jews and countless antifascists, the enslavement of conquered peoples, and the impending global domination by the Aryans of no interest to them? Although Dolgoff defends Rocker against the purist's reproach that he was a supporter of the war, he cannot understand Rocker's uncritical identification with England and France. Was Rocker, Dolgoff asks,

---

63.   Ibid., p. 66.
64.   Ibid., p. 71.

simply refusing to admit that Hitler had received weapons from both countries? He then reminds us of the many crimes committed by the so-called democracies: European colonialism, slavery in the US, and the genocide of the Native Americans—crimes comparable to those of the fascist nations.

Dolgoff also criticizes Rocker for his later rejection of "revolutionary anarchism."[65] He counters Rocker's eulogies of American federalism with the reminder that it is the unscrupulous exploitation of immigrant labor in the US which alone "is responsible for the phenomenal development of American industry."[66] He rejects the rehabilitation of capitalism as a fundamentally peaceful system, reminding us of capitalism's cyclic crises which to this day have been solved only by military production and war. Finally, Dolgoff counters Rocker's hypothesis of the diminishing importance of the class struggle in the face of the atomic threat with his own theory of a newly emerging middle class consisting of scientists, engineers, technicians, and academics who need, among other things, war production as a means of shoring up their class position and social status. Neither old-time German anarchist Augustin Souchy nor Abad Santillan are spared Dolgoff's sharp criticism. Late in his life, Dolgoff complains, Santillan came to see the Scandinavian countries as models for peaceful progress without class struggle, and he proposed a strategy of consumer and producer associations as the path to anarchism. Dolgoff counters this with a Bakunian skepticism of nonrevolutionary cooperatives and adds:

> Anarchists who reject "old tactics," who hold that "not nineteenth century revolution but twentieth century reform is the real revolution," that cooperatives and other schemes make—or can make—capitalism acceptable or superfluous, will be enthusiastically hailed by bourgeois liberals, even "enlightened capitalists."[67]

Dolgoff also disagrees with some anarchists about their actions during the Spanish Civil War: was the decision of the CNT to take part in the government of Catalonia right or wrong? Purists accuse the CNT of collaboration, centralism, bureaucratization, and betraying of the revolution. They say that it would have been better if the anarchists had remained true to their antiparliamentary principles instead of continuing the fight against Franco at any price. For Dolgoff this is a malicious defamation of the Spanish comrades, who were caught in a tragic historical trap. Their only choice was between collaborating with both the socialist and communist antifascist opponents, establishing an anarchist dictatorship over all the other antifascists, or assuming the terrible historical responsibility for a fascist victory. Any choice they made would have been wrong. Here, too, Dolgoff prefers antifascism to principled adherence to dogma.

The New Left fares no better in Dolgoff's judgment. In the "authoritarian elements" of the New Left, "these ambitious, power hungry young Lenins who

65.   Ibid., p. 114.
66.   Ibid., p. 115.
67.   Ibid., p. 118.

want to lead the masses," he sees "the same scenario that I witnessed thirty years before."[68] Although he stresses that he is not belittling the "magnificent struggles of the young rebels against war, racism, and the false values"[69] of the establishment, there is hardly anyone among those antiauthoritarian rebels with whom he can really identify. He was miles apart from their uncritical identification with Third World liberation movements, which are all, in Dolgoff's view, doomed to dictatorship. And he sees such supermilitant groups as the Motherfuckers or the Black Panthers, who referred to Bakunin, as the heirs of Netchaev.

Only the CNT and the IWW escape Dolgoff's wrath. The left radical IWW, founded in 1905, was not associated with any particular ideology. With its decentralized, nonhierarchical, and antiauthoritarian practice, however, it was closely related to anarcho-syndicalism. The "wildcat," as the IWW was nicknamed, preferred direct action and wildcat strikes to negotiations and contracts with employers. Unlike the AFL (American Federation of Labor), the IWW organized unskilled labor, immigrants, and migrant workers. The red scares of the early 1920s and the attraction of Bolshevism almost completely destroyed the IWW, which was considered hopelessly old-fashioned by the time Dolgoff became a member in the late 1920s, when leftists were joining the socialist or communist parties.

Dolgoff speaks proudly of his work with Benjamin Fletcher, a black sailor and unionist who did much pioneering work within the IWW for the integration of white and black workers. He describes wildcat strikes, work slow-downs, boycotts, and self-help actions during the Depression. Unemployed members collected leftover food from the markets to feed themselves and their fellow members. They appealed to employed workers not to work overtime, to demand a reduction in working hours, and to organize demonstrations. In Dolgoff's collection of essays *The American Labor Movement*, the IWW is one of the few highlights that brighten the dark picture his fierce criticism draws of American labor organizations.

Besides the IWW, Dolgoff also honors the early beginnings of the American labor movement in the 1830s when workers read socialist texts to each other while working at their machines. He tells of the heroic climaxes of the class struggle: the huge railroad strike of 1877; the movement for the eight-hour day, which culminated in the general strike on May 1; the subsequent Haymarket tragedy; and other spontaneous strike movements, including the mass walkouts under the banner of the IWW at the beginning of the century, and the sit-in strikes of the 1930s.

In agreement with radical leftist historians like Daniel Guérin, Dolgoff dates the procapitalist—or as he calls it, collaborationist—trend in the labor movement

---

68.   Ibid., p. 101.
69.   Ibid., p. 103.

back to the late 1870s. He cites a speaker of the ITU (International Typographers Union), who, in 1850, still considered it "useless" to "disguise the fact that there existed a perpetual antagonism between capital and labor." Nothing of that insight was left eighteen years later, when the president of the ITU declared that "working men desire no division of property or overthrow of the social system."[70] In Dolgoff's opinion, Samuel Gompers, who founded the AFL in 1886, in the end succeeded in establishing the workers' willingness to cooperate with business, to identify with corporate capitalism, and to accept the ideology that capital and labor are in the same boat. Gompers declared socialism to be "economically, socially, and industrially wrong"[71] and in 1890 founded an alliance of unionists, industrialists, and bankers for the preservation of capitalism. The AFL's "business unionism," suited as it was to laissez-faire corporate capitalism, became outdated in the New Deal era. After the split in the AFL and a corruption scandal exploited by the government, the CIO (Congress of Industrial Organization) was founded in 1935. This strategy of "industrial unionism" fit in with Roosevelt's vision of welfare state capitalism. Dolgoff accuses the CIO's cofounder, John L. Lewis, of having used the powerful strike movements of the 1930s for his own purposes, thus integrating the labor movement into the system. He cites Lewis at the AFL congress in 1935:

> I stand here and plead for a policy . . . that will protect our form of government against the (radical)isms and philosophies of foreign lands, that now seem to be rampant in high and low places throughout the country. . . .[72]

Even more devastating is Dolgoff's judgment of Sidney Hillman, the CIO's vice president. He was the one, says Dolgoff, who broke up the great strike movement on Roosevelt's orders. Hillman negotiated the no-strike agreement (for the duration of World War II) and thus became an appeaser for Roosevelt's policies. There is no principal difference between laissez-faire capitalism and welfare state capitalism, between the AFL and the CIO, and between Gompers and Hillman, Dolgoff says: they were like two thieves who, having fought over the spoils for a while, decided in the end to share it—the result was the AFL-CIO.

The leaders of the labor movement were not only willing to compromise, they had also become corrupt very early on. This began, Dolgoff recounts, with the introduction of the "business agent," an unfortunate cross between employment agent and workers' representative. This go-between between labor and capital had the power to call and to end strikes without consulting the workers. In Dolgoff's words the business agent was a "parasite who usurped the power of the workers on the job."[73] Unscrupulous opportunists like the infamous union official Parks profited from union and corporation alike: they would

---

70.   Sam Dolgoff, *The American Labor Movement.* Champaign, IL: Resurgence, 1980, p. 49.
71.   Samuel Gompers, quoted in Dolgoff, ibid., p. 3.
72.   John L. Lewis, quoted in Dolgoff, ibid., p. 20.
73.   Ibid., p. 9.

blackmail the company by calling for strikes, which they would then call off after being paid off by industry. Others took bribes to break strikes, or as job agents kept a high percentage of the wages of the people for whom they got jobs. In the 1920s and 1930s the corruption in many unions became rampant and included mafia involvement. Gangster bosses and former pimps like Georges Scalese and William E. Malony ruled entire industries with blackmail. Pensions and strike funds were embezzled by crafty swindlers who then invested or speculated with the stolen money. Jimmy Hoffa continued these practices in the 1950s, and when he was finally indicted the union even paid for his lawyer, Dolgoff says angrily.

When Dolgoff talks as a pragmatic unionist and realistic observer of the political events of his lifetime, his positions are almost indistinguishable from those of council communists. His insistence on the industrial proletariat's leading role is at times almost dogmatic. But when he speaks of anarchist principles, he becomes a moralist and idealist like many anarchist colleagues.

> Solidarity on the job and on the picket-line is the economic expression of the inborn feeling for mutual aid. True socialism is much more than an economic doctrine. It is an ethical ideal. It cannot be imposed from above. It grows out of the feeling of brotherhood and is forged in the common struggle for noble aims.[74]

For Dolgoff, the defender of the traditional anarchist "ideal," economics takes a back seat to two higher principles: on the one hand, the inherent goodness of the human being; and on the other hand, the state whose demonic nature inexorably works towards the establishment of the dystopia of Orwellian totalitarianism. And so it happens that Dolgoff, though basically critical of romantic anarchists, often shares their weakness. His praise of the early labor movement with its "network of cooperative institutions"[75] of mutual aid becomes questionable, however, when he advises younger union colleagues to forget about the welfare state. Workers should demand their wages without deductions, set up independent unions, and administer their own social security and health insurance. As understandable as this position may be, considering the history of union corruption and the fact that labor representatives have traded working class rage for the meager benefits of a minimal welfare state, there could be no benefit in rejecting minimal welfare and unions if this strategy never went beyond the stage of a self-destructive boycott. That would simply be to play into the hands of union busters.

The idealization of the good in human beings is as unrealistic as the demonization of both the state and centralism. Thus Dolgoff, a bitter opponent of all naturalist ideologies, sees the federation as the "natural" form of organization, as opposed to the "artificial" form of centralization. He envisions future anarchist society as self-regulating and organic.

---

74.   Ibid., p. 40.
75.   Ibid., p. 42.

Power will not flow from the bottom up or the top down, for the simple reason that there will be no top and there will be no bottom. Power will flow through the whole organism, like the circulation of the blood, constantly revitalizing and renewing its cells.[76]

In his essay *A Critique of Marxism* Dolgoff refutes the theories of historical materialism and the (economic) theory of the state, although unlike other more superficial critics, Dolgoff does not equate Marxism with Leninism, and "real" socialism. Instead he cites economic determinist, evolutionist, Eurocentric, and authoritarian passages especially in Engel's "Anti-Dühring" essay to arrive at a rather un-Marxist interpretation of Marx, similar to the evolutionist theory of German social democracy prior to World War I. He aptly defines pure economic determinism as a "doctrine which in practice saps the revolutionary vitality of the masses" and conditions them "to accept capitalism and to cooperate with their rulers in their own enslavement."[77] In the utopian-anarchistic tradition, Dolgoff proposes, instead, ethical action and mutual aid, which presumably arise from the noble goals and good will of humankind.

Like Bakunin he views the state as the source and perpetrator of domination and inequality rather than as the product of class differences, serving to protect the interests of the bourgeoisie. Accordingly, the state came into being through robbery, conquest, and plunder, and is nothing but institutionalized domination by hordes of troops or gangs of thieves. This is similar to the old bourgeois view that history is created by the actions of powerful individual villains and heroes.

In defending anarchism against Marxism, Dolgoff contradicts himself. For example, he subscribes to Rocker's anti-economic explanation of the origin of wars, and, to a lesser degree, to his revision of class theory. Classes, Dolgoff says in this context, are not the most important agents of social change. The wars in our century have brought about much more social change than have labor struggles. The influence of nationalism on history, he continues, was totally underestimated by Marx and others; and so, like the state, war and nationalism seem like inexplicable plagues, the result of human criminality. It should not come as a surprise, then, that morality holds the promise of salvation.

Dolgoff not only accuses Marx of economic determinism and of establishing an incorrect theory of the state, but also of glorifying capitalism and the bourgeoisie. Marx's statement that the bourgeoisie has unleashed more productive power in one hundred years than all previous generations combined is absolutely wrong, according to Dolgoff. To prove this Dolgoff turns to the past and defends the Middle Ages, free cities, guilds, village communities, the Renaissance, and early socialism. He not only quotes Lewis Mumford's complaint about the cold money mentality of the bourgeoisie, but also refers

---

76.   Ibid., p. 80.
77.   Sam Dolgoff, *A Critique of Marxism.* Minneapolis: Soil of Liberty, no date, p. 3.

to Bakunin's notion of the "instinct of revolt" of oppressed peoples in agrarian societies and the heroic tradition of the peasant wars.

Dolgoff drew more criticism from the New Left for his critique of Castro in *The Cuban Revolution* than for his critique of Marx. After all, the Cuban revolution—with its long-haired, bearded revolutionaries, the legendary march on Havana, the David-vs.-Goliath relationship between Cuba and the US, and its martyr, Che Guevara—had contributed to the politicization of many young people. Later, anti-imperialist solidarity with Cuba often developed into a blind identification: information countering the illusion of Cuba as the only "good," real socialist country in the world was disbelieved. Old left anarchists distrusted Castroism from the beginning, and the victors of the Cuban revolution quickly became demons in their eyes. Many New Left anarchists justified the need for an authoritarian regime, whereas most Old Left anarchists abandoned the Cuban cause and with it all other Third World liberation movements. Some are even said to have supported the Vietnam War. Dolgoff's book on Cuba, which includes documents and eyewitness accounts, begins with a realistic assessment.

> The myth, induced by the revolutionary euphoria of the pro-Castro left, that a genuine social-revolution took place in Cuba, is based on a number of major fallacies. Among them is the idea that a social revolution can take place in a small semi-developed island, a country with a population of about eight million, totally dependent for the uninterrupted flow of vital supplies upon either of the great super-powers, Russia or the US. They assume falsely that these voracious powers will not take advantage of Cuba's situation to promote their own selfish interest.[78]

Dolgoff and his coauthors attack the militarization of Cuban society, the centralist, hierarchical structure of the state, state control of unions and the prohibition of strikes, the fostering of nationalism, the reintroduction of the death penalty, imprisonment and execution of political opponents, the reintroduction of the performance principle of labor, Castro's personality cult, and government control of all aspects of private life from the cradle to the grave. The book's final, biting chapter describes Castro as a political adventurer in the tradition of the *caudillos,* the unscrupulous putschist dictators who plague Latin America. The anarchist and veteran of the Spanish Civil War, Abelardo Iglesias, one of the book's contributors, calls Castro's march on Havana a "military spectacle" and a "vulgar imitation of Mussolini's march on Rome."[79] However, neither Iglesias nor the MLC (Movimento Libertario Cubano), the Cuban libertarian socialist movement and its exiled leadership, which is represented in the book through numerous documents, can be accused of simple bourgeois anticommunism. Iglesias unequivocally rejects both "the reactionary emigré forces and the politicians in exile who would not hesitate to sell their

78.   Sam Dolgoff, *The Cuban Revolution*. Montreal: Black Rose, 1976, p. 23.
79.   Ibid., p. 93.

souls to the devil himself in order to reconquer the political and economic power they lost."[80] The MLC repeatedly states that it opposes Castro's regime as being not revolutionary enough rather than too revolutionary, and that it does not wish to be associated with the "greed and corruption"[81] of the old order. Nevertheless some of the articles by Cubans in exile published in Dolgoff's book have a somewhat reactionary ring. Disappointment with Third World liberation movements led some critics to become allies of US imperialism; Dolgoff tries to avoid this trap by suggesting other solutions to the problems of the Third World.

While his book about Cuba is appealing because of the sheer amount of information it contains, Dolgoff's article "Third World Nationalism and the State" remains hopelessly mired in generalizations. Dolgoff uses examples of the young, independent African nations in an attempt to prove that all political experiments in the Third World since liberation from the colonial yoke have been fruitless. Thus, he says, the independence of the former African colonies brought too little or no freedom to the continent's 420 million inhabitants. Tanzania has more political prisoners than South Africa; a quarter of the population of Ghana lives in exile; at least nineteen African nations are ruled by military dictatorships; and "socialist" national liberators like Bourgiba and Nkrumah are no better than such power-hungry political adventurers as Idi Amin. Dolgoff cites shocking examples of personality cult, corruption, and luxury: Nkrumah's golden bed, the nine palaces for the wives of the Central African Republic's head of state, and the president of Gabon's $600 million palace with revolving doors that disappear at the touch of a button. He speaks of the victims of the bloody wars against the separatist rebels in Biafra and Ethiopia, and of the outrageous human rights violations in other African countries.

As justified as this criticism and the assertion may be that national liberation does not necessarily lead to freedom, it nonetheless is not accurate to equate Hitler, the horrors of the Khmer Rouge, Stalin's USSR, Mao's cultural revolution, Castro's Cuba, Nasser's Egypt, with just about everything that happens in decolonized Africa. Equally unconvincing is Dolgoff's attempt to blame all evil on the state, for to do so is almost to render all economic, historical, or class analyses superfluous. Even less convincing is the utopia of a stateless, decentralized, "natural" or "organic" society.

> In Africa, the new "Third World" countries, to their eternal shame, are obliterating rich, varied cultures on the pretext that they are out to 'modernize and civilize the inferior savages.' But these cultures are in many respects far superior, far more humane, far freer than the authoritarian institutions imposed upon them by would-be "saviors."[82]

---

80.   Ibid., p. 95.
81.   Ibid., p. 141.
82.   Sam Dolgoff, *Third World Nationalism and the State*. Champaign, IL: Resurgence, no date, p. 17.

There follow several passages describing the idyll of loosely federated tribes without a central government and their harmonious village communities in precolonial Africa, culminating in the suggestion that anarchism could be established in Africa by restoring the tribal system. Dolgoff makes no mention of the potential of industrial progress, implying that the solution to the problems of the world's poorest countries is to turn back the wheel of history by several centuries. Ironically, while Dolgoff's critical position toward revolutionary events in the Third World sets him apart from the New Left, his idealization of the tribe resembles the counterculture's romance with Native American tribalism. Is this not merely the other side of the coin bearing Che Guevara's heroic likeness?

While Dolgoff's article on Africa is a kind of journey into the past, his essay *The Relevance of Anarchism in Modern Society* embraces the future, the propitious age of electronics, which will be the age of anarchism. Dolgoff says that technology is in itself a friend of humanity. The advances in productivity will enable society to free itself from scarcity and poverty. Dolgoff prophesies a consumer economy in which purchasing power will no longer be linked to production, making the wage system obsolete. Workers' control would not be obsolete, however, and in the free society of a post-revolutionary future it will express itself through a network of consumer associations and producer's unions. Hence, achievements of technology will for the first time be used to benefit humanity. Thanks to the possibilities of modern communications, internationalism in the form of direct democracy will become possible on a global scale. Centralism and bureaucracy will simply dissolve. Even now, Dolgoff continues, there is evidence of a global tendency toward economic decentralization. He cites renowned economists from East and West, and demonstrates his theory using General Motors as an example. Following Schumacher's slogan "small is beautiful," GM was reorganized into a federation of small companies—only the profits remain centralized. Kropotkin's blueprint of a decentralized economy, Dolgoff concludes, is much easier to realize today than it was in his day, and, in any case, the pollution of the environment makes it inevitable. Contrary to many others who speculate about the future, Dolgoff does not believe in the end of the proletariat. He envisions the "scientific-technical worker," and an army of computer engineers and programmers whose social status and pay is already not much better than that of blue-collar workers and will deteriorate even more as technical education spreads. In addition, Dolgoff hopes that these technicians, forced into monotonous work, will transform their desire for creative work into revolutionary energy.

Dolgoff's vision of the future may be utopian and naively trusting in the benefits of technology, but only two pages later he proves himself an acute interpreter of the present wretched state of affairs:

A highly sophisticated economic system, once viewed as the prerequisite for the realization of socialism, now serves to reinforce the domination of the ruling classes with the technology of physical and mental repression and the ensuing obliteration of human values. The very abundance which can liberate man from want and drudgery now enables the state to establish millions of technologically unemployed—forgotten, faceless outcasts on public "welfare," will be given only enough to keep them quiet. The very technology that has opened new roads to freedom, has also armed states with unimaginably frightful weapons for the annihilation of humanity.[83]

Dolgoff never wavers as he sails between the Scylla of anarchist nostalgia and the Charybdis of anarcho-futuristic daydreams, always arriving back into safe harbor. For despite his ambivalence, he belongs to the more modern social revolutionary anarchists who are in the process of emancipating themselves from utopia. Dolgoff's adherence to seemingly old-fashioned concepts—class analysis, anticapitalism, and social revolution—as well as his courage to stand up for the most unpopular positions, and his defiance of every kind of authority have kept this revolutionary veteran young. His autobiography ends as follows:

> I am only too well aware of my shortcomings, but I have been able to bear up under such circumstances, because people afraid to act because they might make a mistake will never do anything—and that would be the biggest mistake of all.[84]

Noam Chomsky—A "Fellow Traveler" of Anarcho-Syndicalism

Noam Chomsky once said that he usually either stands completely alone in his political opinions or belongs to a very tiny minority. He is known not only as a distinguished linguist, but also as a critic of US imperialism, Stalinism, and Israeli foreign policy. The fact that his social theories have always contained anarcho-syndicalist and council communist positions is usually overlooked.

I met with Noam Chomsky at the Massachusetts Institute of Technology in Boston. Although he holds one of the distinguished positions generally reserved for Nobel prize winners, his study is small and modestly furnished. Chomsky is a friendly, unconventional man; he was wearing jeans, sneakers, and a checkered shirt. He makes his own coffee and treats the institute's secretaries as equals. He is the opposite of how one typically would imagine an famous scientist whose books are translated into at least ten languages. He has the unpretentious manner of a person whose political opinions were formed in real life rather than at Harvard, and he is in fact critical of the elitism of many academics and intellectuals. In his book *America and the New Mandarins,* published in 1969, Chomsky attacks the "abuse of knowledge and technique" in a "society that encourages specialization and stands in awe of technical expertise."[85] He blames power-hungry technocrats, who he calls the new mandarins, for participating in the planning of the Vietnam War. The

83. Sam Dolgoff, *The Relevance of Anarchism to Modern Society.* Minneapolis: Soil of Liberty, 1977-79, p. 20.
84. Sam Dolgoff, *Fragments: A Memoir.* Cambridge, MA: Refract Publications, 1986, p. 167.
85. Noam Chomsky, *American Power and the New Mandarins.* New York: Pantheon Books, 1969, pp. 25-26.

Sam Dolgoff

Noam Chomsky

"counterrevolutionary subordination"[86] of the "house-ideologues for those in power"[87] is not surprising, he says, because ideology is in general merely the "mask for self-interest"[88] in a comfortable position in society. He quotes Bakunin's visionary critique of technocracy and Rosa Luxemburg's warnings about the Bolshevik elite in order to compare the opportunism of Leninist and liberal intellectuals. He uses the Spanish Civil War as an example of how Bolshevism and Western liberalism were united in their opposition to the anarchists' social revolution, and how the historians of these ideologies falsified history. Unlike Bakunin's, Chomsky's critique of intellectuals is directed only against the misuse of intellect and knowledge. He is very vocal in his rejection of the traditional anarchist mistrust of science per se.

Chomsky's critique of successive American administrations begins with their restorative post-war policies which did their best to destroy or dismantle the antifascist resistance movements. He also attacks the plundering of the Third World on behalf of the economic and political interests of the American power elites as well as the demonization as communists of anyone opposed to these policies. He directs his careful analysis and sharp judgment to the economy of military-industrial production and to the sabre-rattling anti-communism of the Cold War with Moscow.

> The ritual denunciation of the so-called "socialist" states is replete with distortions and often outright lies. Nothing is easier than to denounce the official enemy and to attribute to it any crime.[89]

His critique of socialism in its Leninist-Bolshevik form is just as sharp as that of capitalism. He calls Leninism a "particularly obscene variant"[90] of the idea that the ignorant masses must be ruled in their own interest by those allegedly more intelligent. In his eyes, this began with the Bolshevik coup, which followed the early phase of the Russian revolution and its "elements of a potential socialist society,"[91] in order to destroy these elements, i.e., the factory committees, the councils, and the union movement, to militarize work, and to establish a "totalitarian commanded economy run by a kind of new class of bureaucrats and managers."[92] Chomsky says that this society—created by Lenin and Trotsky and perfected by Stalin—never had anything in common with socialism. The assumption that it was socialist survived because of the propaganda interests of both the US and the USSR.

> The Soviet leadership thus portrays itself as socialist to protect its right to wield the club, and Western ideologists adopt the same pretense in order to forestall the

---

86.   Ibid., p. 28.
87.   Ibid., p. 30.
88.   Ibid., p. 72.
89.   Noam Chomsky, quoted in *Our Generation*, vol. 17, no. 2, Spring 1986, p. 48.
90.   Noam Chomsky, interview with the author, 1988.
91.   Ibid.
92.   Ibid.

threat of a more free and just society. This joint attack on socialism has been highly effective in undermining it in the modern period.[93]

Like Orwell, Rocker, and other anarchists, Chomsky criticizes capitalism and state socialism and uses the term totalitarianism to describe both "systems of bureaucratic power." He interprets the Cold War as an understanding between the superpowers to maintain, for its own sake, the fictional threat of mutual destruction.

> Thus the enemies became partners who fully agreed to divide up the world among them. . . . While the Soviet Union could blame their intervention in Afghanistan on the threat of American imperialism, the US blamed the threat of Soviet communism for its intervention in Grenada.[94]

Chomsky, who subscribes to anarchism because, among other things, its theorists are the only ones who have recognized totalitarianism as the "real basis of our age,"[95] never fell into the conservative trap lurking behind this viewpoint. About the late writings of Rudolf Rocker he says:

> I wonder whether he was simply swept up in the extraordinary postwar propaganda campaign organized by the West, by far the most powerful, extensive, and I think, most successful, in history.[96]

At the time of my interview with Chomsky, in the spring of 1989, the US seemed to be gripped by a sort of Gorbachev fever. Even before his visit to the United States, Gorbachev was being widely celebrated as a hero of peace and liberty. Liberals, left liberals, and former New Leftists alike saw the dawn of peace rising in the East, and eulogized his concepts of a mixed economy, *glasnost,* and *perestroika.* Chomsky did not join this chorus. In his view, the Soviet leader's interest in change represented "the recognition that the command system under the totalitarian structure will not enable the Soviet empire . . . to survive in the modern world."[97] Hence *glasnost's* tendency towards opening the political system, whereas *perestroika* would produce an industrial restructuring of the type "forced down the throats" of Third World countries by the International Monetary Fund (IMF). Chomsky says that *glasnost,* as democratic change, and *perestroika,* as a supercapitalist, mandatory industrial reform, are mutually exclusive processes. Chomsky is indeed a political maverick: he offends both traditional and reformed Moscow communists with his categorical rejection of Bolshevism; he scares the conservatives with his unswerving anticapitalism; and to those who believe that a free market and a welfare state can coexist he is a bitter pill to swallow.

Noam Chomsky was born in Philadelphia in 1928. His parents were educators and Zionists deeply involved in Jewish cultural causes. He had working-class relatives in New York, who, for the most part unemployed, were active

---

93.   Noam Chomsky, quoted in *Our Generation*, vol. 17, no. 2, Spring 1986, p. 48.
94.   Noam Chomsky, *Arbeit, Sprache*. Mühlheim, 1986, p. 92. Quoted in *Le Monde Libertaire*, No. 455, Paris, 1982, translated by Danny Lewis.
95.   Ibid., p. 93.
96.   Noam Chomsky, letter to the author, 1989.
97.   Noam Chomsky, interview with the author, 1989.

communists or Trotskyists. Working class culture, he says, was at the time very much alive, and the discussions about Marx, Freud, the Budapest String Quartet, and Shakespeare in this environment could hold water to the Harvard Faculty Club. Beginning at the age of eleven, Chomsky often visited his relatives in New York, worked in his uncle's newsstand, and frequented the used book stores on Fourth Avenue, whose owners were often extremely interesting and politicized people. The libertarian socialists among them impressed him most of all. He had long discussions with them and with the anarchists from the *Freie Arbeiterstimme,* a Jewish anarchist newspaper. During that period he came across Diego Abad Santillan's book *After the Revolution,* which influenced his understanding of anarchism. His first article, published in 1939 in a school newspaper, dealt with the dangers of fascism and its tacit agreement with Western democracies, especially in Spain.

As a youth, Chomsky was also interested in left-wing, antistatist Zionism, which was striving for a bi-national, socialist Palestine and the cooperative labor system of the early Jewish settlers—a political position which today would be considered anti-Zionist rather than Zionist, he adds with resignation. He could not identify with the leftist Zionist youth groups of the day, because they were either Stalinist or Trotskyist. In 1953 Chomsky faced the same problem with his collectivist comrades during a stay of several months in a kibbutz— some of them even defended the late Stalinist purges that were motivated primarily by anti-Semitism.

Early in his life Chomsky personally experienced the fascist variety of anti-Semitism. His was the only Jewish family in a German-Irish-Catholic neighborhood full of anti-Semites and Nazi sympathizers. He and his brother were afraid to leave the house when the Catholics came home from school. These same people, Chomsky relates, became glowing American patriots after Pearl Harbor. Later he was very skeptical about the patriotic interpretation of World War II. He recalls, for example, the sport of high school mates to taunt German POWs across the barbed wire of a camp near his high school. He himself found such behavior repugnant, although he was much more consistent in his opposition to Nazism than his neighbors. Another key experience, he continues, was to watch the political gyrations of his leftist relatives following the Hitler-Stalin Pact and Hitler's attack on the Soviet Union. The political views and insights he gained during that period have been little modified since.

In the mid-1960s Chomsky became active in the movement against the Vietnam War. It was largely impossible at the time to publish views critical of the war, so he spoke at hundreds of events and supported the network of conscientious objectors. He was arrested at the demonstrations in Washington in front of the Department of Justice and the Pentagon in 1967 and spent a night in jail. Chomsky still passionately defends the brave young men who risked exile and prison to protest the dirty imperialist Vietnam War. He was also active in the civil rights movement and in groups supporting the Black Panthers. There were some criminal elements in the Panthers, he says, but it was the representatives of the constructive factions, not the criminals, who were persecuted and murdered by the FBI. This, Chomsky says, was the establishment's answer to the movements of the 1960s whose social and grassroots democratic character were a source of fear for the privileged classes. Chomsky feels that the current portrayals and interpretations of the New Left, to which he credits a "revival of anarchist thinking,"[98] are wrong. Books on the subject are either written by former presidents and other leading personalities of the SDS (Students for a Democratic Society) or by people who fear the movement and its challenge to authority. In both cases the writings on the subject have little to do with what really happened. The New Left itself, however, like all mass movements, had been formed by "people who are unknown and who disappear from history."[99] Later, others who wait until the hard initial work is completed take over and become the leaders, speakers, and teachers of ideas of such movements, thanks to their privilege of education. Looking back, Chomsky says of the New Left:

> It was very diverse in character ranging from real craziness to very courageous and dedicated and constructive work. . . . But the point is that at every point it was part of a challenge to authority.[100]

Everything was questioned, from styles of clothing to music to philosophy and the authoritarian structures of the country—all of which had a permanent effect on US society, which is much more open and free today because of it. As an example Chomsky cites the Iran-Contra affair, during which the Reagan administration felt that it had to do its dirty business "clandestinely" simply because Reagan could no longer afford to do the kind of things openly that Kennedy and Johnson got away with. Chomsky adds that the New Left must be credited with publicizing the treatment of Native Americans as genocide, which until the 1960s had been either silenced or portrayed as "cowboy-and-Indian stories."

Despite his unwavering sympathy with the New Left, Chomsky never shared its unconditional identification with Third World revolutionaries. As a libertarian socialist and internationalist (much like the Old Left anarchists) he rejects the authoritarian Leninism of most Third World revolutionary movements and believes that there is more to be learned from the Spanish revolutionaries; but, unlike others he unconditionally stands in solidarity with anti-imperialist liberation movements, whose libertarian elements, he notes, are always the first to fall victim to imperialism, as can be seen in Cuba and Nicaragua. So the US did not lose the Vietnam War, but attained its objectives, contrary to public perception. This discriminating view, coupled with the fact

98.   Noam Chomsky, *America and the New Mandarins*. Op.cit., p. 19.
99.   Noam Chomsky, interview with the author, 1989.
100. Ibid.

that he could not accept the neo-Leninist cadre groups and the militancy of certain sections of the movement, earned him the reputation among radical activists of being a reformist, while at the same time the establishment continues to fear him—as evidenced by the fact that during the Watergate scandal Chomsky was on Nixon's list of enemies.

In spite of the corporate American media, which accepts Chomsky as a linguist while boycotting him as a political commentator, he has never ceased speaking out against capitalism and imperialism. He was one of very few, for instance, who condemned US cooperation with Saddam Hussein years before the latter decided to bite the hand that fed him—at the time a very unpopular position. "He was a moderate," Chomsky writes bitterly.

> Of course, he had constructed perhaps the most violent and repressive state in the world. He was torturing, murdering and killing Kurds. But it didn't matter, he was good for business.[101]

In the fall of 1990 it was again Chomsky who was one of the first leftist American intellectuals to condemn the Bush administration's double standards. Saddam Hussein, he says, was only perceived as the "new Hitler" because he had stepped on the "wrong toes." Before, during, and after the war Chomsky pointed again and again to the destructive role of the US in the UN Security Council. He refers to Bush's alleged attempts to keep the peace while posing ultimatums as "the rejection of diplomacy," which could only be considered diplomacy in a "post-Orwellian world."[102] He notes that the rulers of the deeply indebted US were not concerned with oil or oil prices, but with oil profits. Chomsky was also the first to call the role of the US in Bush's new world order that of a "mercenary state." Since the demise of the Soviet Union as America's competitor, according to Chomsky's often quoted prognosis, the US will devote even more energy than in the past to playing watchdog to ensure the obedience of Third World countries, because its monopoly on force is practically all that is left to it as a decaying world power. However, Japan and Europe will have to foot the bill, Chomsky adds.

Chomsky refers to himself as a "fellow traveler of anarcho-syndicalism." In his article "Remarks on Anarchism," which became the preface to Daniel Guérin's book *Anarchism* he writes:

> The consistent anarchist, then, should be a socialist, but a socialist of a particular sort. He will not only oppose alienated and specialized labor and look forward to the appropriation of capital by the whole body of workers, but he will also insist that this appropriation be direct, not exercised by some elite force acting in the name of the proletariat.[103]

---

101. Noam Chomsky, *The New World Order*. Westfield, NJ: *Open Magazine*, 1991, p. 5.
102. Noam Chomsky, ibid., p. 9.
103. Noam Chomsky, *Remarks on Anarchism*, in *The New York Review of Books*, May 21, 1970, p. 34.

Here he is recalling Bakunin, who in the program for the revolutionary brotherhood calls for all members to be socialists first and foremost. Besides Rocker, whom he considers to be the last important anarchist thinker, Chomsky refers to the liberalism of the enlightenment, with such representatives as Jean Jacques Rousseau (1712–1818), Emanuel Kant (1724–1804), and Wilhelm von Humboldt (1767–1835), as another source of anarchism or libertarian socialism. They all, he says, fought for the liberation of mankind against the rule of powerful institutions such as feudalism, the state, and the church. Though these writers had in their day no notion of capitalism, with its new forms of power and domination, Humboldt nonetheless anticipated Marx's early writings on the alienation of labor.

For Chomsky, anarcho-syndicalist society will be characterized by production conceived and carried out by the producers and their councils. Another important notion is that the state is in and of itself an instrument of repression. Chomsky also stresses the modernity of anarcho-syndicalist forms of organization as suitable for industrial society. All of this, he says, is very similar to council communism and libertarian Marxism in the tradition of Rosa Luxemburg, Anton Pannekoek, Hermann Gorter, Karl Korsch, and Paul Mattik. "Radical Marxism," he writes, "merges with anarchist currents"[104]—certainly a heretical thought for dogmatic anarchists and communists alike, who agree, most of the time, in their insistence on continuing their age-old feud.

When I asked him about the right-wing versions of anarchism, Chomsky strongly rejected their laissez-faire capitalist antistatism. For him the only legitimate heirs to the legacy of bourgeois liberalism are the libertarian social- ists with their opposition to power per se, not just state power. He attributes the anarcho-capitalists' success to the broken promise of right-wing conservatism in the Reagan-Thatcher era. The neoconservatives hoped to gain greater credibility from the popularity of "right"-libertarian antistatism, for the notion of preserving capitalism without state force is an illusion:

> The predatory forces of the market would destroy society, would destroy community, and destroy the workforce. Nothing would be left except people hating each other and fighting each other.[105]

When asked for a general definition of anarchism, Chomsky referred again to Rocker. He sees a historical tendency towards recognizing and overcoming repressive and authoritarian structures, from slavery to women's repression, and believes that its realization is anarchism. Anarchists are people who radically question the principle of authority everywhere—in the economy, the community, the family—and who consider it "an insult to human nature."[106] In using the term "nature," he is referring to Rousseau's assumption of the innate human

---

104. Ibid., p. 34.
105. Noam Chomsky, interview with the author, 1989.
106. Ibid.

capacity for self-perfection and the latter's evolutionary character. Like Bakunin, Kropotkin, and others he deduces from that principle a human instinct of freedom. Unlike his predecessors, however, Chomsky believes that for the time being we can only speculate about its existence. He hopes that science will one day shed more light on human nature and the kind of society for which it is suited. As a linguist he claims to have only a few answers to one aspect of human nature, language:

> I think it is clear beyond any question that the systems of knowledge that we attain, in particular, knowledge of language, are based on genetically determined structures that are simply realized in the course of development in many respects. Our language is like a circulatory system. It grows in a particular way because of our biological endowment modified a little bit by the environment in which the person develops. And I think the same is true of other systems of common sense understanding and recognition of personality and identification of social structures and so on.[107]

I asked him whether the notion of a predetermined human nature could easily be misused for the purpose of legitimizing that which is given: authority, inequality, exploitation, and racism. Chomsky admitted that though this is often the case, it does not spring from the assumption of a human nature, but from various other assumptions. For example, the assumption that people are different from each other because they are male or female, or white or black, or the moral notion that people should be treated differently according to racial or other norms. Tests show that the ability for language is slightly better developed in women than in men, but, Chomsky notes, to conclude from this that only women should become writers would be idiotic. On the other hand, he continued, one might ask why so many progressive people, including Marx, have declared human nature to be a purely historical product. Why do they prefer to see people as "unshaped matter, formless, unstructured, incompetent?"[108]

Why do they insist on believing this, although all evidence is to the contrary? The fear of playing into the hands of racists is not reason enough to ignore the truth. Chomsky suspects that the real reason for rejecting the existence of human nature is the conclusion that otherwise there would be no moral barriers to the manipulation of humans, thus legitimizing the favorite pastime of intellectuals: controlling people for their own good. If there is such a thing as a natural, instinctive longing for self-determination, then we must find out how much of human ability to judge and discern is rooted in human nature, whether "slavery is wrong because it violates human nature"[109] or because it is economically obsolete. Up until now, Chomsky stresses, we have only been able to draw approximate analogies from what we have learned in the linguistic and cognitive areas; one day, however, these inquiries might produce results which "would

---

107. Ibid.
108. Noam Chomsky, interview with the author, 1988.
109. Ibid.

enable us to ground our moral judgements on something stronger than our moral intuitions."[110]

He who thinks that authority and domination are wrong, says Chomsky, always has moral reasons for this position, reasons that must be based in human nature. In *America and the New Mandarins* Chomsky attributes an "irreducible moral element" to the resistance against the Vietnam War "that admits of little discussion."[111] He hopes that people who engage in nonviolent resistance will "become humans of a more admirable sort."[112] And he quotes Einstein, who referred to the "War Resistance League" of the 1950s as a moral elite. To my skeptical questions about the function of such an elite, Chomsky replied that there is hardly anyone who does not consider himself to be moral. Himmler's speeches, for instance, oozed morality. Though people have always found ways to morally justify anything, no matter how murderous, this is no reason to turn one's back on morality. In an attempt to save Einstein's moral elite from my suspicion of being a self-named avant-garde, Chomsky commented:

> They were saying, we think what is happening is monstrous. And we are willing to suffer for our opposition to it. And we would like you to follow us.[113]

Chomsky has never shied away from criticizing "his own," such as intellectuals or Americans. He criticizes Israel, he once said, not despite of but because of his Jewishness, which makes him feel all the more morally responsible. There is no question that moral indignation and feelings of responsibility have always been the main engine behind the political involvement of privileged intellectuals. Whether this can be generalized, as Chomsky does in the Rousseauian tradition by arguing innate goodness or morality, is, in my view, a more difficult question to answer. Where does the resistance of the disenfranchised, the outcast, the starving, the exploited come from in the end? From physical-economic scarcity or from moral need? And is it not precisely this resistance from below that changes society—as all anarchists from Bakunin to Chomsky believe? What is exactly the relationship between hunger and a sense of justice? How important or unimportant is the morality of intellectuals, how relevant their commitment to action within the framework of class struggles? These questions will most likely not be answered by mere knowledge about the existence or nonexistence of human nature.

Crucial to Chomsky's moral responsibility is his unconditional defense of free speech and the civil rights of everybody whose opinions put him at a disadvantage. His position on this question is similar to the hard-line ACLU's view that it is necessary to defend the rights of Nazis to demonstrate in a Jewish neighborhood, as was the case in Skokie, Illinois, about a decade ago. In line

---

110. Ibid.
111. Noam Chomsky, *America and the New Mandarins.* Op.cit. p. 380.
112. Ibid., p. 375.
113. Noam Chomsky, interview with the author, 1988.

with his principles, Chomsky has signed countless petitions for the protection of civil rights, even when those being protected were religious chauvinists or imperialist war criminals. This basic principle led to a big scandal in the case of the French literature professor Robert Faurisson, who claims that there were no gas chambers in Nazi concentration camps. Faurisson was prosecuted in France for falsifying history and lost his university job. Chomsky signed a neutrally-formulated petition defending Faurisson's civil rights (but not his statements). In the course of the controversy which grew out of this petition, Chomsky was accused of sharing Faurisson's views. At one point Chomsky wrote a letter to a friend who had joined the ranks of those criticizing him. In the letter he made clear that he was concerned only with Faurisson's civil rights, and he accused the French intellectual community of a lack of civil rights consciousness. This letter, written in 1980, was later reprinted in a book by Faurisson in which he defended himself against the charge of historical falsification. Because of the emotionally charged atmosphere surrounding the controversy, Chomsky withdrew his permission to reprint the letter, but it was too late to prevent its publication. The rumor that Chomsky has written a preface to one of Faurisson's books stubbornly refuses to die. In a letter to me about this, Chomsky writes:

> I have only one regret: that when I learned of Faurisson's "memoir," I asked to have my comments on freedom of speech excluded from it. That was unprincipled. If some gangster like Rostow or Henry Kissinger were to be denied a teaching position on the grounds of his activities as a war criminal, or brought to trial because he lies outrageously and denies not only past but—far more importantly—ongoing atrocities, I would have no hesitation (as in the Rostow case) to defend his rights.[114]

Similar to Albert Einstein and Franz Oppenheimer, Noam Chomsky combines scientific brilliance with a social and moral conscience and the courage to be a political activist. He belongs to those people of integrity who have made their mark on the history of anarchism since the days of Kropotkin. His voluntaristic concept of human nature capable of perfecting its innate goodness originates in the utopianism of the 18th and early 19th centuries. Chomsky came to anarchism via early Zionism which was characterized by early socialism. As a realistic critic and social analyst concerned about the here and now he found his way to anarcho-syndicalism; as an antiauthoritarian and an opponent to war he was active in the social movements of the 1960s. His belief in the efficacy of ethical principles reflects the greatest strength and greatest weakness of both anarchism and the American New Left. In modern anarchism he plays the role of a mediator between the Old and the New Left. In his loyal criticism of the Leninist-nationalist ideologies of Third World liberation movements, he moves beyond the dogmatic ignorance of the Old Left and the blind identification of young antiauthoritarians.

114. Noam Chomsky, letter to the author, 1990.

2   ECO-ANARCHISM

An Encounter with Murray Bookchin and the Greens of Vermont

In Germany as well as in the United States, Murray Bookchin is a household name among anarchists and ecologists. Especially in Germany Bookchin's redefinition of anarchism in ecological terms has revived interest in it, and his writings played an important role in the early alternative movement. Today many anarchists and members of the ecology and Green movements believe in the form of anarchism he advocates. In the US many regard him as an important philosopher and activist representative of both the New Left and the ecology movement. The historian of anarchism, Paul Avrich, refers to him with deep respect, Russell Jacoby portrays him in a positive light in his book *The Last Intellectuals,* and Sam Dolgoff, despite major theoretical differences, considered him a "bold thinker."

Social Ecology and Deep Ecology

In the late 1980s Bookchin became known for his critique of irrationalist and antihumane eco-fundamentalism. His temperamental attacks were directed against Earth First!, especially against a faction that evolved around the group's charismatic leader Dave Foreman. Foreman, who in the 1960s belonged to William Buckley's youth organization YAF (Young Americans for Freedom) and worked as an electoral assistant to Senator Berry Goldwater, in the 1970s became a lobbyist for the Wilderness Society. Disillusioned with the organization for its reformism and its corporate hierarchical structure, he founded Earth First! together with four other radical outsiders of the mainstream ecological movement, among them Edward Abbey, the author of the eco-sabotage novel *The Monkey Wrench Gang.*

Civil disobedience, romantic glorification of rough wilderness, hard-drinking male chauvinism, redneck ideology, and Wild West jingoism were the group's outlook—according to its own cherished legend it first met in a New Mexican whorehouse. The group settled in Tucson, founded the newspaper *Earth First!,* and got involved in the protection of old-growth forests. It was organized in a loose-knit structure and used the direct action tactics described in Abbey's novel, including such Luddite tactics of "ecotage" as tree-spiking. In spite of its anticommunist, antileftist, and anti-labor stance, Earth First!'s male-dominated founding generation (not to be confused with the people around Judy Bari) often referred to itself as anarchist and established a matching ideology, which they called Deep Ecology. This term, introduced by the Danish ecologist Arne Naess, originally designated all non-reformist ecological thought including Murray Bookchin's. Until today its prime tenet is ecocentrism as opposed to anthropocentrism. In the Foreman version the idea of biological egalitarianism became misanthropic: "Down with people!" is said to be one of the Earth First!er campfire battle cries. Its critique of technology, in combination with a voracious nostalgia advocating a return to the Stone Age, regards everything since the invention of the pulley as the devil's work. Foreman, whom his admirers like to compare to a bear, wants to preserve the natural world for its own sake, not for any benefit to humanity. He views himself as a "warrior" against the "human pox"[115] on our planet. This goes well with some of his favorite slogans: "back to the Pleistocene, dream back the bison, sing back the swan," and "far too many human beings on Earth (Malthus was right)."[116]

During the late 1980s a string of outrageously inhumane and racist remarks appeared in the organization's magazine. Commenting on one of the most dreadful African famines in recent times, Forman agrees with Thomas Malthus's theory that poverty is the result of the overpopulation of the poor:

> The worst thing we could do in Ethiopia is to give aid—the best thing would be to just let nature seek its own balance, to let the people there just starve.[117]

Neo-Malthusianism, neglectful of the fact that population growth declines as soon as the living standard rises, played a role in the European prefascist and fascist context that fostered racism, social Darwinism, genocidal fantasies, and euthanasia. (The Nazis believed that a life not "worthy to be lived" should be ended, and in the name of euthanasia they killed thousands of imbecile and crippled children, mentally ill men and women, beginning shortly after the fascist empowerment.) During the cold war Neo-Malthusianism was revived by conservative European and American policy-makers who realized that foreign aid to Third World countries would not eradicate poverty and that poverty was leading to social revolutionary, often communist movements and insurrections. From that time on the rulers of the industrialized countries have linked foreign aid programs to population control. This has led and still leads to cruel sterilization campaigns: In India under Indira Ghandi and her son Sanja's regime, men and women were kidnapped and forcibly sterilized. In El Salvador,

---

115. Dave Foreman, quoted in Christopher Manes, *Green Rage*. Boston: Little, Brown and Company, 1990, p.84.
116. Dave Foreman, quoted in *Earth First!*, June 21, 1987.
117. Dave Foreman, in *Simply Living*, vol. 2, No. 12, 1987.

for instance, women have been sterilized without their knowledge after having giving birth in the context of a development program funded and established by the International Planned Parenthood Federation. Others were refused treatment in government hospitals unless they agreed to have themselves sterilized.[118]

As problematic as Foreman's Malthusianism is his view that it is ecologically necessary to put an end to immigration:

> Letting the USA be an overflow valve for problems in Latin America is not solving a thing . . . It is just causing more destruction of our wilderness.[119]

Like Foreman, the late Edward Abbey, who referred to himself not only as an anarchist, but also as a "national chauvinist" or the "Ezra Pound of the ecology movement," is opposed to immigration. He warns against the "brown hordes," which will overrun America:

> It might be wise for us American citizens to consider calling a halt to the mass influx of even more millions of hungry, ignorant, unskilled, and culturally-morally-genetically impoverished people.[120]

Another viewpoint, more global than this familiar kind of national chauvinism, was presented in articles published under the pseudonym "Miss Ann Thropy" (read misanthropy). In a 1987 article, which unleashed a heated controversy in the leftist and left-liberal press, Miss Ann Thropy says that the only way of restoring nature's health is to re-establish the hunter-gatherer society. This requires a decrease in population to 20 percent of its current level in order to successfully disrupt "industrialism," which needs a certain number of producers and consumers to function properly:

> Capital dries up, governments lose authority, power fragments and devolves onto local communities which can't affect natural cycles on a large scale.[121]

According to this theory eliminating both workers and capitalism would destroy industrial capital. The article culminates in hailing AIDS as a cure against overpopulation.

> If radical environmentalists were to invent a disease to bring human population back to ecological sanity, it would probably be something like AIDS.[122]

Just as the plague contributed to the downfall of feudalism, Miss Ann Thropy thinks, AIDS could become an even more potent cure to today's industrialism, for this modern-day plague effects only humans without harming other living

---

118. See Bill Weinberg, *War on the Land, Ecology and Politics in Central America*. London: Zed Books Ltd., 1991.
119. Dave Foreman, in *Simply Living*, vol. 2, No.12, 1987.
120. Edward Abbey, quoted in *Fifth Estate*, No. 12, 1988.
121. Miss Ann Thropy, in *Earth First!*, May 1, 1987.
122. Ibid.

beings and its comparatively long incubation period lets it spread across the globe more slowly, thus more effectively.

To Murray Bookchin goes the credit for being one of the first to call these neo-Malthusian misanthropes what they are: "barely disguised racists, survivalists . . . outright social reactionaries"[123] and "macho mountain-men like Dave Foreman, who writes in *Earth First!*, a . . . journal that styles itself as the voice of a wilderness-oriented movement of the same name—that 'humanity' is a cancer in the world of life."[124]

For them, Bookchin says, nature is like "a beautiful view from a mountain top."[125] He is convincing in his sharp analysis of the primitivism in the theories of ecologists who, he says, utterly abandon any concept of social analysis and equate humans and animals, as well as living beings and inanimate objects. Conflicts of class and race have no place in their theories. Everything is thrown together and cooked into one big potpourri, leaving behind the murky idea of some original sin against nature. Bookchin counters the glorification of the feudal Middle Ages and its alleged exemplary autarchy, simple life, and spirituality with an analysis of the hierarchical nature of feudal society, under whose yoke the vast majority suffered bitterly. He does a great service in his untiring effort to open the eyes of environmentalists ignorant of history to the "problem of overpopulation." He asserts, slightly simplifying matters, that Hitler and Himmler as Malthusians exterminated six million Jews in the name of overpopulation and had plans to exterminate all Slavic peoples as well. After a controversy at the national congress of American Greens in 1987 Bookchin and his followers decided to refer to their own philosophy as Social Ecology to stress their concern about social problems and their conviction that capitalism is the source of both social and ecological destruction. Bookchin has been accused of unfair and unjust criticism of Earth First! because he equates the Foreman/Abbey faction with the whole group and the former's ideology with Deep Ecology. His accusation of "eco-fascism" was quoted in the *New York Times* shortly after Dave Foreman was arrested and charged with conspiracy in June 1989 in the context of an ecotage-action committed by other Earth First!ers.

By the late 1980s the cowboy-and-redneck faction around Foreman and Abbey, whose racist statements caused the neo-fascist Tom Metzger to boast that his own organization "made dents with the Earth First! movement,"[126] was faced with a grassroots opposition rapidly developing in northern California. Mike Roselle, one of the founding members who had been active with the Yippies, became one of the spokespersons of this new faction, together with Judy Bari, a former New Leftist and union activist. These Northern California Earth First!ers

---

123. Murray Bookchin, *"Social Ecology versus Deep Ecology,"* Green Program Project, undated, p. 12.
124. Ibid., pp. 12-13.
125. Murray Bookchin, interview with the author, 1989.
126. Tom Metzger, quoted in *The Village Voice*, July 25, 1989.

combined pacifism, New Age spirituality, and vague ideas of anarchism with a passion for social change. Referring to the founding group, Bari said she was "appalled by this macho image and their anti-labor attitude."[127] She, Roselle, and others distanced themselves from that group's comments about AIDS, Ethiopia, and closing national borders. They even entered into a coalition with the IWW, whose members were attracted to Earth First!'s militancy and direct-action tactics. At the national Earth First! meeting in 1989 some of the new activists burned an American flag, in contradistinction to the cowboy faction, which never failed to hoist it during their meetings. In 1990 Northern California Earth First!ers began their campaign for the protection of the redwood forests which—unlike the forests for whose survival the other faction had fought—were private property. Bari tried to forge an alliance with the loggers who were regarded as natural enemies by the cowboys. The campaign climaxed in the "Redwood Summer" project which drew its inspiration from the Mississippi Summer of 1964. To win over the loggers Bari declared a moratorium on monkey-wrenching and publicly disavowed tree-spiking. Shortly thereafter in May 1990, she and her husband Darryl Cherney were severely injured by a bomb in their car. The homes of other activists were raided by the FBI, supporters were detained, and the two victims were arrested and charged with having committed the attack themselves.

In 1990 Earth First! finally split. The Northern California faction took over the magazine, and the Foreman group, now in the minority, founded the *Wild Earth Journal*. This development went hand in hand with the rise of a new generation of deep ecologists; Roderick Nash, for instance, who views radical environmentalism as a means to include non-human species in the agenda of minorities and exploited groups whose rights must be fought for. Then there is Andrew McLaughlin, who attempts to unite deep ecologists and social activists by holding that deep ecology is compatible with both socialism and anarchism. He mentions the conservation movement in the early Soviet Union, sharply criticizes neo-Malthusians for opposing foreign aid, and insists that radical ecologists ought to side with the poor. Despite adhering to the deep-ecologist principle of the need to decrease human population, he somewhat contradictorily concedes that "the best way to moderate and then reverse the growth of human population is to find ways of providing a decent life for all."[128]

Irrespective of these new tendencies in the American ecology movement, many still believe that Malthusianism is leftist and humanitarian. Activists and authors of the Foreman type are still influential. In 1990 Christopher Manes (aka Miss Ann Thropy) published a book in which he not only cites Dave Foreman's most problematic remarks, but also refers positively to the German eco-reactionary Herbert Gruhl and his book *A Planet Gets Plundered (Ein Planet*

127. Judy Bari, quoted in Susan Zakin, *Coyotes and Town Dogs*. New York: Viking, 1993, p. 353.
128. Andrew McLaughlin, *Regarding Nature*, New York: State University of New York Press, 1993, p. 182.

wird geplündert). Gruhl had unsuccessfully tried to infiltrate the German Greens before he founded the rightwing ÖDP (Ecological Democratic Party) in 1982. Gruhl's vision is a strong nation state which, faced with the ecological crisis, must sort things by imposing its will on various (allegedly unjustified and useless) agendas of individuals and special interest groups. Manes plays off Gruhl's outspoken anti-social politics against the German Green Party with its sense of social responsibility stemming from the New Left:

> The new left has a constituency of the poor and powerless, whose very real present needs sometimes demand policies incompatible with ending industrial growth. [129]

Manes insists on politics designed to reverse population growth because he sees "limits to how many people can live in dignity on this planet." Indeed the majority of humans, the "poor and the powerless," do not live in dignity. Is Manes, who believes that nature's interests are incompatible with those of the poor, suggesting (as Malthus did) that they should be starved to death? Or is he thinking of Pol Pot's successful depopulation and deurbanization of Cambodia? In the book's last chapter, "The Unmaking of Civilization," Manes depicts a desirable future of a drastically decreased world population and quotes Edward Abbey's "scattered human populations modest in number that live by fishing, hunting, food-gathering, small-scale farming and ranching, that assemble once a year in the ruins of abandoned cities."[130]

An Oasis of Enlightenment in Dark Times

I met Bookchin on a cold day in March in his small, wooden Victorian house. He lives in a suburb of Burlington, Vermont, which was once a center of leftist alternative activities—today it is a major yuppie stronghold set in a splendid mountain landscape.

Bookchin's yellow house has the aura of an oasis, filled with the spirit of humanist enlightenment and radical social involvement—a rare treat in our dark ages characterized by the return of clerical authority, social-Darwinist brutality, Puritan moralism, open racism, and misogyny. Bookchin and his friends clearly despise all the things that I feel threatened by on both sides of the Atlantic. They proudly refer to themselves as leftist, anticapitalist, and revolutionary. For hours on end I heard scathing criticism of neo-religiousness and New Age nonsense. Bookchin sadly quoted a like-minded author who has proven that superstition is more rampant in the US today than it was in Europe in the 14th century. He harbors a special distaste for Californian neo-gurus, who he calls "diaperheads." New Age harmony, he explains, leaves no room for controversy. Nowadays, he feels, everything is a question of motives, not reasons;

---

129. Christopher Manes, *Green Rage*. Boston: Little, Brown and Company, 1990, p. 132.
130. Edward Abbey, in Christopher Manes, *Green Rage*. Boston: Little, Brown and Company, 1990, p. 241.

and the rampant therapy mania in America has many running to a psychologist or professional counselor for the slightest problem instead of thinking and deciding for themselves. This, Bookchin complains, just like the nostalgia for the medieval age, the interest in mysticism, or the longing for the Neolithic Age of 10,000 years ago, is all part and parcel of the conservative backlash against the progressive social movements of the 1960s, of which Reaganism was but a symptom. "A whole generation has emerged," he says, "it is beginning to forget the 1960s and is accepting capitalism the way it accepts the snow outside like a natural fact."[131] Proudhon, Bakunin, and Kropotkin would be rolling in their graves if they knew what kinds of people call themselves anarchists today. He also curses his socialist competition in the city council; they are even worse than the German social democrats, he says. Nor does he have anything good to say about Jesse Jackson and the Rainbow Coalition.

I first saw Murray Bookchin when he was lecturing in Germany in the 1970s. He was wearing a loose tunic with a standup collar reminiscent of traditional Russian peasant shirts. His bohemian appearance and passionate oratory gave him the aura of a charismatic 19th-century revolutionary. Bookchin radiates energy, is always focused, and is willing to answer any question. When I met him later in Burlington I thought that he was likeable and interesting, as well as a witty narrator. He still likes to dress wildly. In the car he wore a heavy leather army jacket and a fashionable baseball cap. In the kitchen he wrapped a kitchen towel around his head and asked roguishly whether I thought he looked Jewish or Arab.

Ecofeminism

Later I met Bookchin's companion, the ecofeminist and anarchist Janet Biehl. The former New York actress and painter, about thirty years younger than he, wore an old hand-knit sweater, hiking shoes, a wool hat, and a backpack. Her outfit was misleading: my suspicion that she might be a nature romantic or a health fanatic proved false, as did my suspicion that the younger mate of a dominant person like Bookchin might be his intellectual creation. Biehl admitted to differing with Bookchin, especially on women's issues.

> Murray tends to argue that women's and men's differences are more biological than I am quite willing to allow yet. I think he means this in a very positive way. . . . I am weary of how these kinds of ideas have been historically used against women in the past.[132]

She is outspoken against feminist dogmas which claim that women are morally superior to men, or that misogyny is the root of all repression. She feels that it is not enough to eliminate misogyny, because "women are not going to be free until everybody is free."[133] She vigorously criticizes such conservative tendencies

---

131. Murray Bookchin, interview with the author, 1989.
132. Janet Biehl, interview with the author, 1989.
133. Ibid.

in radical disguise as the Italian concept of *affidamento*, a feminist version of the pedagogic/pederast Eros, or Lacan-disciple Luce Irigaray's theory that femininity is dual because of the labia's double nature.

In her articles Biehl warns against the depoliticizing effect of religion. In "Goddess Mythology in Ecological Politics," for example, she masterfully describes and criticizes the "feminist" religiousness to which large sections of the feminist movement have fallen prey since the mid-1970s. Alienation and stress, she writes, create a need that therapy and mysticism seem to satisfy, but the causes of distress giving rise to this need remain; as a matter of fact, the new religions serve only to stabilize the social conditions that are at the root of alienation. She believes that the new religions, which keep people in the dark, depart from the myth of a Neolithic paradise with its alleged egalitarian matriarchies and mother-goddess religions, and she attributes to the mythopoetic historians a "simplistic philosophical idealism, confusing religious symbols with religious institutions."[134]

In another passage she attacks everything now labeled ecofeminism, a term that Bookchin told me was coined at his Institute for Social Ecology. Biehl defines the original goal of ecofeminism as an effort to combine feminism, anarchism, libertarian socialism, and social ecology. Ecofeminism, she stresses, was once "above all leftist,"[135] but unfortunately did not remain so for very long:

> Ecofeminism has in fact abstracted women and nature out of left political theory and has thereby narrowed itself, dismissing serious critiques of capitalism and the nation-state and emphasizing personal transformation and even goddess-worship as sources of social change. . . . it has become not only antileftist but even reactionary.[136]

Biehl calls for the reintegration of the feminist movement into the political left, i.e., anticapitalist and antistate movements, and she feels that the difference between the sexes has been overemphasized. Social ecofeminism, she says, should take biological differences into account. She does not tell us, however, which differences between the sexes, other than giving birth, menstruation, and nursing, have their roots in nature rather than in society. Unanswered, too, remains the core issue of feminism and patriarchy about the notion that women are by nature nurturing. Biehl claims that women are, in fact, the keepers of the "ethics of care."[137] While she stresses that it is an anachronism to limit women to the home sphere, she insists that it is nonetheless a sphere which needs to be protected from capitalism. The fact that employers are increasingly organizing and paying for child day-care centers and the care of senior citizens is a sign that the principle of caring is being banished from the "private realm"[138] personified by women for thousands of years:

---

134. Janet Biehl, "Goddess Mythology In Ecological Politics," in *New Politics* VII, Winter 1989, p. 91.
135. Janet Biehl, "What is Social Ecofeminism," in *Green Perspectives*, No. 11, Oct. 1988, p. 1.
136. Ibid., p. 1.
137. Ibid., p. 5.
138. Ibid., p. 5.

Many women who would prefer raising children to working to earn a "rotten piece of the pie" . . . find it increasingly difficult to do so. . . . they work not because they want to but because they have to; nor are men any more able to stay home with children. Where once one income sufficed to support a family, two now scarcely do.[139]

Biehl believes that women have been less deformed by capitalism than men. Many of the characteristics that appear to be rooted in nature should be, in her view, preserved by women and regained by men. Biehl's simultaneous rejection of any missionary role for women does not change the two-edged character of her basic theory: it is only a short step from the notions of preserving the home sphere and female nurturing to that of the traditional family and the virtues of the female martyr sacrificing everything on the altar of motherhood.

A Revolutionary in Changing Times

At the beginning of our interview I asked Bookchin to briefly summarize his life. His response was a fascinating biographical, historical, and political sketch. His life and thought, despite obvious breaks, seem like a harmonious reflection of the history of his age. The story of his commitment begins with his grandmother's participation, as a social revolutionary, in the Russian Revolution of 1905. Persecuted in its dark aftermath, she was forced to emigrate. Bookchin's parents lived in New York and, like many Jews of their generation, worked in the sweatshops of the garment industry. During the October Revolution they became followers of Lenin. Bookchin, born in 1921, grew up watching his mother active in the IWW. Pictures of the assassins of Czar Alexander decorated his grandmother's room, and she told him stories about Emma Goldman and Alexander Berkman. He knew more about the Russian revolutionaries than about Robin Hood, "more about socialism and anarchism than . . . about America and American history."[140] At the age of nine he joined the Young Pioneers, the communist children's organization. At fourteen he was promoted to the communist youth group and was active in it until 1935. To my surprise, this eco-anarchist critic of communism painted a remarkably positive picture of the Communist Party of his day:

And I went through the communist movement during a period when the communists were very revolutionary. We used to call this the third period, because that meant the period of proletarian revolutions . . . after the second period which was one of bourgeois consolidation. We were extremely revolutionary at that time.[141]

According to Bookchin it was not until the Hitler-Stalin Pact that the American Communist Party became the reformist party of the Popular Front era, which it remained until World War II.

---

139. Ibid., p. 6.
140. Murray Bookchin, interview with the author, 1989.
141. Ibid.

Murray Bookchin

Janet Biehl

When the Spanish Civil War broke out, Bookchin joined the communists, because he thought that they were the most ardently antifascist. He tried to join the international brigades, but was rejected because of his youth. His skepticism toward the politics of the Popular Front grew, and in May, 1937, he refused to believe that the workers of Barcelona, who were shot down by both fascists and communists, could themselves be fascists. He was also very disturbed by the Moscow trials, and the subsequent execution of many of his "teachers." After completing school Bookchin went to work in a New Jersey steel factory and became active in union struggles. Disillusioned by Stalinism and expelled from the Communist Party in 1939, he worked with the Trotskyists until the late 1940s and wrote for several of their periodicals. One has to remember, he says looking back, that "in 1937 Trotsky stood alone against Stalin" and that he was a "heroic figure."[142] One might, of course, ask *why* that hero stood alone. Or is it not true that he, the butcher of Kronstadt and murderer of anarchists, had, together with his friend Lenin, already neutralized all of Stalin's potential opponents?

During World War II, Bookchin's Trotskyist position was anti-interventionist, or, as he calls it, Bolshevist. He seems to have been part of a small group which, unlike the two major factions of American Trotskyists, did not support World War II. In the union movement he belonged to the "rank and file faction"[143] unwilling to accept the agreement between Roosevelt and the unions to waive the right to strike during the war. He was a member of the UAW (United Auto Workers), which, according to him, was almost as radical as the IWW. Union democracy, he says, was still intact in those days until the three month strike of 1947, which marked a turning point:

> That was the end of the workers movement. When we came back from the strike, we were like servants of the government. We had pension plans, we had unemployment insurance, we had retirement benefits, health benefits. It was like working for the government. We had, in exchange, to work very hard. They increased productivity. . . . union democracy was destroyed. The presidents of the locals were paid by the company; not the union, but the company paid them.[144]

Convinced that the historical role of the labor movement had come to an end, Bookchin put the class struggle behind him. He took an office job, attended evening college, seminars, and courses, including one on the Frankfurt School. He was trained as a mechanic at a technical school. Though the working class, in his view, has degenerated, he has maintained his ties to it.

For him the 1950s were "a period of deep reaction in America. Nothing seemed to be happening, and so it was very difficult to function as a revolutionary."[145] He found a way out of those dark times through his studies

---

142. Ibid.
143. Ibid.
144. Ibid.
145. Ibid.

of ecology. In an essay he wrote in 1949, which seems to foresee all present ecological issues, he pointed out that the use of pesticides, chemical agriculture, and air pollution are serious problems caused by capitalism. At the time these calls in the wilderness went unheard in the US, but raised some interest in West Germany. In 1954 a German edition of Bookchin's writings entitled *Lebensgefährliche Lebensmittel (Fatal Food)* appeared under the pseudonym Lewis Herber. In the 1960s and 1970s, Bookchin developed the theory of ecological anarchism.

> And I felt that the changes that had to be made were not only to clean up the planet, but you had to clean up society. And you even had to clean up the human mind, which was structured around domination.[146]

What it was exactly that converted Bookchin to anarchism in the early 1960s is not entirely clear to me. Kropotkin had not been translated into English, he told me, his first acquaintance with classical anarchist theory was through secondary sources, but he worked out these ideas more and more by himself.

After the dry spell of the 1950s, Bookchin joined the New York chapter of the SDS. In retrospect he sees the student movement as libertarian, anarchist, and, most of all, American.

> The wonderful thing about the SDS was that it has spoken the American tradition. It tried to dig out from America what Americans could feel the idea of the American dream was. And one of the ideas of the American dream was the idea of an utopia, a new world that would be created on this virgin continent. And that ideal was often very anarchistic.[147]

As can be learned from his writings during his SDS period, however, Bookchin did not at the time expound Americanism—he was a defender of revolutionary youth, a critic of the Leninist and Maoist factions, and both an ecologist and anarchist. He founded the group "Radical Decentral Project," and together with his followers began publishing the magazine *Anarchos*. In 1969, the SDS's final year, he and his followers went to Chicago for its last congress and to meet with local anarchists from the IWW. Bookchin told me that the [failed] goal of his *Anarchos* group was to "revive the old SDS, bring it back to the American traditions."[148]

Like many old communists and anarchists Bookchin could identify neither with the liberation movements in the Third World nor with the Black Panthers at home. But unlike Dolgoff and Chomsky, whose positions on these issues differed from those held by the New Left, Bookchin never seems to have been interested in the issues of race or the Third World.

> The Vietnam war had a very bad effect upon the American Left. Everyone began to try on the Left to imitate Mao, or began to imitate Che Guevara and especially

---

146. Ibid.
147. Ibid.
148. Ibid.

Castro coming down from the mountains, that whole mythology of guerilla warfare. I realized that was absurd in America. In fact, 90% of the American people absolutely couldn't understand any of this.[149]

Regarding the fate of his *Anarchos* group he says that

the organization was destroyed essentially by the Marxists and by the Black Panthers, the militant black organization which came in and intervened and sort of guilted the white middle class students into obeying its position.[150]

One might ask whether it was the Vietnam War that had a "bad effect upon the American Left" and whether the Black Panthers really destroyed *Anarchos*. Didn't the American left revive and radicalize itself over the Vietnam War? And is it not true that white racists, not black militants, aroused the guilty conscience of the white middle class, with all the ramifications that followed? At any rate, Bookchin left New York in 1970. Since then he has had a love-hate relationship with his native city. His tales of New York in the 1930s and 1940s, with its diverse political culture, are full of nostalgic charm, and his disgusted description of the poverty, decline, and yuppie rip-off in that modern Babylon are equally riveting.

Burned out by the big city, he moved into his yellow house in Burlington. He studied Aristotle, Hegel, Fichte, the Frankfurt School, and other international classics of philosophy, and wrote his book *The Ecology of Freedom*. In 1974 he founded the Institute for Social Ecology at Goddard College in Plainfield, Vermont. The college provided him a farm, where he and his students built solar energy projects and windmills, did organic farming, and drew up plans for ecological and feminist research projects. Although the farm was later sold, the Institute still exists today.

In the 1980s Bookchin became the most noted spokesperson of the ecology movement in the US and the intellectual founding father of the Vermont Greens. For a while he cooperated with and supported the former socialist mayor of Burlington, Bernard Sanders—a fact he now prefers to overlook. He developed a new political concept called "municipalism," the basis of the political platform of the Burlington Greens.

Bookchin's life appears to fall into three major periods. In the late 1940s he abandoned the labor movement and the Old Left; in the late 1960s he turned his back on urban activism and the remnants of the New Left; and at the end of the 1980s he began settling scores with the heirs of the New Left, the ecology and feminist movements in their currently popular forms. At each juncture, he attacks former colleagues and friends, espouses new theories, and draws a group of people around his new school of thought. This kind of flexibility makes him seem the exact opposite of such anarchists as Dolgoff and Chomsky, whose

---

149. Ibid.
150. Ibid.

political positions have remained consistently rock solid. Anarchism itself seems a philosophy in constant metamorphosis. Perhaps eco-anarchism will prove to be even more mutable: Bookchin, its most renowned theoretical advocate, is one of the most flexible people I have ever met or read, his ability for harmonizing opposites notwithstanding.

Vote for Municipalism

Bookchin's political strategy is based on the traditional New England town meetings. Once a year public meetings open to all citizens take place in all the villages and towns of Vermont. Problems of local government are discussed and decided in an open vote, e.g., school tuition, the construction of a new road, the appropriation of public money for recreational institutions, bicycle paths, and so on. Issues are placed on the agenda by petition. The meetings are chaired by a board of selectmen, which is responsible for implementing the resolutions. Until 1966 all of Vermont's local governments were elected in town meetings. This tradition of direct democracy goes back to colonial times and, according to Bookchin, contributed greatly to the success of the American Revolution. In the revived institution of the town meeting Bookchin and his comrades hope initially to assume the role of a "parallel ethical system of governance"[151] to influence local politics. In the long term they hope to replace capitalism with a decentralized, participatory democracy anchored entirely in public town meetings.

> But the decisions made about the economy are not simply made by the workers, who work in a print shop or by the farmers who work on a particular farm growing cabbages. . . . Quite on the contrary: everybody meets in an assembly. And everyone, no longer thinking of his or her own particular enterprise, thinks of the general good. They discuss what shall we do, how many cabbages do we need. And the people who make the cabbages talk about how many tables we need to make, how many lamps we need to make. They do this in a town meeting, all of them.[152]

The goal of municipalism is life according to the principle: "From each according to his abilities, to each according to his needs"—a peace-loving society in which competition, market economy, and money have been replaced by harmony between people and with nature. Responding to my questions about how this goal is to be reached, Bookchin answered:

> We have to slow up growth, because it is tearing down the planet. This of course is very anticapitalist, because under capitalism if you don't grow, you die. . . . We have to change the city charters, such that we can have community meetings instead of turning everything over to the *Landtag* [state or provincial parliament] or turning everything over to the *Bundestag* [national parliament]. We have to develop regional

---

151. Murray Bookchin, *The Rise of Urbanization and the Decline of Citizenship*. San Francisco: Sierra Club Books, 1987, p. 273
152. Murray Bookchin, interview with the author, 1989.

confederations such that we all send representatives from the different towns and even from the different neighborhoods to a kind of council. . . . People think that bureaucrats have the right to make policy. I say that only the people can make policy. . . . What we can do is, city by city, community by community, village by village to bring them all into confederations based on community assemblies.[153]

Bookchin and his colleagues reject the idea of a Green Party participating in state or national governments, as it has done in Germany. The concept of "libertarian municipalism" provides only for local voter participation. Bookchin refers to this concept as anarchist, pointing out that Bakunin supported the idea of local voting. He explains what he means in two small, simply written newsletters. In "The Greening of Politics" he asserts that today politics is seen as a system of power exercised by specialists, so-called politicians, who have nothing or little in common with the people they allegedly represent. This was not always the case. Prior to the age of absolutism, well into the 16th century, politics meant something different: in communities, villages, small towns, and big cities people took care of public affairs themselves, in popular democratic meetings and with directly elected representatives, similar to the town meetings. Bookchin fails to give specifics, however, either on the historical and economic background or on how exactly this practice of grassroots democracy is supposed to work. Instead, the reader is treated to a golden view of the era preceding absolutism.

Political life extended beyond citizens' assemblies to include a rich political culture: daily public discussions in squares, parks, street-corners, educational institutions, open lectures, clubs, and the like. People discussed politics wherever they came together, as though they were preparing themselves for the citizens' assemblies. . . . The concept of a political culture gave rise to civic rituals, festivals, celebrations, and shared expressions of joy and mourning that provided every locality, be it a village, town, neighborhood, or city, with a sense of personality and identity, one which supported individual uniqueness rather than subordinated it to the collective. Such politics, in effect, was organic and ecological rather than "structural" in the top-down sense of the word.[154]

It is not easy to see how the writer of these nostalgic lines could be the same person who criticizes a certain faction of deep ecologists for looking to the distant past in search of models for the future. Furthermore, the astonished reader learns, these organic and nonhierarchic traditions have survived in some places, especially in the US, which is the real home of local autonomy, self-reliance, and the protection of the individual from state authority. Unfortunately, in recent history these American ideals were capitalized upon by the right, by the acolytes of Ayn Rand, the advocates of "greed, egotism and the virtues of property."[155] The left has not followed them up "because of the lure of European

---

153. Ibid.
154. Murray Bookchin, in *Green Perspectives*, No. 1, Jan. 1986.
155. Ibid.

and Asian traditions of socialism."[156] Bookchin goes on to say that we now need to speak to Americans about these issues in their own home-grown, radical style, not in German Marxist or Chinese Maoist language, for municipalism is an American concept, not a "borrowed and refurbished one from abroad."[157] How is this nationalist rejection of foreign influence compatible with Bookchin's criticism of the conservative backlash of late-20th-century America and with his identification with Bakunin the internationalist? How far can one go, I ask myself, in drawing on images of the precapitalist past for the purpose of creating a future before it ultimately becomes a plain distortion of history?

In the second newsletter, "Municipalization: Community Ownership of the Economy," Bookchin draws a line between his municipalism, on the one hand, and, on the other, the labor movement, class struggle, and classic anarchism, which in his opinion are historically obsolete. Hence the industrial proletariat has lost its significance in the age of computers; no reasonable person can today continue to see the Revolution of 1848, the Paris Commune of 1871, the Russian Revolution of 1917, and the Spanish Civil War of 1936 as viable models. Since the failure of the Spanish Revolution, it is no longer possible to end capitalism through armed uprisings or revolutionary general strikes. Contrary to what he told me in the interview, in this article he has nothing positive to say about the working class. He writes that the "seemingly revolutionary working class"[158] never cared about anything else than a Marxist workers' state or an anarcho-syndicalist confederal shop committee. The labor movement represented "merely class-oriented movements"—not the majority of people, only the minority of factory workers.

He touches only lightly upon the subject of communism, meaning the "nationalization of the economy"[159] and the fact that it has nothing in common with municipalism. Not so the difference between municipalism and anarcho-syndicalism, the "syndicalist ideal of collectivized self-managed enterprises."[160] For Bookchin the traditional socialist critique of anarchism is justified: worker's self-management challenges neither capitalism nor private property—an argument that the Bolsheviks also used after the revolution to close or nationalize factories and businesses of which workers had taken direct control. Furthermore, Bookchin sees the "union controlled"[161] anarcho-syndicalist collectives of the Spanish Revolution as stepping stones toward centralization, bureaucratization, and nationalization of the economy, and he feels that Diego Abad Santillan especially played into the hands of the "Marxist elements"[162] of the Spanish left.

---

156. Ibid.
157. Ibid.
158. Murray Bookchin, in *Green Perspectives*, No. 2, Feb. 1986.
159. Ibid.
160. Ibid.
161. Ibid.
162. Ibid.

This dark picture provides a strong contrast to the bright tradition of "libertarian municipal politics,"[163] which, in freely confederated form, grows to encompass neighborhoods, villages, cities and their meetings, until it reaches its goal, the "continental networks."[164] After taking us on a breathtaking sweep of the history and philosophy of public participation in politics and of anarchism, Bookchin points to citizens' action groups in Madrid during the 1960s and 1970s, local socialism in contemporary England, and citizens' action groups in the cities of Western Europe and the US. Not only do these recent social movements bring challenging issues onto the public agenda, he explains, but they also unite previously seemingly incompatible elements of society: middle class, working class, farmers, city dwellers, specialists, unskilled workers, liberals, conservatives, and leftist-liberals. This is the "potential for a genuine people's movement."

> Implicitly, this kind of movement restores once again the reality of "the people" on which the great democratic revolutions rested ideologically until they became fragmented into class and group interests.[165]

Here, one of the few publicly declared leftists in the US dismisses the historical left as a sum of minority, particularist, and nonpopulist movements, and plays it off against bourgeois "mass revolutions." He declares the classic authors of the anarchist workers movement to be representatives of the "libertarian municipal tradition" of his own historical construct—a tradition that is, if nothing else, clearly bourgeois. It would be unfair to measure the merits of such a prolific author as Bookchin on the basis of these two pamphlets alone. Whether the brew of nostalgia, nationalism, and disavowal of the labor movement as expressed in these pamphlets represents Bookchin's political message is, at this point, still an open question, but its theoretical proximity to the ideology of the *Volksgemeinschaft* cannot be overlooked.[166]

In Bookchin's house I learned that he categorizes the American Greens into three groups: "New Age," "leftist," and "reformist." The first of these factions (including "Earth First!"), I was told, originated in California; the second (leftist) in New England; and the reformists are the supporters of Jesse Jackson's Rainbow Coalition. Additional details of these divisions were explained to me by Howard Hawkins, a young activist and writer for the leftist faction. Hawkins, who came to the Greens through his friendship with Bookchin, was active in the antiwar and civil rights movements. In the 1970s he worked in several social projects in Harlem. He told me that the first Green meeting took place in St. Paul, Minnesota, and was organized by such New Age Greens as Charlene Spretnak and other social democratic or liberal environmentalists. Greens suspected of

---

163. Ibid.
164. Ibid.
165. Ibid.
166. The *Volksgemeinschaft*, or people's community, is a term commonly used by prefascist and quasi-fascist ideologists, whereby the *people* is viewed as an organic and heterogeneous entity.

leftist leanings were specifically excluded, Hawkins said. Many of the meeting's participants expressed an interest in joining the Democratic or Republican Party to establish Green caucuses. Unable to agree on common strategies, the participants set up the "Green Committees of Correspondence." This umbrella organization, which since 1991 publishes its literature under the name "The Greens," now comprises more than 142 local groups holding a variety of beliefs. By 1991 twenty-two Greens had been elected to fourteen local governments. Green parties are being formed in Hawaii, California, Arizona, New Mexico, and Missouri, which intend to run candidates in local and state elections. The long-term goal is to establish a national Green Party-USA.

The back of each newsletter from the "Green Committees of Correspondence" bears the following statement in green letters on white paper: "The Earth is our Mother. Let us start with that."[167] It is followed by a quote from Chief Seattle from the year 1855:

> The fragrant flowers are our sisters. The reindeer, the horse, the great eagle are our brothers. The rocky heights, the foamy crests of waves in the river, the sap of meadow flowers, the body heat of the pony—and of human beings—all belong to the same family.[168]

The Green platform, written in 1991, considers the "corporate market system" rather than capitalism as its opponent. The corporate market system is competitive, profit-oriented, and exploitative; its goal is unlimited economic growth; and it creates domination and greed. The Greens' political alternative is the concept of community. A real community is based on values, and its members are cared for by the community, which assumes a nurturing role. A noncorporate society is constituted of small units—shops, cooperatives, exchange networks, and neighborhood meetings, with a regional system of food distribution—a self-sufficient, autarkic economic network.

In addition, the Greens call for a 95 percent reduction of American military spending and for the establishment of a citizens' militia. They propose a public health care system financed by taxes on alcohol and cigarettes (a suggestion taken up by the Clinton administration) and wish to legalize marijuana. In their views, spirituality means consciousness of human connectedness to the earth and all living things.

The first platform of the Greens' left wing was published by the "Left Green Network" in 1989. In the preamble the authors stress that they are radical, anticapitalist, and grassroots-oriented. Green politics, they write, are "left politics—and are incompatible with the competition, alienation, exploitation, and endless accumulation that characterize capitalism."[169]

---

167. Newsletter of the Green Committees of Correspondence.
168. Ibid.
169. *Left Green Network*, New Hampshire, March 1989, p. 3.

The platform's authors reject irrationalism, New Age religiousness, Malthusianism, and anti-leftist positions, and they support social ecology. They see the ecological crisis as the product of capitalist society based on hierarchy and power, and its "war on the natural world"[170] as an extension of the war of each against all among humans. Social ecology, the politics of human equality and liberty, stands in solidarity with the liberation struggles of women, African-Americans, gays and lesbians, workers, teenagers, old people, people under colonial rule, and all those "who are weighed down by the institutions and culture of domination."[171] Its political goal is the cooperative commonwealth where

> people democratically and cooperatively own and control their economy. Global corporations and centralized state enterprises should be broken up and replaced by individual and family enterprises, cooperatives, and decentralized publicly-owned enterprises. Basic industries and services would be socialized through municipalization into community ownership and control.[172]

A "moral economy" guarantees human rights, including a guaranteed minimum income, a "decent standard of living"[173] for everyone, and the equitable distribution of available employment to all who wish or are able to work. The community provides free education, health care, and public transportation. The leftist Greens see themselves as internationalists who "actively solidarize with non-aligned peace, ecology, democracy, worker, feminist, antiracist, antimilitarist, and anti-imperialist movements in every country—East bloc, West bloc, Third World."[174]

The internationalism advocated by the authors of these words has nothing in common with the original strategy of worldwide cooperation in the struggle to end capitalism. At present, their program of international cooperation is limited to the exchange of information with Greens in Europe and Latin America, and with the native peoples of America and Australia. How limited to a single nation their political practice really is becomes apparent in the platform's concept of the right to self defense. Bookchin and Hawkins support the tradition of the locally controlled militias of the American Revolution, and Hawkins supports the idea of an alternative defense program, adding that "the people should not be disarmed until the state is disarmed."[175]

As I still did not grasp how municipalism will overcome capitalism, I asked Hawkins to tell me who would own the means of production. The key principle, he responded, is the decision power of the "community as a whole":

> Take this GE plant, it produces weapons. Burlington might take it over . . . in our own domains. Tell GE, do whatever they are going to do, but don't bother us and

---

170. Ibid., p. 4
171. Ibid., p. 4.
172. Ibid., p. 5.
173. Ibid., p. 5.
174. Ibid., p. 6.
175. Howard Hawkins, interview with the author, 1989.

start producing something we want in there. The people who work in there have lots of skills, they could help design this alternative production. And basically they would control the day-to-day operations. Any surplus that came out of the operation's enterprise would be controlled by the community as a whole. In other words, they control the capital.[176]

So it seems that these leftist Greens opt to continue the tried and true tradition of capitalists and authoritarian communists alike, that is, to avoid the simple, democratic act of transferring the means of production to those who actually produce; the workers of a communalized factory might, at best, "help" to design an alternative economy. They are supposed to work for a community, which replaces the corporations in "controlling the capital." Hence municipalism seems more "small-capitalist" than "anticapitalist," a mixture of village communism, utopia, and welfare state reformism unified by the populist myth of the community as a whole.

The Town Meeting

On March 7, 1989, the traditional day for town meetings (also the local election day), I attended one of these events in the company of Janet Biehl. Approximately two hundred citizens of Charlotte, a small village near Burlington, had assembled in the Charlotte Central School Gymnasium. The board of selectmen sat on the podium and announced the agenda, chaired the discussions, and counted hands during voting. Bookchin had warned me: "The people," he said, "are very orderly." In the same breath he proudly called the town meeting "our tradition" and a "real arena for political life."[177] I was indeed astonished: it was in every way the most conservative and—lily-white—meeting I have ever attended in the US. I felt that if someone had stood up, said that he or she was a Green, a leftist, or an anarchist, proposed ending capitalism, or even raised the issue of equal rights for African-Americans, he or she would surely have been considered completely crazy. Outside in the hall, where I was looking for potential interviewees, my simple question about their political background alarmed most. No one except for an old lady had heard of the Greens: "Yes," she told me, "they are the environmentalists who want to clean up the rivers and lakes, a very important issue." She said that she was an independent, because she couldn't make up her mind between Republicans and Democrats. "The others," she stated candidly, "are all Republicans: almost everyone in Charlotte is a Republican."

Truly a "real arena for political life." While driving back, Janet Biehl explained to me that the Vermont Republicans are not like Reagan or Bush; they are real "libertarian" decentralists who don't want to have anything to do with government or the [welfare] state, because they are proud and want to live independent lives; but, of course, unlike the Greens they are for free enterprise.

---

176. Ibid.
177. Murray Bookchin, interview with the author, 1989.

However, Biehl felt that the Burlington Democrats' centralistic state philosophy is more dangerous. Back in Bookchin's kitchen, I confessed my surprise about the conservative town meeting. Bookchin explained to me that Vermont is the whitest state in the Union with the freest gun laws, but although anyone can carry a gun, people don't go around shooting each other.

It appears that things are just as they should be in this "whitest state" of the Union: the Greens are on the left, the Republicans are really anarchists in disguise, and the bearers of arms are peaceful citizens. Above this lovely scenario hovers "our tradition," the spirit of the American Revolution. Municipalism lurks just around the corner, regardless of whether we look toward the future or toward the past. I had trouble picturing these upstanding citizens at the town meeting working with feminist, African-American, gay, lesbian, and Native American activists. I imagine that it will be a very long time before the Greens' call for the cooperative commonwealth ever catches on in Vermont.

Later On

My pessimism about the Greens' chances in the Burlington elections was justified. The local group disbanded in January of 1991, whereas the "Left Green Network," expanded by groups from all over the US, is extremely active. It organizes regional and "continental" meetings and congresses, and puts out a bimonthly periodical called *Left Green Notes,* in which we learn that the organization it represents departs from Bookchin's original correct line and makes compromises both to the left and to the right.

For the New York chapter of the "Left Green Network," for example, municipalism is no longer the only acceptable organizational principle. Two other activists point to the under-representation of unions, labor organizations, and the concept of workers' self-management in the theories of the "Left Green Network" and criticize the exaggerated idealization of the founding fathers. There have also been articles on racial problems and multiculturalism, and during the Gulf War they published statements opposing the war. The leftist Greens, however, like the Green umbrella organization, did not dare to take an antiwar stand, nor did Murray Bookchin.

Murray Bookchin—The Philosopher

Eco-Anarchism, the Youth Movement, and the Affluent Society

In 1964, Murray Bookchin (under the name Lewis Herber) published an essay entitled "Ecology and Revolutionary Thought," which he refers to as the "manifesto of the ecological movement." This essay, his first American publication on the topic, is a pioneering critique of the damage and destruction of the environment by air and water pollution, the chemicalization of farming and food, and the over-exploitation of natural resources. Bookchin depicts the disastrous consequences of the irresponsible use of atomic energy, and his prediction of an ozone hole seems almost clairvoyant. With great foresight he also warns of the impoverishment and erosion of farmland resulting from the monocultural industrialization of agriculture. He sees a similar process of simplification and standardization emerging in society at large. Centralization, especially in the form of huge urban conglomerations, makes human relationships totalitarian and unfree.

While he does confront the issues of bureaucratization, alienation, and mechanical standardization, he addresses neither social injustice, class inequality, poverty, hunger, racism, and war, nor capitalism. Instead, one learns that the major problem is bigness and centralization. Only the science of ecology, with its teachings of natural balance, can prevent the destruction of nature and the extinction of the human race. The truth of ecology derives not so much from the "power of human reason" as from a still "higher power, the sovereignty of nature over man and all his activities."[178] That sovereignty has been forgotten by humans who must be seen as a "highly destructive parasite" which "threatens to destroy its host—the natural world—and eventually itself."[179] Bookchin's conclusions differ from those of purist biocentric ecologists who equate humans with parasites and assume that nature would be better off without them.

> The imbalances man has produced in the natural world are caused by the imbalances he has produced in the social world. . . . What we are seeing today is a crisis not only in natural ecology but, above all, in social ecology.[180]

Similar ideas on the reciprocal relationship between society and nature can be found in the—often comically naive—writings of Charles Fourier (1772-1837). This early socialist utopian writer posits a primordial state of harmony between man and nature that was destroyed by the rise of patriarchal, hierarchical "civilization." Nature, originally kind and benevolent, takes its revenge via adverse climatic conditions, food shortages, droughts, floods, and other calamities. Only when mankind straightens out social issues—i.e., puts an end to war, greed, and exploitation, organizes the labor process in a sensible fashion, overcomes puritan morality and the patriarchal family, and re-establishes the rights of children and women—can there be a reconciliation with nature. This reconciliation will, in turn, result in an evolutionary process that will bring about paradisiacal conditions for humanity. Fourier prophesies that the seas will turn to lemonade, that sharks will help load our ships, lions will metamorphose into "anti-lions" and serve as steeds, and that trees will bear twice the amount of fruit. For industry he has detailed plans of an efficient labor force motivated by splendidly decorated manufacturing palaces and by

178.   Murray Bookchin, "Ecology and Revolutionary Thought." Burlington, Vermont: Green Program Project. no date, p. 4.
179.   Ibid., p. 6.
180.   Ibid., p. 6.

glittering balls between the working periods. Agriculture he envisions as pleasant horticulture. Famous are Fourier's detailed ideas of free love with all imaginable sexual pleasures culminating in "decent" orgies without obscenity, violence, and male domination. Inspired by humans one day even the planets will copulate. The smallest unit of Fourier's utopian socialist society is the phalanstery, an integrated housing and work complex enclosed by gardens and trees. Though critical of social injustice and exploitation in the class society, Fourier was not an egalitarian. Convinced that an ongoing benevolent natural evolution would automatically eliminate poverty and drudgery, he didn't see a need for abolishing the laws of inheritance, and differences of income and wealth.

The social and ideological critique contained in Fourier's utopian message, in particular its cultural-revolutionary element with its emphasis on the emancipation of women, influenced both Marxism and anarchism. The message has also been of interest to futurist believers in technology and to modern labor technicians. And it has served to legitimize an agrarian romanticism and quasi-religious worship of nature, thereby turning the vision of joyous labor in the paradisiacal gardens of a pacified, reconciled nature into the sweet poison of romantic illusion.

Bookchin holds that the "integrative, reconstructive aspect of ecology"[181] leads to anarchism whose primordial aspects are anti-urbanism, distrust in technology, and the attraction of village and agricultural life. The farmers' or ecologists' "intimate relationship with the unique qualities of the land on which they grow crops"[182] becomes the life-preserver for the technologically battered human race. "The factory floor must yield to gardening and horticulture."[183] Telephones, teletypes, radios, television, and computers would be reduced to a minimum in the society he envisions. Bookchin draws on Herbert Read, the British anarchist philosopher and critic of modernity, as well as on the "intuitive anarchism" of youth, its "love of nature," and its "intense individualism."[184] His theories of ecology and anarchism also encompass the old liberalist postulate of diversity and variety. Harmony in nature and society can only come about through "organic differentiation, not standardization."[185] The larger the "variety of prey and predators," the more "stable the population."[186] Dangerous ground, this. Theories that strain the parallels between nature and society easily shipwreck on those same rocks where some deep ecologists practice their social-Darwinist rites. Bookchin, however, sees things differently:

> Ranging from community, through region, to entire continents, we would see a
> colorful differentiation of human groups and ecosystems . . . We would witness a

---

181. Ibid., p. 4.
182. Ibid., p. 8.
183. Ibid., p. 11.
184. Ibid., p. 10.
185. Ibid., p. 10.
186. Ibid., p. 11.

dynamic interplay between individual and group, community and environment, man and nature. Freed from an oppressive routine, from paralyzing repressions and insecurities, from the burdens of toil and false needs, from the trammels of authority and irrational compulsion, the individual would finally be in a position, for the first time in history, to fully realize his potentialities as a member of the human community and the natural world.[187]

Just how this anarchist ecosystem is supposed to function politically and economically remains clouded in the fog of utopian promise.

In an article entitled "Towards a Liberatory Technology" published in 1965, Bookchin writes that, while the labor movements of the 19th and early 20th centuries were occupied with the problems of a subsistence economy, things are different today. In a daring blueprint for techno-utopia, he says that modern technology will reduce work to a minimum, or even abolish it all together; it will "replace the realm of necessity by the realm of freedom."[188] The "problems of survival" become the "problems of life."[189] Bookchin identifies here with the Dadaists, those "magnificent madmen" who as early as fifty years ago demanded "unemployment for everybody" at a time when "social-democratic and communist theorists babbled about a society with "work for all."[190] He, who only a few months earlier had been so opposed to technology, was now introducing the principles of computer technology, with the ease and authority he had previously used in introducing the principles of ecology. He speaks about closed and open systems, the development of self-regulating control mechanisms, the dizzyingly rapid reduction of manual labor in the automobile industry, and the imminent end to mining—all thanks to the invention of mankind's newest servant, the computer, the "electronic 'mind'."[191] Computers are faster and more efficient than people, he assures us. The main problem, making sure that this technology is used for the benefit instead of to the detriment of humankind— that it is installed in a decentralized and ecological rather than in a centralized, authoritarian, and destructive way—has almost been solved, too. Soon, Bookchin says, we will not only be producing tiny computers, but also "small 'packaged' factories."[192] Production on a "human scale"[193] can be adjusted to local conditions. Ecologically designed tractors, plows, planters, harvesters, solar devices, wind turbines, heat pumps, electric cars, and single-track trains will free humankind from work. On small farms—separated from one another by trees, hedges, and pastures—each industrially self-sufficient community will exist in ecological, social, and esthetic harmony with its environment; city and country

---

187.   Ibid., p. 18.
188.   Murray Bookchin, *Post Scarcity Anarchism*. Montreal: Black Rose, 1986, p. 115.
189.   Ibid., p. 153.
190.   Ibid., p. 153.
191.   Ibid., p. 123.
192.   Ibid., p. 127.
193.   Ibid., p. 128.

will become one; and plants and animals will abound. Working in the fields will be as easy and fun as gardening. People will become one with their environment and develop "organic modes of thought" and "a new animism." This animism goes not only well with the world of advanced high technology, but, astonishingly enough, even with "controlled thermonuclear reactions."[194] When used ecologically, all technology will become "technology for life."[195] Bookchin's description of agricultural inventions calls to mind Kropotkin's futuristic utopia, with its combination of decentralized small industry, artisan production, and idyllic parks, a simplistic attempt to end the alienation of labor. Yet Bookchin's vacillation between the past and the future is more extreme than Kropotkin's. Similar to Fourier's blueprint for the future, the brave new world of eco-anarchism also has a quasi-religious aspect in that it worships both computer technology and neo-animist nature.

Around 1966 Bookchin turned to New Left activism, current politics, and the historical realities of the labor movement. He developed a concept of anarchism that made him into a kind of authority and role model, especially in New York. His undogmatic ideas offered an alternative to the neo-Leninist trends, popular at the time. In his famous essay "Listen Marxist" Bookchin outlines the history of the Russian Revolution, using as his sources Volin (V.M. Eikhenbaum) and Peter Arshinov, the anarcho-syndicalist historians and eye-witnesses of the revolution. He recounts how the Russian workers and peasants spontaneously organized themselves, describes the Machno movement, the Kronstadt uprising, the solidarity of the workers of St. Petersburg, and revives memories of the "Worker's Opposition," a group that opposed Lenin—information long forgotten or repressed, and at the time not widely known. The article was also significant in its accurate assessment of Leninism and in its condemnation of the neo-Leninist and Stalinist revival. Bookchin accuses the old and new Leninists alike of projecting the image of the authoritarian union leader and Stalinist commissar onto the worker per se.

> One cuts one's hair, grooms oneself in conventional sports clothing, abandons pot for cigarettes and beer, dances conventionally, affects "rough" mannerisms, and develops a humorless, deadpan and pompous mien. One becomes, in short, what the worker is at his most caricaturized worst.[196]

His scathing critique of the PLP (Progressive Labor Party) as a reservoir of middle-class consciousness warms the heart of all victims of Leninist party discipline:

> The authoritarian leader and hierarchy replace the patriarch and the school bureaucracy; the discipline of the Movement replaces the discipline of bourgeois society; the authoritarian code of political obedience replaces the state; the credo of "proletarian morality" replaces the mores of puritanism and the work ethic.[197]

---

194. Ibid., p. 141.
195. Ibid., p. 152.
196. Ibid., pp. 209–10.
197. Ibid., p. 198.

Just as convincing is Bookchin's settling of accounts with the Bolshevik Party, during the period when the workers were replaced by soviets [councils], the soviets by the party, and the party by the central committee—a process whereby the end is divorced from the means. His critique of the cadre party, which he adapted from libertarian Marxists like Rosa Luxemburg, is equally accurate: "a miniature state, with an apparatus and a cadre whose function is to *seize power,* not *dissolve* power."[198]

Bookchin's "critique of Marx" is in many ways similar to the classical anarchist view, according to which Marx is an unbending centralist and advocate of the cadre party who considered capitalism a progressive force in history. Unlike the anarchists of the Old Left, however, Bookchin thinks that Marx's analysis is outdated and no longer applicable to modern affluent society. Ignoring poverty and hunger, especially in the Third World, he says that economic need is no longer a problem. Capitalism, which "itself performs many of the tasks . . . regarded as socialist,"[199] has not only eliminated economic shortages by introducing new technologies, but can also overcome its periodic crises. Thanks to the welfare state, which has bought off the workers, the class struggle has been integrated into capitalism itself.

> To reinforce this class structure by babbling about the "role of the working class," to reinforce the traditional class struggle by imputing a "revolutionary" content to it, to infect the new revolutionary movement of our time with "workeritis" is *reactionary to the core.*[200]

He goes on to explain who is really to blame for capitalism:

> As for the problem of winning the working class to the revolution, we must bear in mind that a precondition for the existence of the bourgeoisie is the development of the proletariat. Capitalism as a social system presupposes the existence of *both* classes.[201]

Is he saying that it may have been a mistake to try to unseat the bourgeoisie? Should perhaps the proletariat have been booted out first? For Bookchin class struggle becomes the root of all evil:

> How often do the Marxian doctrinaires have to be reminded that the history of the class struggle is the history of a disease, of the wounds opened by the famous "social question," of man's one-sided development in trying to gain control over nature by dominating his fellow man? If the byproduct of this disease has been technological advance, the main products have been repression, a horrible shedding of human blood, and a terrifying distortion of the human psyche.[202]

This "disease," he believes, comes to an end in post-scarcity society. The traditional class structure, the patriarchal family, and authoritarian educational

198. Ibid., p. 218.
199. Ibid. p. 202.
200. Ibid., p. 208.
201. Ibid., p. 242.
202. Ibid., pp. 208–9.

methods are all in the process of dissolution. Bookchin's critique of Marxism has come full circle. If it is true, as anarchists argue, that Marx considered capitalism to be a progressive force, Bookchin, as Marx's critic, has outdone the latter. He is convinced both that the capitalist bourgeoisie has the ability to deal with crises and class struggles and that classes within capitalist society will disappear. But how can one disavow the class struggle and be a revolutionary at the same time? The answer: the time for the revolution finally comes after social classes have disappeared.

> Such a social revolution can only emerge from the decomposition of the traditional classes, indeed from the emergence of an entirely new "class" *whose very essence is that it is a non-class,* a growing stratum of revolutionaries.[203]

These revolutionaries, Bookchin explains, are mostly young, and they exist in all strata. He declares modern youth to be the representative of "life-impulses in humanity's nature—the urgings of desire, sensuousness, and the lure of the marvelous."[204] Today's youth, raised in affluence, are hedonistic, disregard taboos, and shy away from work in revolt against the puritanism and work ethic of their middle-class or class-conscious proletarian parents. Since the struggle against need has already been won, what remains is the fight for the cultural revolution. The middle classes, the workers, and society as a whole will follow in the footsteps of the young avant-garde, adopt their bohemian life styles, practice free love, take to communal life, reject work and consumer goods, and "live the revolution in all its totality."[205] The goal of this revolution of the self, of "self liberation," of "self activity," and of the "self-mobilization of the revolutionaries"[206] is the liberation of everyday life; its purpose an end in itself.

> The act of revolution rips apart all the tendons that hold authority and hierarchy together in the established order. The direct entry of the people into the social arena is the *very essence* of revolution . . . There is no theory, program or party that has greater significance than the revolution itself.[207]

Bookchin plays off cultural revolution against social revolution, "self-liberation" against "mass liberation" or "class liberation"[208] and, in the final analysis, the revolution against its meaning—social change. Thus it is only logical for him to reject economics, class struggle, politics, and the anarcho-syndicalist model for council communism in favor of vague ideas of "tribalism and community."[209] Bookchin's articles of the 1960s are works of de-politicization. What begins as a well-stated, leftist critique of Leninism and Stalinism turns into bourgeois anti-communism, bohemian life-style philosophy, and youth-

---

203. Ibid., pp. 207–8.
204. Ibid., p. 61.
205. Ibid., p. 67.
206. Ibid., p. 67.
207. Ibid., p. 275.
208. Ibid., p. 67.
209. Ibid., p. 167.

driven revolution ontology. What could have been a critical discussion of the one-sided determinist understanding of class in economic terms becomes a denial of class struggle and economic misery. The attempt by the New Left to link the social and cultural revolution has in Bookchin's interpretation turned into a one-sided notion of the cultural revolution as an end in itself. His original solidarity with a politicized youth movement during the 1960s becomes an ideology of youth as the personification of the revolution above and beyond its goals. Comrade Bookchin, formerly of the Old Left, cannot overcome the dogmatic habits of his Leninist past and thus is unable to arrive at an undogmatic interpretation of Marx or at a modern understanding of anarchism. Instead, he preserves the revolutionary pathos of the 1930s while inverting Old Left values. He views economics, labor, and class struggle as Puritan, and bad, while he sees Bohème, antiauthoritarian youth, sex, and all things considered to be decadent by Stalinists as life-affirming, revolutionary and good.

The Ecology of Freedom

Bookchin's book *The Ecology of Freedom* begins with the old Nordic legend of Ragnarök describing "the breakdown of the primal unity,"[210] a myth that according to Bookchin depicts

> how the gods must pay a penalty for seeking the conquest of nature. It ends with a social project for removing that penalty, whose Latin root *poenalis* has given us the word pain. Humanity will become the deities it created in its imagination, albeit as deities *within* nature, not *above* nature—as "supernatural" entities.[211]

Bookchin's concept of nature is intended as an alternative to Darwin's. He rejects as anthropocentric, in the sense of a humanization of nature and a transfer of social standards, Darwin's characterization of nature as cruel, stingy, hostile, selective, and hierarchical. He nonetheless assigns to nature such characteristics as fruitful, nurturing, protective, egalitarian, creative, and so on. In his description of the "organic" societies of early human history, nature assumes a nurturing role.

> Nature as life eats at every repast, succors every new birth, grows with every child, aids every hand that throws a spear or plucks a plant, warms itself at the hearth in the dancing shadows, and sits amidst the councils of the community . . . Ecological ceremonials validate the "citizenship" nature acquires as part of the human environment.[212]

He also speaks of "the blood that flows between the community and nature" and of the "unity that edges into the intimate intercourse of sexuality, birth and the interchange of blood."[213] Singing animist praises of nature, he finally rejects a religious approach to nature in favor of a vision of nature as teacher.

---

210. Murray Bookchin, *The Ecology of Freedom*. Palo Alto, CA: Cheshire Books, p. 17.
211. Ibid., p. 11.
212. Ibid., p. 47.
213. Ibid., p. 48.

His deduction of ethics from nature is equally fraught with contradictions. According to Bookchin, natural evolution develops toward an increasingly meaningful whole, the individual elements of which are all part of a great organism from which "spirit" and ethics derive. Nature itself has an implicit ethical structure. Mutualism and freedom are not exclusively human achievements; they also exist in the greater organic, cosmic context. However, nature is not "a model of ethical behavior," but rather "a source of ethical meaning."[214] What, I wonder, is the difference between the former and the latter? Both notions could stem from a conservative thinker, who uses metaphors of nature to justify social injustice and misery. For instance, how we are to interpret statements like the following?

> A wolf has no business lying down with a lamb. The imagery is trite and in its own way repellent. The "pacification" of nature does not consist in its domestication.[215]

Elsewhere we are told that a pack of wolves kills a sick caribou to "remove an organism that can no longer function" for the purpose of "organic renewal and ecological stability."[216] Likewise, the brief pain that a hunter inflicts on his prey, Bookchin continues, is rarely as cruel as the suffering that human society inflicts on healthy human beings and animals—suffering that could only have originated in the "cunning of the hominid mind."[217] Zealous environmentalists, having generalized the hunter-prey relationship between species and the ecologically necessary elimination of the weakened old caribou, might be tempted to revive the principles of the survival of the human fittest and euthanasia.

Bookchin views rationality as he does ethics, something that humankind cannot itself create, but can only imitate from nature. Reason derives from the subjectivity of evolutionary nature. The evolutionary process brings forth the spirit, a term Bookchin often uses interchangeably with rationality and subjectivity. A major problem of modernity is that spirit, rationality, and subjectivity are relegated to the "realm" of the head. To feel them within the body is now possible only in fantasy, play, art, intuition, creativity, sexuality, and during childhood and adolescence. Bookchin's critique of instrumental reason differs dramatically from that of the Frankfurt School, despite their common basis. Dialectic is replaced by a moralizing dualism that claims to overcome "the evil" in "every good" and to regain the positive aspects of that which has been lost in history—the "sociality" in "solidarity of kinship," the "rationality in primal innocence," the "willfulness in patriarchy," and the "personality in individualism."[218] As an alternative to instrumental or "authoritarian reason" Bookchin suggests

---

214.   Ibid., p. 278.
215.   Ibid., p. 277.
216.   Ibid., p. 362.
217.   Ibid., p. 362.
218.   Ibid., p. 268.

a "libertarian rationality"[219] which "bears witness to the symbiotic animism of early preliterate sensibilities without becoming captive in its myth and self deceptions."[220] A metaphor used to explain this "libertarian rationality" is the mother-child symbiosis.

> For it is not only love that the mother ordinarily gives her child but a rationality of "otherness" that stands sharply at odds with its modern arrogant counterpart. This earlier rationality is unabashedly *symbiotic*.[221]

Here again women face the same old question: is not the mother-child symbiosis, as both an ideal and a permanent condition, an extreme state of dependence, characterized by inequality, helplessness, and power? What a frightening thought—the passive-exploitive greed of the infant and the omnipotence of the mother over her helpless offspring as an eternal, unalterable condition! Is not this concept of rationality in the end simply the recognition of all that is given, natural? Couldn't the "rationality of otherness," for example, become the rationality of domination and hierarchy in a caste society? Furthermore, what good, one might ask, is rationality at all if, set out over and against the notion of instrumental reason, it disappears under a multitude of irrational attributes?

For Bookchin, not only ethics and reason, but even "human nature" is based on the "prolonged process of physical maturation" as a "biologically constituted form of consociation." Though he allows that "cooperation, mutual support, and love" (which he attributes to human nature) are also products of culture, in his view the major impetus comes from biology and nature. "Nature," he says, "does not merely phase into society," it "is there all the time." "Cooperation, mutual support, and love"[222] thus do not represent a mature, voluntary form of altruism arising from cultural insight between rational equals, rather from an instinctive, childlike sense that we are all dependent on one another. Hence human nature is a sentiment more passive than active, more felt than learned, and more a part of the past than of the future.

In *The Ecology of Freedom* the relationship of human beings to nature is as passive as the concept of human nature. Bookchin says that the "principles of social ecology require no explanation, merely verification":

> They are the elements of an ethical ontology, not rules of a game that can be changed to suit one's personal needs. A society that cuts across the grain of this ontology raises the entire question of its very reality as a meaningful and rational entity.[223]

The ethics of ecology help humans to differentiate between what serves natural evolution and what does not. The self-organization of nature includes human

---

219. Ibid., p. 307.
220. Ibid., p. 303.
221. Ibid., p. 306.
222. Ibid., p. 317.
223. Ibid., p. 365.

development and history only as long as that process is not disturbed. Therefore having sinned against mother nature for the last 10,000 years, it is now time to rejoin natural evolution. We would be arrogant if we were to create our history ourselves, because nature is not ours "to use," it only "legitimizes"[224] us. It is not surprising then, that the prehistoric humans whom he depicts in the chapter on organic societies are the ones best suited for the "ontological association with the natural world."[225] Although Bookchin fiercely criticizes the passive nature worship of such ecologists as Dave Foreman, in this, his most important work he tends to privilege an age when "nature as the grand leveller"[226] ruled over inorganic and organic matter, animals, the environment, people, tools, and goods as a unity within diversity. The human being has but to find his place within a benevolent natural environment, to adjust ecologically, and be content with the world as it is. He did not mean it quite that way, yet in his poetic vision, nature assumes a god-like position and is therefore sovereign.

Bookchin attempts to refute Marx's theory of class, which he equates with that of a vulgar Marxism defined purely in economic terms. Stripped of all Marxism's inherent emancipatory content, the goal of a classless society resembles either the distorted bourgeois nightmare of communism (where everyone gets everything taken away from him) or the post-Stalinist real socialism societies of the East bloc. Rather than developing a more differentiated understanding of class, Bookchin drops the idea altogether. As understandable as this may be— considering the misuse of the term and the taboo against it in America— Bookchin's substitute term "hierarchy," restricted as it is to the realms of suprastructure and culture, goes to the other extreme, thus not only denying the potential emancipatory content of an economic analysis of society, but also the economic roots of social phenomena that cross class lines.

In his reconstruction of ancient history Bookchin attempts to prove that the rule of the old over the young is even older than that of the male over the female, which, in turn, is older than class rule and exploitation. The prehistoric age is for him a "mine of data, provocative issues, and imaginative possibilities."[227] One such "imaginative" possibility is Bookchin's generalizing definition of all prehistoric communities as organic societies. According to his theory, these "ecocommunities" were characterized by an "intense solidarity internally and with the natural world."[228] Having an "active sense of participation"[229] in the environment and natural events, they were securely embedded within their surrounding ecosystem. "Usufruct," "complementarity," and a guaranteed subsistence income formed the basic social principles. The original gender-

224. Ibid., p. 365.
225. Ibid., p. 48.
226. Ibid., p. 232.
227. Ibid., p. 245.
228. Ibid., p. 44.
229. Ibid., p. 46.

based division of labor in such societies was suitable for an "economy that acquires the very gender of the sex to which it is apportioned." Women's work was women's work because of the female "sense of concern over the integrity of their richly hallowed responsibilities and their personal rights."[230] Bookchin's description of the pivotal role of Stone Age women in creating the community is full of such terms as origin, source, blood, and bond, which to me, especially in their German translation, have a frighteningly familiar ring. Contrary to the "predatory" male, he asserts, women were "more domestic, more pacifying, and more caring," the embodiment of "mythology's ancient message of a lost 'golden age' and a fecund nature."[231] The "primal division of labor,"[232] however, is also based on a "hard biological reality"[233]—the assumption of women's natural physical inferiority—which predetermines men as the protector of the family and the group. Approximately 10,000 years ago, Bookchin states, nomadic hunters and gatherers invented horticulture and established the neolithic village communities. "From the male hunter," social imagery shifted to "the female food gatherer, from the predator to the procreator, from the camp fire to the domestic hearth."[234] Female fertility, proximity to nature, and the development of the principle of sharing "a universally social phenomenon"[235] created a kind of paradise characterized by human and natural goodness. All this changed with the decline of internal solidarity in that "matricentric" agricultural society. This decline began among those at a natural disadvantage—the elders, and the men. As the "most dispensable members of the community," the elders were the first to develop a need for "hierarchical social power."[236]

> The aged, who abhor natural necessity, become the embodiment of social necessity; the dumb "cruelty" that the natural world inflicts on them is transmitted by social catalysis into the conscious cruelty they inflict on the young. Nature begins to take her revenge on the earliest attempts of primordial society to control her.[237]

As educators in the spirit of repressive rationality, the elders began to exert their power. They abandoned animistic religion, became medicine men or shamans, and established early forms of religion and priestly rule based on magic rites. Having once drunk from the "magic fountain of wisdom," the shaman became a "specialist in fear." While the woman, as the gatherer, was still the "specialist in nurture," the man, as the hunter, became the "specialist in violence."[238] As the male's self-esteem was threatened in a world dominated by women, male identity finally developed "its most warped expression in warfare, arrogance,

---

230. Ibid., p. 53.
231. Ibid., p. 60.
232. Ibid., p. 77.
233. Ibid., p. 77.
234. Ibid., p. 58.
235. Ibid., p. 59.
236. Ibid., p. 81.
237. Ibid., p. 82.
238. Ibid., p. 82.

and subjugation."[239] From that point on, priestly rule, religion, and patriarchy destroyed matricentric society whose characteristic complementarity of the sexes was replaced by repression. This led to the founding of cities and the establishment of the state—first the "inner state," the super-ego marked by guilt, followed by the real, external state.

Like his utopian blueprint for the future, Bookchin's imagined ancient history is basically a religious construct. The story of the alienation of humankind from nature, delineated as a revolt against the nurturing mother, is yet another version of the fall from paradise, in which the apple from the tree of wisdom is replaced by magic as the precursor of repressive rationality, and in which Eve is first systematically praised and then made to suffer, guilty of a perfection that sent men reeling in a permanent identity crisis. Not only is history retold in a quasi-religious way, but Bookchin also asserts that social development is a product of religion and human consciousness. Hierarchy, class, and state are the result of the psychological drives of envy and compensation for weakness. Reality is determined by consciousness. What is labeled "complementarity" as the basic social principle is, in effect, stark sexual dualism in which women are reduced to the mindless nature principle of ancient creation myths. Not to mention that his emphasis on "hard biological realities" really speaks the language of the patriarch delineating his role as the protector of women. It should not come as a surprise, then, that the ecofeminist theory of some of Bookchin's former followers has sunk into the ideological swamp of femininity.

This is not the only example of Bookchin's pan-harmonious humanism turning into its opposite. His tale of the neolithic elders turned wicked because of their natural disadvantage, and its implication that the old ought to resign themselves to their frailty and declining social position, could lead a naive reader to believe that euthanasia might be useful, after all. This biologistic projection of the [bourgeois] cliché of the bad old man onto a Stone Age society perceived as gentle and nurturing throughout totally ignores the injustice and cruelty to which the elderly are subjected. This, and not the curse of nature, is perhaps what makes them grumpy and mean.

Besides class theory, Bookchin's other main point against Marxism (and classical anarchism) is the former's relationship to nature. The postulate of control over nature, he feels, legitimizes the concept of domination in general, which, in turn, becomes a kind of prerequisite for freedom, thus making possible the idealization of capitalism as a "progressive" force. Progress is portrayed as the development of domination, technocracy, and inhumanity after the oneness of humankind with nature has been destroyed; social progress and human achievement seem to be of a purely cultural nature, and then only in precapitalist society. Bookchin principally identifies the orientation of Marxism or classical anarchism toward reality and the respective social blueprints with Victorianism and plays

---

239. Ibid., p. 251.

the former off against hedonism, imagination, the romantic worship of nature, and utopian visions. To emphasize the issues of the economy, exploitation, and class society seems only to spread the very disease one was trying to cure.

> Almost every critique of the "bourgeois traits" of modern society, technics, and individuality is itself tainted by the very substance it criticizes. By emphasizing economics, class interest, and the "material substrate" of society as such, such critiques are the bearers of the very "bourgeois traits" they purport to oppose.[240]

Hence money and politics must be dirty. Anyone defending economic interests is greedy. Anyone trying to liberate himself from the yoke of class rule is himself a potential ruler. And anyone analyzing society in economic terms becomes a bourgeois materialist. Not even the Frankfurt School fares better: Bookchin dismisses its critical theory as Marxist and Freudian, unwilling to "invoke the claims of nature."[241]

Bookchin is categorically opposed to psychoanalysis, which he credits with an "extraordinary reactionary content." Freud, he says, ignores the fact that the reality principle in an organic society is determined by the limits of nature itself.

> It is displaced by a mythic "pleasure principle" that be constrained by guilt and renunciation. Cooperative nature is turned into predatory nature, riddled by egoism, rivalry, cruelty, and the pursuit of immediate gratification.[242]

Like most critics of classic psychoanalysis, Bookchin (mis)interprets Freud's description of the bourgeois psyche as a prescription for action and prefers to envision the human being at his most uncorrupted: the way nature made him, uninfluenced by civilization. That spoilsport Freud, on the other hand, threatened to "destroy our dreams."[243]

Bookchin's criticism of Marxism focuses on Marx's concept of primal communism, as well as on his labor and commodity theories. He rejects Engel's version of original communism because it allegedly includes the ideas of collective property and of a natural shortage of goods and counters it with the notion of sharing as an integral part of human nature and with the principle of usufruct. He interprets Engel's version of matriarchy as the rule of women over men. His view of Marx is even worse: according to Bookchin, Marx proposed to subject nature to man in the manner of a patriarch, thus despiritualizing not only labor, but also the product of that labor, the commodity. Marx's concept of labor, he asserts, is a utilitarian one that ignores the autocreative, subjective, or spiritual nature of abstract matter. Labor as "the materialization of play" and utility-value as the "materialization of desire" have since been left to "the utopian imagination."[244] Bookchin (mis)interprets Marx's analysis of the commodity as a

---

240. Ibid., p. 217.
241. Ibid., p. 273.
242. Ibid., p., 117.
243. Ibid., p. 270.
244. Ibid., p. 230.

justification for the consumer society, while he himself ontologizes the commodity and its "essence,"[245] that is, its utility value. In organic societies, Bookchin says, labor is a "sacrosanct activity," and "procreation"[246] and production are the child born of the marriage between humanity and nature. The "self-realization of matter is analogous to gestation and birth"[247]—a notion that calls to mind the copulating planets of Fourier's utopia.

With their "hypostatization of labor," their belief in science and technology, their "myths of progress," and their "commitment to proletarian hegemony," socialists, communists, and anarchists were completely off the mark, Bookchin states. It was not the "scientific socialists," but the utopians who recognized imagination to be a "socially creative power,"[248] which, Bookchin believes, should be revived in an artistic-literary manner or as an "evocation of tradition." "Utopian *dialogue* in all its existentiality must infuse the abstractions of social theory."[249] Hence, according to this view, it would seem that the cultural supersedes the social, the existential the abstract, tradition change, and utopia reality.

One of the utopian philosophers Bookchin admires is the Marquis de Sade, in whose writings can be found an elaborate theory of nature; in Sade's view, as in Darwin's, however, nature is cruel and without compassion, and only the fittest survive. Despite his claim to ethical principles, Bookchin ignores this contradiction and extols the virtues of Sade, one of the most outspoken philosophical apologists of amorality, who believes that pleasure belongs only to those who have the power to inflict suffering on others.

> His orgiastic appeal to a new sensibility... stands sharply at odds with the strong emphasis on "self-discipline" that the emerging industrial bourgeoisie was to impose on the nineteenth century.[250]

The question is whether de Sade's depiction of orgies, whose ritualized tortures were planned down to the nitty-gritty, attacked the virtues of bourgeois self-discipline, or whether in the end they only copied it. Try as I might, I am simply unable to detect any such "new sensibility" in de Sade's writings; Fourier, the master of idyllic orgies, seems a more likely candidate to me, but in Bookchin's view Fourier is primarily a "social ecologist" and only secondarily a cultural revolutionary.

> His phalanstery can rightly be regarded as a social ecosystem in its explicit endeavor to promote unity in diversity... the phalanstery must try to compensate in psychic wealth and variety for any inequalities of material wealth existing among its members.[251]

245. Ibid., p. 229.
246. Ibid., p. 231.
247. Ibid., p. 232.
248. Ibid., p. 325.
249. Ibid., p. 334.
250. Ibid., p. 327.
251. Ibid., p. 331.

Emphasizing as he does that freedom is more important than equality, Fourier's insistence on property, inheritance, and unequal income is music to Bookchin, an apologist for "unity in diversity." A "feast of diversified, qualitatively superb delights" makes the differences in income "irrelevant."[252] It is here that social ecology shows its real colors and reveals itself, as a liberalist rather than a socialist doctrine. It is no coincidence that Bookchin, who straddles the left and the right, is so enthusiastic about Fourier's concept of "absolute doubt," which, in its abstract radicalism, easily changes into its counterpart, conservatism. Bookchin is also atttracted to Fourier's eclectic combination of pseudo-science and vision, yet he hesitates to follow his predecessor's cultural revolutionary trail to the end, to Fourier's radical settling of accounts with the bourgeois family and his critique of the mother cult—the more or less indirect repression of women that celebrates a comeback in Bookchin's theories.

The Ecology of Freedom is a utopian work. The social and political reality of the past, present, and future are pretty much faded out, and capitalism is neither mentioned nor criticized. Anarchism is discussed only as a negative example of what we *don't* want. Not much of the revolutionary pathos of the 1960s has remained by the 1970s.

Long Live the Past

In *The Rise of Urbanization and the Decline of Citizenship,* published in 1987, Bookchin describes the eco-community not as a village, but as a city of the pre-capitalist age. He begins with the Cätal Hüyük society of the 7th century B.C. in Asia Minor, continues on through the Athenian *polis,* the free cities of medieval times, and the Italian city states of the Renaissance, down to the Puritan townships of New England in the 18th century. The unifying basis of these societies is not the mother-child dyad, but the *agora*, the people's assembly in ancient Greece. Morality and ethics are not longer derived from nature, but from an urban code of values rooted in their "citizenship" that proves itself by participation in community life. Citizenship is regarded as the social equivalent to "biotic involvement"[253] and civic history as the social equivalent to natural history. Bookchin contrasts this society with modern urbanization, an unnatural way of life. A "cancerous phenomenon,"[254] urbanization not only devours the countryside, turning it into a suburb, but also the city itself, by robbing it of its historical qualities.

While the book is most informative in its many details about the origin and history of various cities, its often glaringly generalized postulates derived from that history border on the speculative, especially when they are subsumed to

---

252. Ibid., p. 331.
253. Murray Bookchin, *The Rise of Urbanization and the Decline of Citizenship.* San Francisco: Sierra Club Books, 1987, p. x.
254. Ibid., p. x.

the book's main thread, the dualism of a good past and an evil presence. Without hesitating to lump together Cätal Hüyük with both ancient Athens and the cities of the Middle Ages and the Renaissance, Bookchin describes life in these places as follows:

> The good life by no means meant the affluent life, the life of personal pleasures and material security. More often than not, it meant a life of good*ness*, of virtue and probity. . . . Love of one's city, a deep and abiding sense of loyalty to its welfare, and an attempt to place these sentiments within a rich moral and ecological context, whether God-given or intellectual, clearly distinguishes the majority of cities of past eras from those of present ones.[255]

He compares the "traditional religious, cultural, ethical, and ecological" qualities of old with the quantitative, often "ethically neutral"[256] character of modern cities. What Bookchin has to say about the cities of the past seems to be more characteristic of his own idealistic view of history. It is no coincidence that he repeatedly laments and attacks the materialist viewpoint that perverts our urban ancestors as much as it does us. Historical materialism, like the egotistical political economy of the industrial bourgeoisie itself, lacks ethical values. It "slaps not only the face of philosophical idealism but also the high spirit of European romanticism" in order to "disenchant the world"[257] and to annihilate the past. Bookchin's message, that in the past humans were more ethical, moral, amicable, responsible, altruistic, and closer to nature than people today, becomes a simple believe-it-or-not exercise.

Bookchin posits that history knows no "structure"[258] comparable to that of the democracy of the ancient Greek *polis*. He credits Greek democracy with a "high level of consciousness, civicism, commitment, and esthetics,"[259] and praises the "vision of *eleutheria* [freedom] based on equality."[260] He attributes to the *agora* a "direct, almost protoplasmic contact, full participatory involvement and its delight in variety and diversity," and he defines it as a "genuine ecological community within the *polis* itself."[261] The *polis* owes this not only to its consciousness of civil virtue, but also to the notion of *paideia,* a term that for Bookchin is closer to the German concept of *Bildung* than to the English word "education" and includes connotations of "shaping," "forming," "improvement," and "character-building." The *paideia* of a young man, the reader learns, is a "creative integration of the individual into his environment" and calls for "individual responsibility."[262] After a lengthy description of the unifying effects of religious rites, Bookchin's eulogy of the *polis* culminates in the definition of citizenship as a drama in the

---

255. Ibid., p. 6.
256. Ibid., p. 7.
257. Ibid., p. 208.
258. Ibid., p. 40.
259. Ibid., p. 35.
260. Ibid., p. 44.
261. Ibid., p. 61.
262. Ibid., p. 59.

service of ethos, art, and cult, in which collectivity, solidarity, responsibility, and sense of duty are preserved. However, Bookchin is little bothered by either the elitist men's club nature of ancient Greek society or by the fact that its economy was based on war, slavery, and the subjugation of women. He makes a half-hearted attempt at criticizing its misogyny, xenophobia, and slavery, but excuses these spots on the democratic vest of Athens by pointing to the "compelling realities of ancient urban life" in the middle of a "world of chaotic uncertainty and mindless barbarism."[263] One of the realities, war, is laconically referred to as a "fact of life in antiquity."[264] The morality Bookchin ardently invoked earlier in rejecting materialism evaporates as soon as his idealism capitulates to the social realities he so detests. His sympathies for the Greek aristocracy should surprise no one. He stresses the noble ancestry of all the great Athenian democrats and praises Solon the legislator, who never advocated the political and economic supremacy of the people or the removal of the aristocracy from power. The ancient Greek aristocrats' ideals of friendship, their code of honor, and their contempt for material things were incorporated into the "puritanical virtues"[265] of democracy, which, in turn, rejected luxury, splendor, and culinary pleasures. The belligerent masculinity of the aristocracy was translated into civic loyalty, personal dignity, and virtue.

In this book, Bookchin redefines the terms city, state, political, and social. Equating "citification" with urbanization and banishing the city from the history of ideas, he asserts, led to a disastrous confusion between state and society, and between government and society. As a result, politics is usually equated with the politics of the state. The separation of the social and the statist, however, was one of anarchism's most important contributions to political theory. Bookchin's definition of "social" includes "family, workplace, fraternal and sororal groups, religious congregations, unions and professional societies."[266] From there he develops a concept of politics claiming to be derived from the smaller, ethical unit of the city rather than from a centralized bureaucratic state.

The Athenian *polis,* he states, is both a representative example of this concept of politics and the incarnation of the Aristotelian political model. Bookchin quotes Aristotle's warning of a political unit that is too large and non-self-sufficient, thus loosing its "true nature,"[267] as well as his plea for modesty and a sense of community. He also seems to identify with Aristotle's horror of the "rule of the many over the few," or even of "the poor over the wealthy."[268] Separated from their economic base, morality and ethics become ends in themselves; and the political and social, reduced to the private, becomes

---

263. Ibid., p. 87.
264. Ibid., p. 73.
265. Ibid., p. 66.
266. Ibid., p. 32.
267. Ibid., p. 37.
268. Ibid., p. 39.

meaningless. The result is the double standard and social blindness of someone who, while glorifying ancient "democracy," fatalistically justifies its war-economy, inequality, and slavery. Antistatism thus becomes a local, narrow-minded, antisocial ideology, and its attendant politics an upper-class patriarchal game. Democracy degenerates into a mere "structure" suitable only for the perfection of certain individuals, rather than for the welfare of humanity.

According to Bookchin, the forces that turned organic traditional societies into the victims of centralist modernity first appeared in Europe as a new economic development. Since that time, both the accumulation, expansion, and competition of trade and the profit motive have continuously evolved into activities that are ends in themselves. The older, local exchange of goods had more in common with barter than with modern trade. Despite these changes, he continues, trade relations remained relatively limited and "ethical" for quite a long time.

> Trade on a small, local scale between closely associated communities and individuals fostered cooperation rather then competition.[269]

In the Age of Absolutism, however, the nation state's goal of centralism worked against the small, local scale of medieval society and brought about the destruction of the evolutionary forces of nature and society. Diversity and complexity disappeared, and localism gave way to nationalism; community government evolved into bureaucracy, and the people turned into a population of isolated monads and passive subjects. A "corrosive global market economy"[270] has ruled ever since, personified by the English Puritans and dominated by "a moral imperative that made greed an end in itself."[271]

The "history of civic freedom,"[272] however, Bookchin stresses, did not end with the 14th century. Not even absolute monarchs were able to completely destroy the economic and social diversity of the old world.

> It was precisely the rich social features of the sixteenth, seventeenth, and eighteenth centuries—the extraordinary diversity of social life and its forms, the creative tensions from which so much mobility in status, cultural, and intellectual fervor emerged— that makes the era so fascinating and provocative.[273]

Well into the 18th century, Bookchin claims, there existed a "mixed economy," composed of elements of simple commodity production, feudalism, and capitalism. These elements were "not simply 'modes of production,'" they were "ways of experiencing the world and organizing it artistically and intellectually."[274]

Until well into the 20th century, the absolutist modern tendencies of standardization were opposed by communal political and social movements,

---

269. Ibid., p. 197.
270. Ibid., p. 135.
271. Ibid., p. 207.
272. Ibid., p. 114.
273. Ibid., p. 186.
274. Ibid., p. 199.

beginning with the Peasant Wars and their heroes Thomas Müntzer and John Ball, through the communal elements of the French Revolution, down to Emilio Zapata's Mexican Revolution, and the centers of communication of modern labor movements. All of them had one thing in common: a desire to preserve the "village community, its insular lifeways, its networks of mutual aid, its common lands and communitarian economy."[275] What most harmed the village community (which is, in the final analysis, what Bookchin's urban ideal boils down to) is the expansion of trade, communication, and commerce. A centralized road system was built between 1850 and 1860, making possible totalitarian rule, capitalist monetarization, and industrialization. According to Bookchin, it is "growth" that differentiates capitalism from the earlier economic systems including its own earlier forms: "the expansion of pavements, streets, houses, and industrial, commercial, and retail structures over the entire landscape."[276]

Nonetheless, Bookchin feels that the heritage of the previous age was still alive in the 19th century and was recreated in the form of sub-cultural communities of ethnic minorities resembling villages in the industrial cities of Europe and the US. In New York, for example, in areas like Little Italy, Chinatown, and the working-class slums of the Lower East Side, a proletarian culture developed which was held together by a communal network of mutual self-help organizations. Bookchin stresses the "broadly social, even utopian concerns" into which "class conflicts often spilled over beyond economic issues."[277]

Things did not really begin to go downhill, says Bookchin, until the end of World War II, when capitalism triumphed on all levels. The development from a market economy to a market society is reflected in the culture of the 1920s with its "personal greed and vice"[278] and its glorification of urban life. It took the economic depression, he continues, to bring people to their senses, at least in the US. Agrarian, precapitalist values—which in the New World found their expression in the pioneer's republican pride and which were renewed by the influx of new immigrants from the villages of Europe—experienced a revival. Agrarian and small-town life styles were rehabilitated in the "social vitality"[279] of the 1930s.

It is capitalism's growth, Babylonian immorality, and unlimited greed that makes Bookchin hate capitalism and modernity. He seems to despise industry more than industrial exploitation, the greed of the exploiter more than the plight of the exploited, the materialistic mentality of capitalism more than its unjust and murderous reality. The alternatives are the tribe, village, handicrafts, small trade, small capitalism—everything that is limited and confined. Bookchin's backward-looking and moralistic critique of capitalism swings like a pendulum

---

275. Ibid., p. 185.
276. Ibid., p. 202.
277. Ibid., p. 214.
278. Ibid., p. 222.
279. Ibid., p. 219.

between its progressive and reactionary elements. One cannot help but be reminded of the caste particularism of the fascists, their differentiation between working capital and greedy capital, their glorification of the past, and their moralistic vision.

In the book's last chapter Bookchin develops his brand of municipalism through a portrayal of 18th-century New England townships. These settlements of the Puritans, whom progressive historians have described as bigoted fanatics, are for Bookchin the "centers of social rebellion, civic autonomy, and collective liberty."[280] It is surprising to find that what they set out to do was to re-establish the tribal society of the Hebrews. In a "social as well as religious purification"[281] they attempted to return society to its original egalitarian, collectivist structures. They strove to attain the simple life, fairness, mutual aid, and "communitarian values" instead of the "fetishization of change."[282] They subscribed not to the market and the economy, but rather to a *moral* society and a *moral* economy. Because New England Puritanism rejected the church hierarchy, in Bookchin's eyes, it became an "utterly anarchic conception of Christianity," and the "periodic meeting[s] of the entire male [!] population"[283] were a model for future town meetings. He claims that women had high status in this society, and that accusations of Puritan patriarchy reflect a historical bias. This former advocate of hedonistic youth culture, who turned his back on the proletariat because it was too puritanical for him, now considers the Puritan state of God as the real model for an anarchist society. Having spared no effort in defending Puritan morality against material greed, economism, and Marxism, he is led by that same Puritan morality back to the very source of the money ethic that he so bitterly opposes. Bookchin makes yet another interesting theoretical loop to arrive at the resolution of this particular dilemma: it is not the virtuous New England citizens who are responsible for the money ethic, but rather the New England merchants whose orientation toward expansion and accumulation led them to abandon the "aristocratic values"[284] of traditional commerce and to exploit their own communities. Both accusations spring from the traditional critique of capitalism from the right, which blames the merchant for the materialistic decline of morality and criticizes capital's unpatriotic behavior. The Nazis turned this into the scapegoat theory of the Jewish merchant and his global conspiracy with the international labor movement.

Bookchin not only is aware of his proximity to fascist ideology, he even feels that an "ecological society . . . of free, autonomous, and organic communities"— although entailing perhaps the risk of "becoming a 'folk community' in the

---

280. Ibid., p. 233.
281. Ibid., p. 232.
282. Ibid., p. 234.
283. Ibid., p. 236.
284. Ibid., p. 240.

parochial, even fascistic sense of the term"—at the same time offers the opportunity of "producing a highly fecund terrain for promoting the development of deeply individuated and richly creative personalities."[285] In his view, National Socialism opportunistically exploited this "utopian content of that popular yearning for a sense of place and community."[286] Countering nationalism with local identity, Bookchin concludes:

> The conflict—more precisely, the tension—that exists between a localistic vision and a nationalistic reality is the most important basis for a new politics that we can redeem from the present crisis for which "urbanization" is a metaphor.[287]

In the book's final section Bookchin relates the concept of municipalism to his own experience in Vermont. He begins with the following appeal:

> Never has it been so necessary to place every innovative practice in the light of a visionary ethical ideal . . . liberal and radical causes are still mired in economistic and productivistic panaceas. Their moral message . . . has given way increasingly to strictly material demands. Far more than the right . . . the political middle ground and the left avow a solid bourgeois gospel of bread on the table and money in the bank.[288]

Bookchin combines his complaint that the right has co-opted the values of the American Revolution—freedom, decentralism, federalism, and individualism—with harsh criticism of the internationalism and anti-imperialism of the left:

> It will be an unpardonable failure in political creativity if a movement that professes to speak for a new politics does not try to occupy that landscape but rather, in a self-indulgent "hate America" mood, debarks to a "Third World" ideological ghetto abroad with shrieks about the "mad dogs of imperialism," snarling perpetually at its most natural allies at home—the ordinary citizen desiccated by his or her own spiritual poverty.[289]

"Ordinary people" become "ordinary citizens"—plain middle-class—small-town patriots who have always responded more aptly to nationalism than to internationalism. They make no economic demands, because that would place them on par with the lower classes. But they are religious—and above all moral.

With his message of disdain for economic panaceas, Bookchin has created a demagogic pied-piper strategy for some future profiteer of crisis. A well-fed person is just a money-grubbing, greedy bourgeois; to feed the world's hungry or even demand "prosperity for all" is bourgeois-materialistic, that is, immoral and unethical. How conservative this sort of morality is becomes even clearer near the end of the book:

> "Revolution" originally meant the restoration of traditional rights in the context of a changed world, a legitimation of emancipation by the power and dignity of tradition.[290]

---

285. Ibid., p. 253.
286. Ibid., p. 254.
287. Ibid., p. 255.
288. Ibid., pp. 277-78.
289. Ibid., pp. 281–82.
290. Ibid., p. 287.

The Utopia of the Third Way

Eco-anarchism as presented by Murray Bookchin—despite its (and his) metamorphoses
from the 1950s to the present—had from the beginning little in common with classic
anarchism, and nothing at all with modern anarcho-syndicalism.

In his 1977 book about the Spanish anarchists, which provides a wealth of
material and information, Bookchin makes clear that his sympathies with
Spanish anarchism are with its cultural revolutionary and utopian aspects. Thus
he is most impressed by the Spanish anarchists who took up vegetarianism,
anti-alcoholism, nudism, and ecological gardening. His heart warms to the
communalist-localist village anarchists and their clan-consciousness. These
anarcho-purists, Bookchin stresses, were not organized in unions or workers'
councils, but in *grupos afinidad* (affinity groups), tiny groups that grew out of
the *tertulia,* the "traditionally Hispanic group of male intimates."[291] He sees the
entire FAI (Federación Anarchista Iberia) as a consolidation of affinity groups.
The climax of the Spanish Revolution, according to this view, was the CNT
congress in Zaragossa, at which the utopian faction of the anarcho-syndicalists
won the day. Here Bookchin is in agreement with the utopian Malatesta, for
whom the unionist version of anarcho-syndicalism was a defection from "pure"
anarchism. Following the argument of the historian Vernon Richards, which
was bitterly challenged by Sam Dolgoff, Bookchin interprets the CNT's wavering
between revolution and compromise with historical reality as reformist
Realpolitik. Having himself organized local elections for the American Greens,
he accuses Abad Santillan, the anarcho-syndicalist, of betraying his principles because,
faced with an impending fascist victory, he called for participation in elections.

Bookchin's anarchism, inspired in particular by Fourier, pays tribute to the
idea of two paradises, the original one and the final one, between whose poles
the world continuously deteriorates. Following this reversed model of progress,
he never tires of complaining about the decline of values and custom:

> We believe that our values are worse than those held by people of only two or three
> generations ago. The present generation seems more self-centered, privatized, and
> mean-spirited by comparison with earlier ones. It lacks the support systems provided
> by the extended family, community, and a commitment to mutual aid.[292]

Whenever the good old days are invoked, the acceptance of inequality is not
far behind as is apparent in Bookchin's most recent book:

> What is problematic about justice "equal and exact," however, is that all people
> are *not* equal naturally, despite the *formal* equality that is conferred upon them in
> a "just" society. Some individuals are physically strong; others may be born weaker,
> by comparison. Still others differ markedly from each other by virtue of health, age,
> infirmities, talent, intelligence, and the material means of life at their disposal.[293]

---

291. Murray Bookchin, *The Spanish Anarchists.* New York: Harper and Row Publishers, p. 116.
292. Murray Bookchin, *Remaking Society.* Montreal: Black Rose, 1989, p. 20.
293. Ibid., p. 98.

Natural differences such as age are not only equated with other allegedly natural ones like intelligence, but even with disparities in income and wealth. What is natural is good, and should be preserved precisely for this reason. Thus it is hardly surprising that Bookchin, despite his critique that part of the feminist movement has become regressive and reactionary, increasingly falls prey to a theory of gender dualism that posits essential differences between the sexes that are caused by hormones.

> Males . . . produce significantly greater quantities of testosterone than females—an androgen that not only stimulates the synthesis of protein and produces a greater musculature, but also fosters behavioral traits that we associate with a high degree of physical dynamism.[294]

Any theory of "inequality," whether in the name of liberation or feminism, whether justified by notions of "diversity" and "complementarity," is intrinsically undemocratic and beats a path straight to the political right. Bookchin's desire for harmony leads him back to what he hates most—our present society. Although he believes that he wants to change everything, in the end everything is likely to stay just as it is: the economy, class relations, the inequality of the sexes, bourgeois ideology, and Christian morality. His ecological concepts waver between an unrealistic notion of communism-on-an-island and the acceptance of things as they are. How easily hedonism turns into asceticism, liberationist activism into passivity, democracy into aristocracy, respect for women into patriarchal ideology, reason into irrationalism, enthusiasm for the future into nostalgia, individualism into crazy-quilt feudalism, and equality becomes inequality.

But Bookchin does not want to be a conservative. And his moral integrity does, in fact, prevent him from being so. His attempt to delineate a third way between the left and the right, however, fails simply because there is no third way.

It is true that the inventor of social ecology has repeatedly distanced himself from antihuman, blood-and-soil naturalism, mysticism, and New Age religiousness. It is also true that in rejecting the international proletariat and in calling for the solidarity of the middle class in the national tradition, Bookchin does not mean the *Volksgemeinschaft* (see note 166). And in his annoying idealization of some fictitious matriarchy, he has never called upon us to worship the Goddess. Despite the fact that he sometimes comes dangerously close to social Darwinism, he would be the last to support it as a principle. But his nature ontology, patriotism, and tolerance of inequality, however, have helped pave the way for conservative developments in the ecology movement. Like Pandora, he will not be able to recall the spirits he has set loose.

---

294. Ibid., p. 55.

3   ANARCHO-CAPITALISM

Murray Rothbard—A Visit with Mr. Libertarian

Speaking to me in German, Sam Dolgoff had described Murray Rothbard as "repulsive." I pictured the intellectual father of anarcho-capitalist philosophy and libertarianism, known in insider circles as Mr. Libertarian, as efficient and urbane, in a fancy setting. The apartment building on the Upper West Side with its elegant lobby and exceedingly polite doorman fulfilled my expectations, but the apartment itself was smaller and much plainer than I thought it would be. Mrs. Rothbard led me into the living room, cleared the sofa of numerous folders so that I could sit down, and disappeared. There was no air conditioning, only a small electric fan. Modest pre- and postwar period furniture; yellowed walls, improvised electrical outlets, lots of dust, and everywhere books, brochures, and junk, stacked up, bundled, and loose. In the bathroom an ancient lamp, its switch jammed, stood next to the toilet. A glance into the professor's office revealed stacks and stacks of books, and here and there a pile of junk.

Rothbard is an elderly gentleman with an easy-going, slightly faded elegance, as unconventional as he is cooperative. His manner was pleasantly unpretentious for an academic, without a hint of vanity and schoolmasterly paternalism. Born in 1926 into a middle-class Jewish family, Rothbard spent his childhood and teenage years in New York. He had two pairs of aunts and uncles on both sides of the family who were members of the American Communist Party (CPUSA). In fact, he recalls, almost everyone he knew was a communist. Moreover, most middle-class intellectuals of the time were card-carrying party members, or at least fellow travelers. Rothbard's father and the latter's sister were politically active anarchists and supporters of Emma Goldman before World War I. His father later lost interest in politics and, though still an individualist, became a conservative liberal. Rothbard is proud of his family's political tradition. His parents had met at an "anarchist ball,"[295] he told me.

---

295.   Murray Rothbard, interview with the author, 1989.

When Rothbard began studying economics at Columbia University he was one of the few Republicans on campus, almost everyone else was either a communist or a socialist. One of his first confrontations with libertarianism was at the college bookstore. There he was impressed by slogans such as "Taxation is Robbery" and "The Enemy is the State" printed in big red letters on the cover of a book by his future teacher Frank Chodorov. Later Rothbard discovered laissez-faire and the Austrian School of Economics. During World War II he joined the political coalition opposing the New Deal and considered himself part of the "extreme right," but by 1949 he had become an anarchist, that is, an anarcho-capitalist. During the Korean War, Rothbard went on to say, there were only two antiwar fractions, the communists and the isolationist "extreme right" of the Republican party, with which he could identify. The Republican right did not become prowar until 1952 when it entered its fateful alliance with the CIA. By 1955 Rothbard had begun looking for a third party, and in 1959 he broke completely with the right. When William F. Buckley stated on the occasion of Khrushchev's visit that he would not shake the hand of the "bloody butcher of the Ukraine," Rothbard was outraged. In a letter to Buckley he reminded him that the Republicans certainly didn't seem to mind shaking Churchill's hand, the "bloody butcher of Dresden." In 1958 Rothbard joined the Rand group.

Ayn Rand (1905–1982) was the self-proclaimed founder of objectivism, a populist version of laissez-faire philosophy. Photographs show an elegant, slightly eccentric woman, often holding a cigarette holder. Her emblem is said to have been the dollar sign, which she liked to wear in the form of a diamond pin. In the 1950s, together with her manager and lover Nathaniel Branden, she founded a political institute in New York, which flourished into the center of the period's conservative in-crowd. She is said to have been as dictatorial as a sect leader. All this came to a sudden end in 1968 when Branden broke off his turbulent love affair with Rand, who was twenty-five years older than he. She retaliated by excommunicating him, an action that led to an irrevocable split among their followers. She herself remained a cult figure. Generations of teenagers since then have devoured her dramatic novels-with-a-message propagating capitalism.

Rothbard was expelled from the Rand group after six months. Even though he shared Rand's principles of individualism, laissez-faire, natural law, and classical esthetics, he could not cope with the organization's sectarian inflexibility nor with Ayn Rand's dictatorial airs. Many of her followers, he told me, changed their Russian or Jewish names to Anglo-Saxon-sounding ones. Rand's real name was Alice Rosenbaum. When I pointed out the cryptic anti-Semitism in one of Rand's novels he seemed at first both surprised and curious. When I went into detail, he agreed:

> That might be right . . . I never thought of that. Yeah, the bad guys are all loose-lipped and whatever, and the good guys tall, sort of Gary Cooper types, Anglo-Saxon . . . [the bad guys] dark and sort of slobbery, yeah, yeah, that's right . . . handicapped, watery eyes, . . . the good guys are all perfect.[296]

Rothbard got his Ph.D. in economics in the late 1940s and was a disciple of Ludwig von Mises. Along with other libertarians from a study group called the "Bastian Circle" he began drifting toward the New Left. In the late 1960s the group began publishing the magazine *Left and Right*; it urged all libertarians, as opponents to the Vietnam War and the draft, to join the New Left. During that period, Rothbard emphasizes, he learned a great deal from his new comrades, especially about the responsibility of the US for the cold war, and it was obvious that he took great pleasure in recalling his collaboration with opponents of the Vietnam War and with the SDS. For him this must have been the libertarian's heroic period. He told me proudly that, thanks to his new connections, he joined the faculty of the Brooklyn Polytechnical University in 1966 where he taught for twenty years in a department in which almost everyone was a Marxist. In 1971 Rothbard, who is now a professor at the University of Las Vegas, became one of the twelve founding members of the Libertarian Party, to which, despite differences, he still belongs.

Rothbard explained that the party's decline during the 1980s resulted from the disastrous impact of Reagan's politics. "This fantastic damp of soft soap and charisma"[297] has corrupted almost the entire movement, he said; many "semi-libertarians" viewed Reagan as a heroic figure, especially after being paid off with government positions. A kind of corruption of both intellect and language, he explained, led people to believe Reagan's promises about freedom and reduction of government, but luckily all of that was limited, thanks to the presidency's two-term limit—in Rothbard's view the Republicans' only wise measure since World War II.

> Otherwise Reagan would have been there forever, they could have mummified him like Lenin in the tomb, prop him up, have a ventriloquist shake his head and imitate his voice.[298]

Since Reagan's retirement there is hope once again, Rothbard stated. He also felt that the developments in the Eastern bloc were grounds for optimism. Six months before the Berlin Wall came down he predicted that the communist system would collapse: "It's like a revolutionary implosion. We are living through a revolutionary moment in history. Just marvelous to see it."[299] And thanks to Gorbachev's disarmament policy, he added, the cold war is over, too.

---

296. Ibid.
297. Ibid.
298. Ibid.
299. Ibid.

They will be trying to find some other enemy, of course. The war against drugs.
That is a beautiful war, because they can never win it. It is a perfect war from the
point of view of the state.[300]

The principles of laissez-faire and opposition to war appear to be the
cornerstones of Rothbard's political convictions. The libertarians, in his eyes,
constitute "the vanguard of classical liberalism" and are "unterrified Jeffersonian
democrats."[301] He explains what anarchism means to him: "I am an abolitionist.
If I could abolish the state by pushing a button, I would push the button."[302]

Rothbard has little in common with the social revolutionary anarchists in
the tradition of Bakunin and Kropotkin. He points out that their motivation
for being anarchists is diametrically opposed to his own. While for them the
need to abolish the state arises from it being the basis and source of private
property, for him it arises because the state is private property's greatest enemy.
Furthermore, he believes in neither collective decision-making processes nor
the possibility of human cooperation without a market economy and trade.

Responding to my question about the equality or difference of men and
women, Rothbard spoke of "natural" differences. He cited the example of a
highly intelligent woman who had studied at Harvard and who had achieved
great professional success. At the age of thirty she decided to have children,
gave up her career, and evolved into an "earth mother" giving birth to one
child after the other.

When asked about his opinion of the ecology movement, Rothbard referred
to their philosophy as "evil" and delivered a scathing critique of ecological
antihuman biocentrism which he equates with the entire movement.

Before I left, Rothbard gave me the addresses of other libertarians. In a
paternal gesture he wrote them out meticulously on several pieces of yellow
paper. He is indeed the most likeable reactionary I have ever met.

The Anarcho-Capitalist Family Tree

Individualism Between Harmony and Dog-Eat-Dog

Murray Rothbard is viewed in anarcho-capitalist circles as the latest addition to
their hall of fame. The founder of individual anarchism is Max Stirner (1806–
1856), the author of *The Ego and Its Own,* a book Marx criticized at length in
The German Ideology. Marx's "Saint Max" shares with the social revolutionary
anarchists not only the same main enemy, the state, but also the same cardinal
virtue, individualism. But he differs with them in that he believes in abolishing
not only the state but also society as an institution responsible for its members.
Society is to be replaced by a "Union of Egoists," whose functions Stirner

---

300. Ibid.
301. Ibid.
302. Ibid.

neglects to describe. In contrast to Bakunin and his heirs, who view property as theft and individuality as an altruistic achievement, Stirner derives his identity solely from property, an arch-bourgeois concept that made him the ancestor of laissez-faire liberalism. Only a little softened through the "Union of Egoists," the property question in his world of the Ego is settled by "the war of all against all,"[303] a model borrowed from Hobbes and based on a concept of an unalterably competitive human nature. As a radical egoist Stirner despises morals, altruism, pity, and above all the common weal, which he views as "the furthest extremity of self-renunciation." He is an unconditional supporter of the belief in natural human inequality.

> Nay, the born shallow-pates indisputable form the most numerous class of men. And why, indeed, should not the same distinctions show themselves in the human species that are unmistakably in every species of beasts? The more gifted and less gifted are to be found everywhere.[304]

Elsewhere, he refers euphemistically to "a new severance or singleness" as a "new equality" or "unequal equality."

As a critic of all bourgeois morals, Stirner is an advocate of free love. But unlike Fourier and the social revolutionary critics of licensed marriage and monogamy, Stirner reduces the relationship between lovers—and human relations in general—to the question of their "usefulness" or "necessity," thus making prostitution the most consistent model of interpersonal relations. Nevertheless many bohemian free lovers from the post-1848 circles around George Sand up until Emma Goldman referred to Stirner. During the 1890s a debate about similarities in Stirner's and Nietzsche's works rose among European intellectuals. In Germany prominent conservative figures of the generation before World War I, among them Chancellor Otto von Bismarck and Rudolf Steiner, founder of anthroposophy, were impressed with Stirner. From the turn of the century until the late 1920s many anarchists, for instance the novelist B. Traven, were impressed by Stirner's individualism. But there were just as many forerunners of the Nazi movement, such as the Strasser brothers, prominent intellectual leaders of the brownshirts, who admired Stirner's contempt for the masses and his approval of the law of the jungle. Indeed some of Stirner's comments can easily be interpreted in a fascist and imperialist light:

> Thus the communists affirm that the earth belongs rightfully to him who tills it, and its products to those who bring them out. I think it belongs to him who knows how to take it, or who does not let it be taken from him, does not let himself be deprived of it. If he appropriates it, then not only the earth, but the right to it too, belongs to him. This is egoistic right: it is right for me, therefore it is right. [305]

---

303. Max Stirner, *The Ego And Its Own*. London: Rebel Press, 1982, p.260.
304. Ibid., p. 213.
305. Ibid., p. 191.

After World War II Stirner's critique of bourgeois morals was rediscovered by the existentialist bohemians who lashed out at the hypocritical altruism, humanism, and moralism of a brutal and immoral bourgeoisie.

Perhaps Stirner's most enthusiastic follower was John Henry Mackay who discovered him in the 1890s. Mackay was a naturalist poet and bohemian who belonged to a more radical faction of social democrats who had abandoned social democracy and became communist anarchists and advocates of the propaganda of the deed. In 1891, under the influence of Stirner's writings, Mackay, who had already made a name for himself with sentimental didactic poetry, published his bestselling opus *The Anarchists* in which he distances himself from his former leftist views. The book was translated into seven languages; In 1992 a new edition was published in Leipzig, eastern Germany. The novel—not very convincing in literary terms—is set in London in the 1880s and describes the labor struggles and the revolutionary immigrants' intellectual disputes. Mirroring the author's own political about-face, the protagonist, Auban, transforms himself from a social revolutionary into an individual anarchist. He breaks with altruistic philanthropy, democratic egalitarianism, revolutionary class-struggle, and the anarcho-putschist belief in the usefulness of violence, embracing instead nonmonopolistic Manchester capitalism in which, thanks to the abolition of interest and inheritance rights, every individual is potentially a small capitalist. The anarcho-communist utopia is replaced by "anarchy," a stateless environment of free competition for all. Under closer scrutiny, what appears to be an overall rejection of violence turns out to be merely rejection of revolutionary violence. Auban/Mackay advocates the "struggle of each against all" and the forcible defense of property at any price.

> I would not be capable of killing a man, whether in war, in a duel, or in some other "legally" permitted way. But I would not hesitate for a moment to put a bullet in the head of a burglar who breaks into my house with the intention of robbing and murdering me.[306]

The former revolutionary justifies such vigilante justice with the resigned comment that "anarchy is not heaven on earth." He states that people have to recognize "their true nature and its needs"[307] in order to be free. Hence there is no need for change. Mackay's development is typical for the intellectuals of the 1880s who, rebelling against the state, the church, and bourgeois morality, sought to establish links to the proletariat, only to end up ten years later as elitist despisers of the masses, semi-religious dreamers, regressive agrarian romantics, or laissez-faire rationalists. Feeling equally threatened by monopoly capitalism and the labor movement, they searched for a "third way." However, both as a supporter of free love and as one of the first semi-open homosexuals,

---

306 . John Henry Mackay, *Werke in einem Band*. Berlin: 1928, p. 859, translated by Danny Lewis.
307. Ibid., p. 859.

Mackay also saw in Stirner the prophet of self-realization in same-sex love. Many first generation representatives of the gay movement were also followers of Stirner and subscribed to a pederast and, for the most part, elitist ideology. It was from this point of view that Mackay wrote his gay Sagitta novels in the 1920s. Named after his pseudonym, these novels enjoyed a small renaissance in the US where in the late 1980s a John Henry Mackay Society was founded in New York.

Mackay was a commuter between the left and the right, as well as between the Old and the New World. In 1893 he undertook a pilgrimage to the Haymarket monument. On his journey through the US he was warmly received not only by individualists, but also by social revolutionary anarchists like Emma Goldman. Only the elderly Johann Most dared to criticize this cult figure, calling him a bourgeois anticommunist—particularly when it soon became apparent that Mackay was in agreement with Benjamin R. Tucker (1854–1939), Most's liberalist opponent and a typical representative of American individualism, in which liberty means freedom of trade, justice is the freedom to make contracts, and democracy is equality before the law and in the market. Josiah Warren and Lysander Spooner, two followers of Proudhon, combined this credo with economic demands such as the abolition of interest and the maintenance of the gold standard, and called this mixture anarchism. Spooner (1808–1887), an abolitionist also opposed to the state and to all institutions, was one of the first to refer to the collection of taxes as theft. In the 1840s and 1850s Warren (1798–1874) founded several individualist colonies, the most famous of which was "Modern Times" on Long Island (1859–1862). Antimonopolist free-market ideology and absolute pluralism in life style and clothing were seen as the safeguards of the principles of nonintervention and fairness.

Benjamin R. Tucker spent his life as a private scholar, writer, and bookseller. From 1881 to 1908 he published his periodical *Liberty*. Though influenced by Stirner and Proudhon, Tucker was a proud patriot. His goal was an antimonopolist, just, laissez-faire capitalism of small entrepreneurs, small farmers, and craftsmen. He defines anarchism as a society without a government in which "all the affairs of men should be managed by individuals or voluntary associations."[308] The antithesis of state monopoly is universal competition—the free market. Tucker considered the book *The Right to Ignore the State* by the American guru of laissez-faire, Herbert Spencer, an anarchist classic. For him, an anarchist is first and foremost a Jeffersonian democrat. Unlike Mackay's dog-eat-dog concept of freedom, Tucker defines his ideal society within the spirit of early socialism as a form of virtuous harmony. The protection of private property and of the person by means of voluntary associations and cooperation is, according to him, only a temporary necessity, because with the realization of his utopia poverty and with it "crime will disappear from the

---

308. Benjamin R. Tucker, *State Socialism and Anarchism*. Colorado: Ralph Myles Publishers, 1972, p. 16.

world."[309] Tucker also rejects bourgeois morality. "Mind your own business" is for him the only law of ethics as well as freedom, which is itself a "sure cure for all the vices." But on the other hand, "attempts to arbitrarily suppress vice" are "in themselves crimes."[310]

Tucker feels that to establish anarchist liberty it would be sufficient to abolish monopolies, which are the means by which the state grants privileges to certain people. The most important of these is "compulsory taxation," "the life principle of all the monopolies."[311] Then there is the state monopoly of money, which is nothing other than the restriction of the right to act as a banker. Without this monopoly, Tucker says, interest, the scourge of the common man, would cease to exist. With the abolition of land rent, that is, of private land ownership for anyone neither living on nor cultivating land, usury would have "one less leg to stand on."[312] Finally, the abolition of the customs and patent monopolies that restrict competition, together with the abolition of monopolistic, universally binding guidelines for religion, medicine, and education in favor of the competition in the market, would bring about the attainment of full liberty. Tucker equates the state with the principle of majority rule. His antistatism, like that of Stirner, thus has an antisocial and antidemocratic connotation. Attacking Kropotkin and Most because of their demands for the expropriation of capitalists, Tucker accused the social-revolutionary anarchists of "falsely call[ing] themselves anarchists,"[313] for in the end, their program envisioned a despotic state socialism.

Laissez-faire Liberalism and the Austrian School of Economics

Anarcho-capitalists of all shades lay claim to the philosophies of classical liberalism of the 17th and 18th centuries, to the theories of John Stuart Mill or John Locke. In fact, however, the beliefs of these right-wing anarchists have little in common with classical liberalism, which looks to foster political change and social reform. They are much more closely related to the laissez-faire liberalist thought of the 19th century. In laissez-faire liberalism, rights, prosperity, and liberty are guaranteed by unhindered competition in the context of a self-regulating market whose laws are "natural" and tolerate no interference. Government's only responsibility is therefore the protection of the market, of contracts, and of property. Everyone's chances at success being equal, whoever is unsuccessful in the marketplace is himself to blame, thus legitimizing the wretched condition of the working classes as well as the brutal reality of social inequality in the name of free trade and competition. In the 1870s, at a time

---

309. Ibid., p. 27.
310. Ibid., p. 21.
311. Ibid., p. 21.
312. Ibid., p. 19.
313. Ibid., p. 22.

when the labor movement and the reform-minded representatives of the bourgeoisie were clamoring for revolution or reform, the laissez-faire theorists outdid each other with cruel solutions. In England, Thomas Malthus, who was one of the first to apply Darwin's evolutionary laws to human society, called for a drastic reduction of the human population. According to his theory, poverty results from a lack of food, which, in turn, is caused by the overpopulation of the poor, and not from an unjust social structure. Neither the rich nor the government can be called upon to take responsibility for this state of affairs: any attempt at a redistribution of wealth, for example, through taxes, only robs the one to give to the other. Kropotkin tells us with remarkable clarity:

> It was precisely when the ideas of equality and liberty, awakened by the French and American revolutions, were still permeating the minds of the poor, while the richer classes had become tired of their amateur excursions into the same domains, that Malthus came to assert . . . that no equality is possible; that the poverty of the many is not due to institutions, but is a natural law.[314]

Popular in the US were the theories of the social Darwinist Herbert Spencer, in which he applied the laws of evolution and natural selection directly to economics. In his view, social reformist measures such as the regulation of working hours, minimum wages, or free education for the poor, are attacks on both natural evolution and social freedom. The artificially induced survival of the weak is to the detriment of the strong; those who prove themselves to be the most capable in the undisturbed market are the true benefactors of humankind. While the free market inevitably leads to an evolutionary higher development in the sense of social progress, state regulation is a throwback to the "static" society of the Middle Ages.

Another version of laissez-faire capitalism originated with the marginal utility theory of Carl Menger (1840–1921). Menger is considered the founder of the Austrian School of Economics, which continued to refine its theory of monetary value until the middle of the 20th century. The most prominent descendant of this school of thought is the monetarist Milton Friedman, the economic authority for such politicians as Richard Nixon, Ronald Reagan, Margaret Thatcher, and others. The subjectivism of the marginal utility theory, which claims to explain price mechanisms and to provide the means for determining market prices, reflects and extends the individualism of laissez-faire. This modern theory of value was originally directed against the classical theory of the value of labor with its social implications viewed as opening the way to socialism. The main representatives of the third generation of the Austrian School of Economics, Ludwig von Mises and F.A. Hayek, eventually became authorities for the libertarians.

F.A. Hayek, who received a Nobel Prize in 1974, just as progressive social policies were being abandoned by governments the world over, had made a

---

314. Peter Kropotkin, *Fields, Factories and Workshops.* New York and London: Putnam's, 1913, p. 158.

name for himself in 1944 with his theory of totalitarianism. Hayek equates fascism and socialism, justifying his theory on the ground that both are enemies of liberalism. Further, Hayek states that both socialism and fascism use state planning, and he insists that the socialist tactic of fomenting class divisions paved the way for fascism. Hayek embraces the idea that a dualism of good and evil is anchored in national traits. He categorizes the English as good, because they display the individualist virtue of tolerance, reject power, respect others, and are intellectually independent. In his opinion it is precisely these characteristics that are typical of the merchant and not of the warrior or military man. Typical of the latter is the collectivist-minded German, who displays ruthless thoroughness, blind obedience to authority, and a senseless willingness for self-sacrifice. (Incidentally both Hayek, the critic of totalitarianism, and his colleague Friedman, who also won a Nobel Prize, were to support the Pinochet dictatorship in Chile.)

The modern classic for all capitalists, right-wing liberals, libertarians, and anarcho-capitalists is Ludwig von Mises (1881–1973), a professor of economics. Rothbard notes that he was a victim of Austrian anti-Semitism as early as the 1920s and escaped to the US in 1940; his library was destroyed by the Nazis. He died in exile in 1973, one year before his doctrines made a belated comeback. Mises's main opponent after World War II was John Maynard Keynes, the intellectual father of the American New Deal and the European postwar social democrats.

Mises first drew attention with his book *Die Gemeinwirtschaft—Untersuchungen über den Sozialismus* (*The Market Economy: A Study of Socialism*), published in 1925. In this book he lays claim to reason, utilitarian thinking, democracy, equality before the law, pacifism, and tolerance as the main principles of liberalism. He rejects both war and revolution, and asserts that society was initially formed by the appropriation of private property and by occupation—primitive man, competitive and violent, grabbed whatever he could get. In the course of civilization, this primitive rule of force developed into law, or rather into property law, through the introduction of contracts. Small groups of people concluded social contracts, which gradually evolved into international law. The contracts guaranteed property and the division of labor, thus enabling the rise of commerce, money, and capital. When people tend exclusively to their (property) interests under such legal conditions, Mises continues, an automatic mechanism of market and society comes into being; it is this mechanism alone that can guarantee the happiness of individuals. The division of labor and the necessity for private ownership of the means of production derive from inequality among humans and the differences in their living conditions. Mises praises the "manifold variety of nature" and of "outer space with its endless, limitless richness in variety."[315] Despite this diversity, it seems that most human beings

---

315. Ludwig von Mises, *Die Gemeinwirtschaft.* Jena: Gustav Fischer, 1932, p. 262, translated by Danny Lewis.

are uniformly intellectually inferior, with the result that the world's wealth needs to be distributed among a very few of the human varieties:

> The masses do not think. This is precisely the reason why they follow those who do think. The intellectual leadership of mankind is a position held by the very few who are able to think.[316]

The few he is referring to, we are told, are the entrepreneurs, who lead and guide the production process for the benefit of all.

The sexes, too, are unequal, Mises tells us. According to his liberalist myth of the primitive horde, relations between the sexes were initially governed by the law of the jungle: Primitive man, greedy and horny, took control of defenseless primitive woman "like an object without any will of its own."[317] It was only the advent of capitalism that changed these conditions. According to Mises's theory, monogamy resulted from a "capitalist way of thinking and calculation"[318] in the family, giving rise to ordered relationships. Equal rights, however, are not the point, since "a woman . . . is simply the lover and mother who serves the sexual drive,"[319] and the radical women's movement is the "spiritual child of socialism." As late as 1925, Mises saw no need for female suffrage, for the "highest state of female happiness"[320] in any case lies in motherhood.

Mises's concept of labor is just as bleak. Work, by definition, is not pleasurable, and there is no direct relationship between work and value. The socialist demand for full compensation for the products of labor is dismissed with the clever assertion that this compensation is determined by the market price. The worker receives this price for his labor in the form of wages. The piece-work method of calculating wages is thus the most desirable, whereas wages based on time are the least desirable, "because wages rise along with the increase in the minimum labor output."[321] Human beings are reduced to a measurable quantity of labor and society is seen as a kind of *perpetuum mobile* whose existence is its own justification. It is most important that no one interfere with this mechanism, be it the state, labor unions, or other representatives of allegedly antisocial special interest groups. Mises's callous justification of the misery in 19th-century factories is but an illustration of this view: he claims that the inferior production capacity of women and children, being all that was available at the time, made long working hours necessary.

The development of a sense of social responsibility and the "expansion of care for the poor"[322] bring great dangers with it, according to Mises. The same applies to accident and health insurance which produce "accidents and illness,"

---

316. Ibid., p. 472.
317. Ibid., p. 68.
318. Ibid., p. 72.
319. Ibid., p. 80.
320. Ibid., p. 78.
321. Ibid., p. 150.
322. Ibid., p. 442.

"prevent healing," and "in almost all cases make them worse and last longer."[323] Unemployment insurance is equally bad, because it is said to foster unemployment; in fact, Mises states that unemployment does not really exist at all, preferring instead the term "wagelessness."[324] Since workers, he asserts, are interested in wages, not in work, then what they are really lacking is not work, but rather a wage for which they are willing to work. The modern worker, spoiled by reforms and unwilling to slave long hours under hideous conditions, is thus viewed as being responsible for unemployment and the economic crises of capitalism.

The liberalist pacifist position is at first glance convincing and an apparently fundamental difference between liberalism and conservatism. Mises criticizes social Darwinism and militarism by noting that society is "always peace, never war."[325] In the doctrine of the division of labor, he continues, the struggle is replaced by "mutual aid."[326] Mises subsequently gives a positive assessment of social Darwinism: the private ownership of the means of production, he claims, replaces the "elimination of human surplus through the struggle for existence . . . with the limitation of progeny for social reasons."[327] He continues along this line of reasoning by stating that liberalism fights only those who "prefer the unions' deadly struggle" to "peaceful cooperation," as well as "criminals" and "savage peoples."[328] Should barbarian communism win even a partial victory, the free nations will be forced to "bring backwards peoples into the realm of civilization or . . . to destroy them,"[329] for the capitalist system must bring the entire world into its system of divided labor. So much for liberalism's alleged devotion to peace. Liberalism is a philosophy that wants us to believe that only "economic livelihoods" are destroyed in the "competitive struggle" and that in capitalism there is "bread and room for all."[330]

Mises's approach to racism is similar to his approach to social Darwinism. He opposes racist ideology only when it preaches racial struggle; when it is linked with the dogma of inequality, however, its "scientific"[331] results are said to confirm liberal social theory rather than to disprove it.

> It is perfectly legitimate to assume that the races are different in their cognitive abilities and in their willpower and accordingly are unequally suited for the task of setting up societies, and that the better races are characterized in particular by their special ability to strengthen social bonds.[332]

---

323. Ibid., p. 443.
324. Ibid., p. 450.
325. Ibid., p. 285.
326. Ibid., p. 28.
327. Ibid., p. 288.
328. Ibid., p. 291.
329. Ibid., p. 476.
330. Ibid., p. 292.
331. Ibid., p. 298.
332. Ibid., p. 297.

Having said this, it is not surprising that Mises has nothing but praise for British colonialism. According to his view, English liberalism can pride itself in having established England's colonial rule to the benefit of the subjugated peoples, in fact, of the entire world.

Socialism itself, behind which the "overwhelming majority of mankind"[333] is aligned, seems irrational to him, unscientific, and backwards; he perceives it as a romantic-mystical ideology that wickedly seduces the ignorant masses, who (using a Nietzschean phrase) "only count because they are numerous."[334] And the class struggle—measured with the same yardstick as the theories of race and nationalism—is viewed as a war of annihilation, thus becoming an heir to social Darwinism. Mises's almost paranoid fear of a socialist victory is also fueled by his unbroken belief in the rule of ideas. The proletariat, he proclaims in all seriousness, is not united by its class predicament, but by socialist ideology. Marx, he asserts, created slogans that "whip up the mob" of factory laborers into "attacking private property," "rationalize their resentment," and "transfigure their instincts of envy and revenge into a historical mission."[335]

The Queen of Reason: Ayn Rand

After World War II several arch-conservative adherents of the Austrian School of Economics made a name for themselves in the US; the most famous of these was Rothbard's former teacher, Ayn Rand. Though she never considered herself an anarchist, and though most anarcho-capitalists dissociate themselves from her, the influence she had on the movement is undisputed. She advocated a state that does not have any social functions and whose power derives from the police, the judiciary, and the military. She defended the economic interests of big industrialists and was determined to fight communism at any cost. In the 1960s she called upon the state to use its power against the New Left.

Though Rand, celebrated by her followers as the "Queen of Reason," considered herself a radical rationalist, she was influenced by Nietzsche's ontology of power and his disdain for weakness and compassion. In Rand's theoretical and literary writings, social Darwinism, the Nietzschean superman, and laissez-faire take on a quasi-fascistic taint. Contempt for people, the survival of the fittest, racism, and communist witch-hunting are stripped of the tolerant pluralist facade with which liberalism usually disguises them. With amazing openness Rand divides people into two categories: on the one hand, "The Few," the creators of progress, who use their intelligence and think and act in an independently creative way; on the other hand, "The Many," the dull members of the herd, who either do not think at all or are parasites, merely emulating the intellectual products of the creative few. The connecting link between the two

---

333. Ibid., p. 3.
334. Ibid., p. 39.
335. Ibid., p. 457.

is the market, which must be free in order to institute justice. Based on private property, the market ensures that the "intellectual giants" are able to blossom undisturbed so that they may uplift the rest of society to the level of their own accomplishments. The "intellectual parasites" and imitators "are constantly being beaten by the innovators,"[336] because the "man at the top of the intellectual pyramid" gets nothing except his material payment but benefits all. The man at the bottom of the heap, however, is so inadequate that if left to himself he would not survive. He "contributes nothing to those above him,"[337] he only reaps others' profits. Rand is perhaps the most open theorist of the purpose of capitalist property rights: they exist to grant privileges to a small minority, thus turning the property rights into a class right. Rand also tells us who the most important of the upper 10,000 are: the tycoons, "a *very small* minority, compared to the total of all the uncivilized hordes on earth."[338] They are the symbol of a free society which would be doomed without them. Borrowing from the progressive rhetoric of minority protection, Rand portrays big businessmen as victims of the anti-trust laws.

In her best-selling novel *The Fountainhead*, she brings to life her rigid scheme of human types. Those who are victorious "on the battlefield of ideas"[339] are proud, eccentric outsiders who suffer under the mediocrity and herd-like mentality of their day. Sensitive esthetes, and good-looking to boot, they love only themselves and their work and allow no interference from anyone. They never ask for help, detest cooperation of any kind, and never grovel, nor do they waste time on friends or have a social life. But they are intellectual aristocrats, arch-geniuses and supermen. If it weren't for their obsession with work and their misanthropic outlook, one might mistake Rand's heroes for left-wing bohemians. They are always Anglo-Saxon Americans. For Rand, a Russian in American exile, the US, with its individualist tradition, is "the noblest country in the history of men."[340] The protagonist of *The Fountainhead*, the genius-architect Howard Roark, is a blondish American with Anglo-Saxon-Teutonic features. He looks very manly and slightly brutal:

> His face was like a law of nature—a thing one could not question, alter or implore. It had high cheekbones over gaunt, hollow cheeks; grey eyes, cold and steady; a contemptuous mouth, shut tight, the mouth of an executioner or a saint.[341]

Roark's rival, the mediocre architect Peter Keaton, who represents the intellectual parasites, has dark hair and soft features. He and his kind are contemptuously characterized as:

---

336. Ayn Rand, *Capitalism: The Unknown Ideal.* Chicago: Signet, 1967, p. 26.
337. Ibid., p. 28.
338. Ibid., p. 61.
339. Ibid., p. 267.
340. Ayn Rand, *The Fountainhead.* Chicago: Signet, 1971, p. 684.
341. Ibid., p. 16.

the person who loves your beauty and the women he sees in a subway—the kind that can't cross their knees and show flesh hanging publicly over their garters—with the same sense of exaltation. I mean the person who loves the clean, steady, unfrightened eyes of a man looking through a telescope and the white stare of an imbecile—equally.[342]

Below the mass of average people are the retarded and the crippled, subhumans whose elimination would be legitimate. Roark, who built a temple in honor of the (super)human race, is the victim of an intrigue and is forced to witness his temple being turned into a home for retarded children—

a grinning child who could not be taught to read or write; a girl born without a nose, whose father was also her grandfather . . . their eyes staring vacantly, the stare of death before which no world existed.[343]

The embodiment of evil is the communist Elsworth Toohey, an architecture critic and Roark's enemy. His purpose in life is to establish the primitive rule of collectivism, to put an end to the work of great men, thus causing society, in the name of equality, to be dragged down to the lowest common denominator.

Let progress stop. Let all stagnate. There's equality in stagnation. All subjugated to the will of all. Universal slavery—without even the dignity of a master. Slavery to slavery. A great circle—and a total equality. The world of the future.[344]

Just as disastrous as Toohey's ideal of equality is his altruism, rooted in the Christian cult of suffering and compassion. Toohey, whom Rand models after the British (Jewish) socialist Harold Lasky, is described as a frail-looking, elegantly dressed man with a wedge-shaped face, ears that stick out, a long, thin nose, and dark eyes sparkling with intellect—in short, a personification of the left intellectual or the Jew. To round out the clichés, it is suggested that this demon of a man may even be homosexual.

The love story between superpeople Howard Roark and Dominique Francon reveals Rand's contradictionary, yet ultimately reactionary, concept of women. The beautiful blond heroine is intelligent, independent, professionally successful, and—fitting a misogynist stereotype—frigid and unsensual. The former qualities enable her to compete with and fight against men. Indeed, competition seems to be the "liberated" element in her relationship with Roark, but competition is always linked to private property and domination: Dominique falls in love with Roark when he looks at her disdainfully, in an "an act of ownership."[345] She weakens and expresses female emotions for the first time in a sudden outburst of hatred. The next time she sees him she is sitting on a horse, from whence she whips him in the face, inducing him to rape her in their next encounter. Roark takes possession of her like "a soldier violating an enemy woman. . . . not as love, but as defilement,"[346] an act of violence that dissolves

342. Ibid., p. 445.
343. Ibid., p. 386.
344. Ibid., p. 640.
345. Ibid., p. 206.
346. Ibid., p. 218.

into ecstasy. Rand, the strong woman, shares the patriarchal view of sexuality's violent nature and of women enjoying subjugation and rape.

How It All Began

Laissez faire, laissez faire,
Everybody's talking about laissez faire
People over here, people over there,
Everybody's talking about laissez faire.
. . .
Sell the roads and bridges, cut off foreign aid,
You all gotta work if you're gonna get paid.
. . .
Well, people so happy they abolished all the tax,
Pot so cheap you can buy it by the packs.
. . .
Like my ole gramma used to say, she said,
"Son, don't sleep in the draft, or you'll catch your death."
So I sing, Ma, not under
Laissez faire, laissez faire . . .[347]

This song with its white working-class overtones was popular in 1969 with the conservative youth organization, "Young Americans for Freedom" (YAF), which was originally the political arm of William Buckley and his arch-conservative *National Review*. YAF's libertarian faction soon acquired the reputation of an *enfant terrible*. During the 1960s anarcho-capitalism developed an antistate and antiwar ideology in the tradition of objectivism. Before Murray Rothbard, the supporters of the new laissez-faire movement drew from three best-selling sources: Hayek's anticommunist classic *The Road to Serfdom*, Rand's *Atlas Shrugged*, and Robert Anson Heinlein's *The Moon is a Harsh Mistress*. Heinlein, one of the most famous science-fiction authors of the 20th century, is politically controversial because of the often militaristic overtones of his work. *The Moon is a Harsh Mistress* depicts a utopian version of the American Revolution, where the lunar colony liberates itself from the imperialist shackles of the Earth. The first intelligent computer becomes a revolutionary and is modeled after the French neoliberalist Robert Lefevre. The lunar revolutionaries' slogan is "TANSTAAFL," which means, "There ain't no such thing as a free lunch," a saying attributed to Milton Friedman. Libertarian members of YAF used this slogan on banners adorning the walls of the YAF conference rooms—much to the chagrin of their political foster parents, the Republican Party. Many young followers of laissez-faire also supported Republican Senator Barry Goldwater, whose speechwriter Karl Hess converted to anarcho-capitalism and became known among anarcho-capitalists as a "leftist" and eccentric. Goldwater, defeated in the 1964 presidential election, embodied a traditional American individualism

---

347. *New Libertarian Notes.* Costa Mesa: New Libertarian Company of Free Traders, 1974, p. 29.

that values personal privacy and self-made success and has a deep mistrust of government, politicians, bureaucrats, and tax collectors.

The moment of truth for anarcho-capitalists came in 1969. The libertarian faction (to which Dave Foreman, the founder of Earth First!, belonged) was expelled from the YAF convention in Denver. Perhaps both the World Science Fiction Congress, which was being held there at the same time, as well as the last SDS convention in Chicago, helped the re-energized laissez-faire ideology attain its breakthrough. From then on, these libertarians demonstrated with left-wing antiwar activists, refused military service, demanded the legalization of marijuana; some even adopted a counterculture life style. Karl Hess made friends with Murray Bookchin, and the student leader Carl Oglesby met Murray Rothbard and spoke at anarcho-capitalist conventions. In Berkeley, libertarians participated in the free speech movement, and at the University of Kansas they organized themselves as an SDS chapter. The libertarian historian Leonard Liggio not only published an anti–Vietnam War journal, but also chaired the Bertrand Russell Peace Foundation. In 1969, Rothbard and Hess organized the first anarcho-capitalist convention in New York, which was raided by the FBI; according to inside gossip, Rothbard left before the raid, while Hess led a small demonstration to City Hall. In 1971, when there were about 10,000 libertarians, the student group "Freedom Conspiracy" was founded at Columbia University in New York, an event symbolized in color on the cover of *Time* magazine in the form of a huge fist with "Laissez Faire" inscribed on it.

The Libertarian Party was founded in Denver in 1971. One year later, the first candidates ran in two states, and received 20,584 votes. In 1976, the party was represented in thirty states for the presidential election and received 171,200 votes. At the end of the 1970s, Wichita oil millionaire Charles Koch began to develop an interest in the political program of the laissez-faire anarchists. His donations were generous and the party was somewhat successful in local elections. The libertarians nurtured hopes of becoming the third party. Ed Clark, who in 1972 had received a respectable 5 percent of the California vote, won a total of 920,700 votes (1 percent) in the 1980 presidential elections, the libertarians' biggest electoral success to date. In 1984, the number of votes dropped to 226,100, only to rise again to 420,000 in 1988. In 1992 the party was represented in all fifty states with about one hundred publicly elected officials. The party newspaper, founded in 1973, is called *Liberty*.

In libertarian political terminology, "right" means limited government in the social arena, patriotism, and a strong defense. The advocates of these principles are mostly orthodox or moderate followers of Ayn Rand, either within or outside the party. Justice, law and order, and responsibility are their maxims, the American constitution is their bible, and the defense of America is their religion. "Peace through strength" was their slogan until recently—that they get on famously with the military-industrial complex is no coincidence. It also follows that they greeted the Gulf War with enthusiasm. For the advocates of limited government, the tyranny of mob majority is a nightmare. Hence, their ideal society would be a republic, rather than a democracy. Robert Poole of the Reason Foundation, the most prominent right-wing libertarian, is the founder of the North American privatization movement, and Margaret Thatcher is said to have much to thank him for.

"Left" in libertarian political terminology means anti-interventionist foreign policy, abolition of the state, and laissez-faire economic policy. To the left of the advocates of limited government are the ex-Randians who have become "anarchists," and for whom the self-regulating market is king; its queen is freedom and its princess competition. No government is needed, the state must be completely abolished, and its functions, including the judiciary and the police, must be privatized. Anticommunism takes a back seat, and foreign policy is nonaggressive. The libertarians of the right ascribe to these "anarchist" colleagues an exaggerated love of liberty and accuse them of being frivolous libertines. Rothbard, who left this faction, is said to have dubbed it the "Sane Sober Anarchist Center." Anarcho-capitalists to the left of this group are opposed to political parties and are somewhat sympathetic toward the New Left or its remnants. Like the latter they are stigmatized as atavistic.

Close Encounters of the Libertarian Kind

In the summer of 1989 I traveled to the West Coast in order to meet the anarcho-capitalists in their strongholds. I talked with two women professors, a bookstore owner, a dealer in gold coins, and a counter-entrepreneur. All but one referred to themselves as anarchists.

Objectivism vs. the Civil Rights Movement and Feminism

At Stanford University I interviewed Anne Wortham, a sociology professor at the Hoover Institute, generally considered an arch-conservative think tank. Since libertarianism is a white, middle-class movement, I was surprised to learn that professor Wortham is African-American. She began by explaining that she was neither an anarchist nor a feminist. At the time of the interview she was doing research on cultural marginalization and on the minority situation of young intellectuals on the political right. Her first book, *The Other Side of Racism,* was published in 1981.

Born in 1941, Wortham grew up in the segregated world of Jackson, Tennessee. Her mother died when she was nine. Thereafter she ran the household and took care of two younger siblings. Her father must have been the African-American embodiment of the American dream: he was the hard-working, self-made man who works himself to the top without complaining so that his children will have a better life someday.

Ann Wortham

Sharon Presley

> Discrimination is terrible, but you've got to live, you've got to put your kids through school. You can't waste psychological energy on feeling downtrodden. Man, you've got to get up in the morning.[348]

Mr. Wortham apparently led his life according to these principles, and, as a good Christian, he could not hate white people. If he hated anything, it was the government. He worked his way up the ladder, became an independent salesman, built a house, and sent all his children to college. He taught them that success is always measured by achievement, regardless of the color of one's skin. Wortham's father did not like the forerunners of the civil rights movement. She related that once he wrote to the NAACP activists that instead of boycotting supermarkets they would do better to find out how to establish their own supermarkets. His daughter later wrote: "We went forth, lured by the American dream and willing to pay the price of being twice as good as our white counterparts in order to compete with them."[349] While she was in school Wortham worked as a maid for white people. Her classmates voted her "most likely to succeed." Later she attended the Tuskegee Institute in Alabama, founded by Booker T. Washington. She did not support the emerging civil rights movement, which a majority of the students joined, and did not feel comfortable there. In 1963, she joined the Peace Corps and went to Tanzania in East Africa. Someone recommended that she read Ayn Rand, and Wortham devoured *The Fountainhead* and *Atlas Shrugged,* sent for material from the Nathaniel Branden Institute, and became a Randian. In 1965 she moved to New York, hoping to work for the Institute. When the Institute arrogantly rejected her, she found a job at a magazine, where she was the first and only African-American on the staff. She attended Rand's and Branden's lectures. She told me that Rand's philosophy of objectivism broadened her intellectual horizons immeasurably. She was finally able to justify her individualism, apply it, and develop a qualified critique of the civil rights movement. Nonetheless, her criticism of the objectivists' personal behavior and pedagogy is scathing. Among these intellectual snobs, whom she believed to know everything and to have read everything, she felt enormous pressure to achieve.

> They read all of Aristotle, they read all of Plato, they knew who the bad guys are, they read all of Kant, and they know why Kant is evil and why Rand calls him the most evil man who has ever walked here. They know why he is evil. And I am not so sure why he is evil. . . . There is an inner circle, and they all sit up front and they all look very sort of stodgy, and they are dressed, there is not a wrinkle anywhere, the sort of people you think don't even sweat, they are so cool. . . . They look to be the embodiment of rationality.[350]

---

348. Anne Wortham, quoted in Bill Moyers, *A World of Ideas.* New York: Doubleday, 1989, p. 131.
349. Anne Wortham, "A Decision Against Meritorious," in *The Freeman*, Oct. 1978, p. 613.
350. Anne Wortham, interview with the author, 1989.

Less advanced supporters who asked harmless questions were yelled at and humiliated. She hated this "extremely barbaric behavior"[351] just as much as she despised the cliquishness of the objectivists and later of the anarcho-capitalists. This was one reason why she never joined the party; another was her belief in the necessity of a limited law-and-order government to protect individual rights and private property. Instead of becoming active in the party, Wortham continued to study on her own and was the first African-American woman to publish articles opposing the civil rights movement.

Her father had instilled in her the pride of a self-made man and the ideology of achievement; Rand taught her egoism, the (alleged) unimportance of empathy, and a hatred of the New Left. Wortham wrote in 1966 that segregation was followed by forced integration that benefited group rights at the expense of individual rights, for example, the right to discriminate. The Civil Rights Act of 1964, which Wortham considers an unnecessary repetition of the Constitution, enabled the government to more strictly control property and production. This and the governmental welfare policies resulting from the civil rights movement are deemed to have subjected the entire nation to a new form of slavery. Congress was forced to accept the principle "from each according to his capabilities, to each according to his needs." Wortham accuses the collectivist black and white activists of the 1960s of lacking self-confidence, and of being weak and masochistic. She denounces Martin Luther King's message of selfless love and brotherhood as a demagogic attempt to exploit the nation's feelings of guilt, by promising it redemption if it saved the blacks. In the militant year 1967, Wortham progressed to hateful tirades approaching those of her teacher Rand.

> A race of people is strangling this nation . . . at the expense of the rights of others. When a man chooses to use force to obtain values, he is no longer to be dealt with as a man; he is to be dealt with as the brute he is.[352]

For Wortham government welfare programs and the "forced tax" levied to pay for them were—and are—as violent as leftist militancy. She told me that her father was a freer person in the 1950s, when the market was less regulated than she herself is today, and that the segregated schools of the time were better than today's integrated ones. The individual successes of blacks were accepted instead of being considered a gift from the government. She emphasizes that now more than ever, the national economy has been severely damaged, by measures providing benefits to underprivileged African-Americans.

> You cannot save the minority community by destroying America. . . . You cannot save those young black kids in the ghetto who don't have jobs by destroying the American economy.[353]

---

351. Ibid.
352. Anne Wortham, "Because I am Individualist," in *The Freeman*, Nov. 1967, p. 2.
353. Anne Wortham in Bill Moyers, *A World of Ideas*. New York: Doubleday, 1989, p. 136.

Here we see the principle of "the common good before the individual good," which demonstrates the classic conservative dynamic between egoism and patriotism. At the same time, Wortham's arguments are often convincing because of that tiny grain of truth on which leftists would do well to reflect. Despite the absurdity of her accusation that the early civil rights movement was racist, I agree that race consciousness, which she aptly criticized in her earlier writings, can be problematic. The same applies to cultural feminist consciousness, which Wortham attacks with similar arguments. Nonetheless, her opposition to the Equal Rights Amendment, which feminists have been demanding since 1923, is reactionary: not only because she lashes out against social equality in the name of freedom, but also because her trust in the American constitution is naive, if not completely blind.

Wortham demonstrated impressive loyalty to her own principles during the Clarence Thomas–Anita Hill controversy. In a letter to a group called "Women for Judge Thomas," Wortham distanced herself from Thomas. Unlike other opponents, both from the women's movement and from the left, she did not criticize him for his misogyny, his opposition to abortion rights, and other reactionary positions, but for his wavering commitment to the principles of natural law and individual rights. She also refused to go along with some women supporters of Thomas who attempted to characterize him as an advocate of the women's movement. In response, she wrote that she considered women's rights to be "a concept of injustice used to undermine the legitimacy of individual rights."[354]

Wortham has sacrificed the humanist portion of her individualism on the twin altars of capitalism and the struggle for existence. Solidarity, social equality, and the political struggle for emancipation are not matters of concern to her.

Moderate Anarchism

In San Francisco I met Jim Peron in his bookstore "Free Forum Books." An articulate man in his late thirties, he has run for election as a Libertarian Party candidate several times. He is openly gay and became interested in anarcho-capitalism through a libertarian gay group. In the past few years, his bookstore has been harassed by the police more often than the leftist gay bookstores in this ostensibly tolerant city. It was first raided in response to an initiative launched by Peron and his staff calling for the abolition of the vice squad. The second raid was triggered by an affair between one of his employees and a fifteen-year-old boy. Like his leftist colleagues, Peron is critical of US government AIDS policies, which have closed gay bathhouses and banned certain treatment drugs or made them extremely difficult to obtain. He is in agreement with Anne Wortham, however, that antidiscrimination laws are destructive.

---

354. Anne Wortham, letter to Ms. Howell of Aug. 14, 1991.

The Statue of Liberty graces the cover of a libertarian brochure entitled *Liberty Reclaimed,* copublished by Peron in 1984. In it he describes the great American Revolution and the Founding Fathers' libertarian spirit. The republic they created was by no means a democracy, but the country has in the meantime degenerated into one. Democracy means rule of the majority, and majorities are infamous for denying and destroying the rights of minorities.

Peron equates the Nazi doctrine of property rights and economic order with Marx's position and the politics of such liberals as Ted Kennedy and George McGovern. At the same time Peron is an uncompromising supporter of isolationist foreign policy; he emphasizes that wars are just as damaging to society as is the welfare state. Not even the Civil War, despite its noble purpose of abolishing slavery, escapes this judgment, since it was, in his opinion, simply an opportunity to broadly expand federal power. The Cold War, too, was destructive and senseless, the only effective weapon against communism being trade. And so Peron is committed to "anarchism," which he regards as a laissez-faire society without government and with private, competing court systems and prisons. Like almost all libertarians, he believes that one hundred years ago American society was more free and more just than it is today; he goes so far as to include black ghettos, which in his opinion were brimming with life and opportunity, places where poor people could reach for the stars by working as vegetable vendors, hawkers, and day laborers.

When I asked Peron about his relationship to left-wing anarchism, he praised Emma Goldman and her article "The Place of the Individual in Society," which he had republished. However, he distanced himself from those social revolutionary anarchists who are "motivated not by a commitment to liberty but by a hatred of peoples' success."[355]

In connection with my question on political and economic solutions to the problems of the Third World, Peron told me that he planned to go to South Africa to work for Leon Louw, a libertarian at the Free Market Foundation in Johannesburg. "Apartheid is the antithesis of free enterprise,"[356] he explained. In his opinion, economic sanctions and boycotts are the worst possible way to bring about the abolition of apartheid; foreign investments are a much better way to improve the lot of the workers and the unemployed. He showed me a book by Leon Louw and his American wife Frances Kendall entitled *After Apartheid: The Solution for South Africa.* I was told that the book was a bestseller in South Africa, which is said to have a flourishing libertarian movement—a claim that leftist South Africans deny.

The book makes clear why free-marketers are opposed to antidiscrimination laws, democracy, and majority rule. Kendall and Louw supported the release of

---

355. Jim Peron, interview with the author, 1989.
356. Ibid.

Nelson Mandela, and define themselves as pluralistic, tolerant, and antiracist. However, there is no mention whatsoever in the entire 250 pages of the rascists' terror regime, where schoolchildren, democrats, and opponents are whipped and executed. Instead, the authors repeatedly emphasize the government's will to reform. In a fictitious final chapter which paints the picture of a better future for South Africa, the sinister ex-president Botha appears as a hero of democratic change. Apartheid is defined as the sum of all laws that limit economic mobility and prohibit whites and blacks from doing business with one another. According to Kendall and Louw, whites in South Africa must deal with an incomplete form of capitalism, while blacks live in a "socialist world" of government control, in "black socialism."[357] In contrast, physical segregation is apparently not all that bad: According to the authors, a visitor from Mars would not view the South African legal system as racially discriminatory, and if apartheid were purely a system of physical segregation, South Africa would be a rich and content country. Moreover, the authors insist that the state-interventionist aspect of apartheid places whites at a disadvantage as well. The market rewards the absence of prejudice:

> If a factory owner refuses to employ black labor, he will have to pay a higher price for white labor. Provided the market is free, someone will see the opportunity to undercut him by employing black labor and cutting costs.[358]

Therefore the scandalously low wages of blacks are just as acceptable as their ghettoization. The long-term consequences of this sort of free market are aptly illustrated by the cheap, illegal taxi companies operated and owned by blacks, and the prediction that "Durban's colorful rickshaws"[359] will return. Of course Kendall and Louw are also strictly opposed to government welfare programs, minimum wages, and antidiscrimination laws, and they recommend entrepreneurial unions as the ideal form of worker representation. They suggest that the cure for South Africa's ills would be a drastic political and economic "decentralization"—the dismantling of state intervention in favor of the free market. They assure us that this would result in the "de-politicization" of labor and racial conflicts, thus pacifying the country. After all, as Master Mises taught us long ago, a depersonalized market serves the interest of those in power better than does a despotic government. And the following cynical statement sounds like a set of instructions on how to improve the racist South African regime:

> It is ironic that every major wave of unrest in this country has resulted from government controls regarding bus fares, rents, transport, education, and wage rates, none of which were necessary for the maintenance of apartheid.[360]

---

357. Frances Kendall and Leon Louw, *After Apartheid: The Solution for South Africa*. San Francisco: ICS Press, 1987, p. 63.
358. Ibid., p. 91.
359. Ibid., p. 200.
360. Ibid., p. 73.

But despite their lip service to antistatism and decentralism, their solution for South Africa is a set of compulsory measures decreed by a central government. The current government, according to their plan, would entrust a commission of governing judges to partition the country into 305 small regional states. These cantons, similar to the ones of "blissfully depoliticized" Switzerland[361] would be held together by a central government with strictly limited functions. To abolish apartheid, all laws dealing with "compulsory integration or segregation"[362] would either be declared invalid immediately or gradually phased out over a period of ten years. In both cases, people with the requisite funds would be free to reserve private restaurants, swimming pools, and other institutions for a certain segment of the population. The only social function of the future South African government would be to distribute social vouchers as proposed by Milton Friedman. No mention is made of a redistribution of wealth, of retirement benefits, health insurance, or educational grants. Instead, Kendall and Louw ease the white minority's fears as regards their privileges in a future pseudo-democracy by referring to still-existing tribal differences and the class differences among blacks. Their remark that capitalist Swaziland flourishes and that half of the country belongs to whites despite a black government only adds icing to the cake.

Back to Jim Peron: Our conversation then turned to another political hobbyhorse of the anarcho-capitalists: revisionist history, as they call it, the principally worthwhile endeavor of liberating history books from the lies of those who use them for political purposes. However, the libertarians' interest in revising history is grounded in the questionable tradition of American isolationism.

Isolationism, the principle of nonintervention in the affairs of European nations, dates back to the Monroe Doctrine of 1823; the abandonment of its isolationist aspect in World War I produced an opposition movement, among whose supporters were left-wing liberals with pacifist and anti-imperialist views. There were just as many, however, who interpreted the Monroe Doctrine as a means of US exploitation of Latin America. The first revisionist historians were German-American isolationists who had been working since the 1920s to absolve their fatherland of its guilt for World War I and to make a corresponding revision of American history books. After 1933 many of them collaborated with the American Nazis. Their influence reached all the way to the Congress, where isolationists espoused fascist, pro-German, and anti-Semitic positions. The embarrassing Germanophile statements of such prominent citizens as automobile magnate Henry Ford raised quite a few eyebrows; star pilot and isolationist activist Charles Lindbergh accepted a medal from Göring. The heirs of the German-American isolationists are still active today, attempting to revise the history of World War II.

---

361. Ibid., p. 121.
362. Ibid., p. 151.

When I asked him about World War II, Peron began by criticizing the American intervention. Asked what he thought would have happened if the US had not countered German plans to conquer the world, he answered with a variation on Ernst Nolte's theory of Soviet fundamental guilt. Peron said that the Germans were not the biggest warmongers and imperialists, that Austria voluntarily joined the German Reich, and that the Sudetenland in Czechoslovakia was "heavily German." That leaves Poland. He said he didn't understand why everybody always blames Germany, considering the fact that the Soviet Union invaded not only Poland, but Lithuania, Latvia, Estonia, and Finland as well. The rest of Europe, which was invaded by the Nazis, apparently does not count, as these crimes took place "only after war was declared on them."[363] No, the Germans' only real concern was Russia: they wanted neither a Western front nor a war with England. The Holocaust, Peron says, would not have been necessary if the US had not interfered in Germany's war against Russia. To compensate, the Germans took their revenge on the Jews. US intervention only helped the Russians and the English: "They at least should have waited until the Soviets and the Germans had fought to a point where they were both very weak."[364] Instead, the US enabled the Soviet Union to dominate Europe and assisted it in gaining technical know-how for nuclear power. Germany, the only European country that could have stood its ground against Russia, was divided. I was horrified. Was he saying that it would have been better if the Nazis had stayed in power as a bulwark against communism and that the ability to build atomic bombs should have remained a German or American monopoly? It was slowly dawning on me what a friend of mine had meant when he predicted that my German accent would assure me great success with libertarians.

My next interview was with George Resch, director of the Center for Libertarian Studies and of a gold coin dealership named "Camino Coin." Resch said that he couldn't make up his mind whether the so-called Operation Barbarossa was a defensive or an offensive war. However, he could imagine that "in Germany, if someone systematically presented that thesis, that they would have a hard go of it."[365] Appalled by the controversy over the old Nazi Wilhelm Stäglich, he complained about the lack of freedom of speech in my country. Stäglich, whose book claims that the Holocaust did not occur, was stripped of his doctorate; according to Resch this action was officially justified by a measure "signed into law by the *Führer* himself in 1939."[366] Resch photocopied an article from the party newspaper Liberty and gave it to me; it was an elegy on Ernst Nolte written by the revisionist historian Ralph Racio.

---

363. Jim Peron, interview with the author, 1989.
364. Ibid.
365. George Resch, interview with the author, 1989.
366. Ibid.

The "Trotsky of the Libertarians" and Holocaust Revisionism

The main figure of the MLL (Movement of the Libertarian Left) is Samuel Edward Konkin III. A "leftist" anarcho-capitalist who lives in Long Beach, California, a city where miles of white sand beaches provide the backdrop for an eerie skyline of innumerable oil rigs and towers—which perhaps explains in part why Konkin III, who is an avid science-fiction fan, chose this city as the site for his so-called anarcho-village and his Agorist Institute (from the Greek *agora* marketplace). I had pictured the anarcho-village as a kind of free-trader colony of young aspiring businessmen. I found Konkin's street in a neighborhood of shabby, flat-roofed houses and rang the bell; the door was opened by a young Latino who showed me into a tiny apartment consisting of a single room. I thought I must be in the wrong place—aren't libertarians supposed to be comfortable, if not affluent? A quick phone call revealed that Konkin III lived in a similar house next door which was part of the anarcho-village comprising five apartments in the neighborhood. Konkin III's appearance was as unconventional as his dwelling was makeshift. He is a Canadian in his early forties, of stately stature, hair combed back close to his head. Dressed entirely in black, with a turtleneck sweater, a metal belt, cowboy boots, and a silver medallion around his neck, he looks like a cross between a leather guy, a catholic priest, and a romantic fascist. He announced proudly that he was preparing "real German coffee" and introduced me to two other inhabitants of the anarcho-village, who tried to speak German with me. A poster of Trotsky adorned a wall. Konkin III explained to me that Murray Rothbard, who likes to think of himself as the Lenin of the libertarians, once compared him to Trotsky. Despite what I expected from their individualism, as typified, for instance by Ayn Rand's characters, the inhabitants of the anarcho-village appeared to be as poor as church mice, and as sociable as bohemian collectivists.

Konkin III believes that the black market is the key to the abolition of the state and the creation of a pure laissez-faire society. He considers himself a "theoretician and practician of countereconomics"[367] and cultivates the image of a rebel. Any illegal act is sacred to him, even if it merely entails jaywalking. "We break the law," he then declares passionately. The Agorist Institute, the headquarters of the MLL, is located in an office building in downtown Long Beach, a city whose numerous palm trees lend it a tropical flair. The office consists of two cramped rooms equipped with two computers. Science-fiction posters cover the walls. The institute, I learned, is "technically legal," a non-profit, tax-deductible project "supported by libertarian business people who feel guilty for being too honest and legal." But the movement publication, the *New Libertarian Magazine,* is "completely countereconomic,"[368] he says. It

---

367. Samuel Edward Konkin III, interview with the author, 1989.
368. Ibid.

unequivocally breaks the law, simply by printing the stock market index without being registered with the state. At the end of the interview, Konkin III presented me with the organization's official brassard: a white circle on a red background, with a black flag above the letters MLL, encircled by the words "agora," "anarchy," and "action." To me, both the color combination and the design were somewhat reminiscent of fascist emblems, and the movement's acronym could have had a Stalinist model. Konkin III, who hinted that his political beginnings had been in the "far right," studied during the late 1960s in Wisconsin, a state with a strong German heritage. Converted to laissez-faire anarchism by Heinlein's *The Moon is a Harsh Mistress* and by the expulsion of the YAF's libertarian fraction, he and three yippies founded a libertarian group at the university. He told the yippies that they could throw as many rocks as they wanted, as long as they threw them only at government buildings, not at private corporations or businesses. In 1970 Konkin III went to New York City where he moved in leftist anarchist circles and founded the magazine *New Libertarian Notes*. As a revolutionary yet apolitical rebel he opposed the founding of the Libertarian Party, but in 1974 he, in turn, set up an organization of countereconomists, the "New Libertarian Alliance." Shortly thereafter he established the anarcho-village, and for ten rather unsubversive years worked as a typesetter in the office of a libertarian pornographer. "Remember, sex and anarchy, they seem to go together."[369] Since then Konkin III has published various magazines, brochures, and newsletters.

The most effective "counterattacks" against libertarianism, Konkin III assured me, have come from within its own ranks—be it the reformism of corrupt intellectuals, the founding of the party, or the donation to it by the oil billionaire Koch, which in the eyes of Konkin III was a corrupt payoff.

As a laissez-faire purist Konkin III is a true believer in the "market process." The "political process," that is, the type of politics where a party "takes over," means nothing to him. No matter what the political content or the historical context, he says, political power always leads to the sell-out of principles.

> The communists come to power in Russia. They shoot all the Bolshevists. The National Socialists take over in Germany, they shoot all the brown shirts, the ones who actually believed in this philosophy. The Jacobins, the French, take over. Robespierre, who probably was a good Jacobin, ended up with his head cut off after Thermidor.[370]

Konkin III strove to emphasize that his MLL is a progressive force. In his publications he places himself firmly in the tradition of the anarchists of the First International and of the left in general. He says that consistent libertarians want "to abolish the state and its parasitic class of bureaucrats, politicians, subsidized businessmen, privileged labor leaders, and military mass murderers."

---

369. Ibid.
370. Ibid.

Nonetheless, this position, he says, is libertarian left, not socialist left, and socialism does not have a "monopoly on the term Left."[371]

In Konkin III's view, society is not based on the commune, but on the market, and the latter makes possible a harmonious alliance between workers and entrepreneurs, much in the same way as it was envisioned by early socialists up to Tucker. Like Mackay, he conceives of a stateless petty capitalism consisting exclusively of small businesses. However, Konkin III insists that his social vision is not to be confused with capitalism, which is synonymous with the abuse of state power and is wholly unrelated to the idea of the free market. In his opinion, Ayn Rand (whose followers were the first to call themselves anarcho-capitalists) rehabilitated capitalism. Konkin III prefers the term "agorism," which he thinks has an anarcho-communist ring to it. His philosophy shares social-revolutionary anarchists' desire for unity among themselves, as well as the utopian desire for an all-encompassing harmony.

> We witness to the efficacy of freedom and exult in the intricate beauty of complex voluntary exchange. We demand the right of every ego to maximize its value without limit save that of another ego. We proclaim the age of the market unbound, the natural and proper condition for humanity, wealth in abundance, goals without end or limit, and self-determined meaning for all: Agora.[372]

The society Konkin III envisions will result from the gradual establishment of the countereconomy. He defines the latter as the sum of all nonaggressive acts prohibited by the state. His list of lawbreaker-saviors includes tax evaders, smugglers, drug dealers, pornographers, prostitutes, and other "sexual enterprisers," midwives, owners of weapons, barterers, illegal immigrants, and food hoarders. The function of the Agorist Institute, he emphasizes, is comparable to that of the black market avant-garde, "who is actually living the life of the purely free enterpriser."[373] The "statist regression of the populace,"[374] according to Konkin III, will pose the main threat to agorist society in its early phase. In the last phase, the *New Libertarian Manifesto* asserts, it is the state itself which will "unleash its final wave of suppression."[375] And that will be the hour of the revolution.

When I asked him what he thought of social-revolutionary anarchists, Konkin III said he shared their main goal of abolishing the state, and with that as a point of departure he could get along with anybody—all kinds of people can represent anarchy—Bakunin, Rothbard, Chomsky, and others. Like many libertarians Konkin III misinterprets Chomsky's critique of American imperialism, seeing it as isolationist historical revisionism. Konkin III beamed

371. Samuel Edward Konkin III, *MLL Pamphlet 1*, 1989.
372. Samuel Edward Konkin III, *New Libertarian Manifesto*. Long Beach, California: 1983, p. 30.
373. Samuel Edward Konkin III, interview with the author, 1989.
374. Samuel Edward Konkin III, *New Libertarian Manifesto*. Long Beach, California: 1983, p. 26.
375. Ibid., p. 27.

when he said that he is in agreement with Chomsky on almost all points, whether it concerns the Middle East, Latin America, Vietnam, Cambodia, or his critique of the media, except that what Chomsky refers to as capitalism, he prefers to call statism, monopoly, or anti-free-tradism. He pointed out that he, too, "defended Robert Faurisson" blurring once again the defense of someone's civil rights with the support of his principles. Konkin III also said that he is encouraged by what he reads in the left press nowadays: the heyday of dogmatic ideologues now seems to be over, while some have even begun contemplating "market socialism."

Konkin III has another secret love besides the New Left, and in his opinion both of these loves are not at all dissimilar. He says that the most principled activists and enemies of the power elite are to be found on the extreme left and the extreme right, only the terms are different, while political moderates are opportunists. Which alternative to the existing system is actually envisioned by those hostile towards the power elite does not appear to count, an attitude that in the past has often enough led leftists into suicidal coalitions.

For Konkin III the present system of economic control in the US is "democratic fascism." In Europe, he says, it was the social democrats who first came out in favor of governmental economic control; in the US it was the Progressives, from whom the Nazis learned a great deal.

> Certainly during the war time it was very difficult to tell the difference between National Socialists and New Deal America. They both had tremendous control over the economy. People were in concentration camps on both sides.[376]

The New Libertarian Magazine published an article by the moderate revisionist historian Jeff Hummel on political repression within the US before and during World War II. His research on government measures against communists, Jehovah's witnesses, black Muslims, Japanese, and fascists shows that there can be no good war, a view to which one could hardly object, if only the author did not at the same time play down the dangers of American and German-American Nazis, almost to the point of sympathizing with them. People such as Sylvester Viereck, the extremely influential pro-German isolationist publicist, or Fritz Kuhn, the leader of the powerful American Nazi organization "German-American Bund," or Ezra Pound, the poet and propagandist of the Italian fascists—in Hummel's view they are but helpless victims of government repression, never allies of fascist (state) criminals. The same issue of the *New Libertarian Magazine* contains a critique by Robert Faurisson of his moderate colleague David Irving. Konkin III, the journal's editor, comments:

> The "cutting edge" of Revisionist History is that of World War II atrocity stories. For our time, defending the free speech of the Holocaust Revisionists ... is the difference between defending free speech and just mouthing off. ... Robert

---

376. Samuel Edward Konkin III, interview with the author, 1989.

> Faurisson . . . is a rare treat to defend: a determined, committed scholar, willing to be a martyr for his cause . . . willing to challenge his fellow Revisionists, especially for being insufficiently hard-core (our kind of guy!).[377]

Faurisson's article was originally written for the *Journal of the Institute for Historical Review* (IHR), which declined to print it. Konkin III was listed as a member of the advisory board in an institute leaflet dated 1985, along with Robert Faurisson, W.A. Carto, the right-wing founder of the institute, Wilhelm Stäglich, the German Nazi judge, and other German and German-American Nazi sympathizers. *The New Libertarian* contains a large ad for the IHR, which is located in Costa Mesa, California, the global capital of revisionist history.

I called the IHR and requested informational material, my German accent reaping the friendliest of tones at the other end. The surprise packet from the IHR arrived two days later, discretely posted in an unmarked envelope. The first item to grab my attention was a photograph of Göring's biographer David Irving posing in front of an enlarged picture of his hero. I began reading the material and learned that the IHR is a nonideological and nonpartisan institution dedicated to the prevention of war and to the discovery of the truth. Yet the language used bespoke quite a different story: the mass murder of six million Jews was referred to as the "so-called holocaust" and a "Zionist myth"; accounts thereof were belittled as "the holocaust story" and eyewitnesses as "the holocaust lobby"; and the existence of concentration camps questioned by referring to them as "so-called extermination camps." The IHR's book catalog features all the classics of Holocaust revisionism and includes numerous accounts of the trials and tribulations of revisionist authors and professors in courts of law. The list also contains a large selection of publications about Russian and Allied atrocities against the Germans during and after World War II, sometimes referred to in this literature as the "holocaust on the Germans." It appears that the bestsellers are militaristic and nostalgic Nazi trash novels set in the 1940s. A few works of serious scholars such as Victor Marchetti, Edward Said, Christopher Hitchins, as well as Chomsky's *The Fateful Triangle*, are included. Cynically the IHR seems to attempt to equate their positions with its own in order to create confusion.

Holocaust revisionism is the subject of a flood of publications, from David Irving's comparatively harmless "Hitler-did-not-know" view of history to Faurisson's "there-were-no-gas-chambers" version, up to tracts by historians such as Arthur R. Butz which completely deny that the Holocaust ever took place. My IHR cornucopia also included five leaflets full of invectives against what is called "one-sided holocaustomania." One of these leaflets, written by Theodore J. O'Keefe, publisher of the *Journal of Historical Review,* claims that the concentration camp inmates all died of typhoid fever, and that the gas chambers were intended for showers and delousing; if there was any brutality in the

---

377. Samuel Edward Konkin III in *The New Libertarian*, Aug. 1986, p. 24.

camps at all, it was perpetrated on prisoners by their fellow communist inmates, who "eliminated their foes with Stalinist ruthlessness."[378] Equally macabre was the leaflet containing the *Leuchter Report* by Fred A. Leuchter, "Americas leading expert on the design and fabrication of homicidal gas chambers."[379] At Faurisson's request, this expert on execution engineering, who also manufactures gallows, electric chairs, and executionary injection kits for US prisons, examined the remains of the gas chambers in Auschwitz, Birkenau, and Majdanek and came to the conclusion that executions could not possibly have taken place there.

No less blood-curdling than these documents and the corresponding book titles in the IHR book catalog are such bed-time stories for Nazi fans and militarists as,

> Campaign in Russia: The Waffen SS on the Eastern Front, by Leon Degrelle ... his masterfully written saga of the battle for Europe on the Eastern Front where the heroism and determination of the all-volunteer Waffen SS were without parallel in the annals of military history.[380]

Available to interested collectors are such videotapes as Leni Riefenstahl's film of the *Reichsparteitag* in Nuremberg, or the pre-war Nazi propaganda film "Yesterday and Today ... a comparison of the prosperity under National Socialism with the despair and moral distress of Weimar Germany,"[381] or another film which demonstrates "the joy of the German worker after years of Weimar unemployment."[382] Sensitive neo-Nazis can order "the private film collection of Eva Braun":

> Spectacular Alpine panoramas highlight scenes of Nazi leaders, foreign diplomats, and local visitors. Candid views of Hitler in war and peacetime chatting with children, conferring with subordinates, relaxing after victories, and recovering after Stalingrad offer a unique picture of the Fuehrer's private life.[383]

Last but not least, the package included *66 Questions on the Holocaust,* which confront us with such puzzling questions as: "If the Nazis cremated six million people, then where are all the ashes?"[384] Anyone curious about the answers to such intriguing questions need only send a self-addressed stamped envelope to the IHR—a pleasure I decided I could do without.

Feminism and Communalism

I was surprised to find the name Sharon Presley in the brochure advertising the Anarchist Convention that took place in San Francisco in July 1989. She was the only anarcho-capitalist active at the convention, taking part in a panel

---

378. IHR Leaflet, 1989.
379. IHR Leaflet, 1989.
380. IHR Catalog, 1989.
381. Ibid.
382. Ibid.
383. Ibid.
384. *66 Questions on the Holocaust,* IHR.

discussion on anarchism and sexism. When I asked both leftist anarchists and libertarians about any ideological overlapping of the two persuasions at the convention, they emphatically denied such a possibility.

Sharon Presley is a pleasant, attractive woman who teaches social psychology at the University of Long Beach. I interviewed her in her simple apartment where three beautiful cats kept us company. Presley read Ayn Rand in the mid-1960s, was a member of the YAF, participated in the Goldwater campaign, and has been a libertarian from the beginning of the movement. She studied at Berkeley and got her doctorate at New York University where she was a student of Stanley Milgram, the author of the famous book *Obedience to Authority*. In her dissertation Presley researched the opposite, the rejection of unjust authority finding that such rejection was motivated by the rejection of political and social authority, by a sense of greater responsibility to one's conscience than to the law, and by a lack of religiousness. It seems to me that she was describing herself as well: her antiauthoritarian attitudes, her social conscience, and her conviction that the world can be changed through enlightenment. She explained to me that obedience to authority was the main scourge of humanity.

> People's feelings that we must have a government to solve our problems is really another variation of that, because they don't believe they can solve their own problems, because they have been always told to look around and obey authority or look to see what other people are doing. And so most people are not encouraged to be individualist in a psychological sense. They are not encouraged to be critical about what's going on.[385]

Presley did not join the Libertarian Party, because she thinks that its style of activism concentrates too one-sidedly on electioneering. But she was active as a spokesperson of the libertarian movement at party conventions and elsewhere. Her main concerns are social psychology and feminism, two issues that are unpopular with anarcho-capitalists. In the mid-1970s she and a number of other women staged a feminist uprising at a Libertarian Party convention. They complained about the lack of women speakers and women's issues, and founded the Association of Libertarian Feminists (ALF). When I asked her whether Rand had been a feminist, Presley was not afraid to criticize the heroine of her youth. Rand had spoken out against the idea of a woman president of the US. "Appalling, just appalling. We were all really upset."[386]

To my surprise Presley and I were in agreement on almost all feminist issues. Contrary to the majority of the women's movement in both Europe and the US, she continues to believe in the equality of the sexes. "There are no inherent sex roles,"[387] she stated categorically. From the scientific standpoint, she continued, there is little evidence to support the possibility of biological gender

---

385. Sharon Presley, interview with the author, 1989.
386. Ibid.
387. Ibid.

differences that influence gender psychology. However, numerous myths, for example the one about testosterone being the source of male aggression, are almost impossible to dispel. As a psychologist, Presley considers the feminist notion that women are better people than men to be "sexism in disguise." And she has the following to say about the theory of moral superiority as a result of female-specific socialization:

> Women more caring and compassionate and men those cold inhumane bastards? . . . I don't think its true. I think that it reinforces in a very subtle way the idea that somehow men and women are different and that maybe it is biological.[388]

As a feminist, Presley is critical of both cultural feminism and libertarian women's politics. Contrary to one of the primordial principles of anarcho-capitalism, she supports the ERA. Unlike Anne Wortham, she believes that a constitutional amendment would abolish the laws that discriminate against women rather than cause discrimination against men. Presley's opinion that antidiscrimination laws help bring about the equality of sex and race is even more heretical. She exclaimed heatedly that discrimination was rampant at the university and that the situation there is like a good-old-boys' club. White men feel most comfortable around other white men, she says; you have to force them to hire women and people of color; if you don't, nothing will ever change.

Her view of laws against pornography and abortion is in line with the libertarian platform, but her rationale for the right to abortion attacks a sacred cow of anarcho-capitalism: the property argument—whether in the feminist claim that "my body belongs to me," or in John Locke's concept of "self-ownership." Presley expounded her view in an article written in collaboration with Robert Cooke, an attorney. The authors argue, first, that the mechanistic idea of one's body and person as property encompasses "the curious equation that self-slavery equals liberty."[389] Second, the authors assert the right of self-determination, the point is women's interest in as opposed to ownership of the body, the appropriate question being: does she want to become a mother or not? They also take issue with a most grotesque libertarian ideological cocktail that mixes rationalistic confidence in technology with the property fetish: the idea that the fetus trespasses on foreign territory and/or property, and that the woman is therefore allowed to kill it in self-defense without being punished. Presley and Cooke expose this idea as the perverse twin of the argument used by anti-abortionists. Countering that the fetus is not a person because it has no consciousness, there could be no justification whatsoever for removing it "alive" and keeping it for medical purposes, as suggested by the prominent libertarian Walter Block—an idea that would throw the door wide open for genetic engineering.

---

388. Ibid.
389. Sharon Presley and Robert Cooke, "The Right to Abortion." ALF Discussion Paper, 1979.

In contrast to cultural and socialist feminists, women anarcho-capitalists support neither abortions covered by health insurance nor free child-care centers. According to them, looking to the state for help is tantamount to recognizing a certain form of patriarchy. The state is *per se* authoritarian and controls everything within its power, from registered marriages to the public school system. Atypical in terms of her political heritage, Presley talked about her concern for poor women who can afford neither an abortion nor child care. In principle, she, too, considers taxes to be theft. But, when asked if she would abolish welfare tomorrow if she could, she said she would not. Her alternative is that of voluntary self-organization in the form of alternative institutions such as rape crisis centers.

At the end of our interview, Presley talked about Ron Paul, then the Libertarian Party candidate who opposes abortion. She complained bitterly about this "conservative" gynecologist with the affected manner of a stiff businessman who has a "terrible position on women."[390] In her opinion, the Libertarian Party must have really gone downhill if a man like that could be its candidate; obsessed with foreign policy and economics, he embodied everything for which she criticized the party. In her view many libertarians make the serious mistake of attempting to both explain and solve every problem in economic terms. Like Murray Bookchin, she separates economic and social issues. The latter occupy the center stage in her idea of a libertarian future, in which she envisions the peaceful coexistence of supporters of limited government, anarchists, and advocates of "voluntary communism."[391] She believes that all social services could be organized at the local level by those concerned. Like Bookchin, she draws a line between these ideas, on the one hand, and socialism and Marxism, which for her mean coercion and authority, on the other. It is no coincidence that Presley is a big fan of Emma Goldman. Her feminist rebellious sense of social justice and equality, coupled with her humanistic morality, make her positions appear more left-liberal than anarcho-capitalist.

However, Presley believes in communalism, as well, and this concept has a number of supporters among libertarians. One of them is David Thereaux, the director of the Independent Institute in San Francisco, whose colleague Jeff Hummel wrote the revisionist historical article in *The New Libertarian* quoted above. Thereaux, too disagrees with libertarian economic determinism, but compensates for this view by leaning toward utopianism. He explained to me that libertarianism does not necessarily lead to capitalism, for the anarchist "decentralized communal arrangements"[392] fit neatly into the libertarian framework. He considers Bookchin's "small is beautiful" to be a "healthy idea" that has "a lot to it," and believes that Germany's Green idea also has "a libertarian

---

390. Sharon Presley, interview with the author, 1989.
391. Sharon Presley, AFL Discussion Paper, 1974.
392. David Thereaux, interview with the author, 1989.

sentiment to it."[393] In Thereaux's opinion, the libertarian future will be one of regional communities, similar to those in Josia Warren's anarcho-individualist experimental colonies. Autonomous regions controlled by the Black Panthers, for instance, with their own economies and self-defense would be equally conceivable. It is computer technology, however, that offers the most unimaginable opportunities for modern society. Communities and communication networks will arise independent of where people live. I was very surprised when Thereaux, asked about Kendall's and Louw's ideas about South Africa, explained with shining eyes that a true solution for South Africa and the Third World as a whole needs to be much more radical. The colonizers and their indigenous successors, the latter blinded by Marxism, had disregarded "existing territories or lifestyles or workings of the native people"[394] for far too long.

> The only real solution to the problems of Africa is to essentially eliminate these different regimes that exist there, which are imposing these incredibly barbaric systems and let the people set up their own indigenous communities regardless of existing boundaries.[395]

Murray Rothbard—The Philosopher

Property and Human Nature

At the beginning of his standard work, *For a New Liberty: The Libertarian Manifesto,* Rothbard states that all true libertarians are strict followers of their own principles, which are based on natural law as derived from insight into human nature. Rothbard compares human nature with the nature of raw materials, like copper, iron, or salt, and of both plants and lower and higher animals. According to him, all of these "units" possess certain typical characteristics, just as do humans, for whom reason is the definitive trait.

> Possessing no automatic instincts, each man must learn about himself and the world, use his mind to select values, learn about cause and effect, and act purposively to maintain himself and advance his life. Since men can think, feel, evaluate, and act only as individuals, it becomes vitally necessary for each man's survival and prosperity that he be free to learn, choose, develop his faculties, and act upon his knowledge and values.[396]

Each human is a lonely being, with only his reason to keep him company. The individual has no claims on society except the freedom to measure his abilities against those of others. In Rothbard's view, human nature, like the nature of copper or an animal guided by instinct, is static and unalterable. "Inequality and division of labor"[397] are innate characteristics. Rothbard freely

---

393. Ibid.
394. Ibid.
395. Ibid.
396. Murray Rothbard, *For a New Liberty.* New York: Collier Macmillan Publishers, 1978, p. 28.
397. Ibid., p. 50.

admits that as a libertarian he is not an egalitarian, and he feels that the gifted few will always lead the less gifted many. He too, emphasizes the variety and diversity of mankind, and "seeks to give that diversity full expression in a world of complete freedom."[398]

Like human nature, natural law is for Rothbard "absolute, immutable, and of universal validity for all times and places."[399] In contrast to tribal law, or to state law demanding and compelling unconditional compliance, natural law has its origins in human reason and is thus the "most nobly and fully human"[400] principle, the "most potentially revolutionary" alternative to the status quo, and a "mighty force for radical change."[401] Like all laissez-faire theorists Rothbard reduces the concept of natural law to property rights. He claims to be the heir of John Locke, Lysander Spooner, and Thomas Jefferson. Quoting the Declaration of Independence, Rothbard reminds us that for the Founding Fathers happiness and property were interchangeable:

> that all men are created equal, that they are endowed by their Creator with certain unalienable Rights, that among these are Life, Liberty and the pursuit of Happiness (the more common triad at the time was "Life, Liberty and Property".)[402]

He says that the right to self-ownership and to homestead are the basic libertarian principles. As in classical liberalism, the right to one's own person is viewed as the basis from which is derived the right to the possession of one's labor and everything produced out of what was previously unused and unpossessed. The pioneer owns his claim, and the settler the land on which he has built his house and planted his vegetables. In libertarian thought human rights—often referred to as "civil liberties"—freedom of speech, of the press, of assembly, and the right to commit "victimless" crimes are inseparable from and unthinkable outside the context of property rights. These civil liberties, like all property rights, are guaranteed and protected by the axiom of nonaggression or noninvasion of the person or property. The state is notorious for being the greatest perpetrator of daily crimes against these principles: by enforcing the military draft, it is guilty of slavery; by advocating atomic warfare, it commits mass murder, and by collecting taxes, it is a thief. The focus of the left critique of the state—the class discriminatory and antidemocratic function of the state to the advantage of the propertied class—is of little concern to the anarcho-capitalist, because for him justice and property are identical. The libertarian concept of the human right to free speech, for example, is

> simply the property right to hire an assembly hall from the owners or to own one oneself; the human right of a free press is the property right to buy materials and then print leaflets or books and to sell them to those who are willing to buy.[403]

---

398. Ibid., p. 303.
399. Murray Rothbard, *The Ethics of Liberty*. Atlantic Highlands: Humanities Press, 1982, p. 17.
400. Ibid., p. 17.
401. Ibid., p. 19.
402. Ibid., p. 23.
403. Murray Rothbard, *For a New Liberty*. New York: Humanities Press, 1978, p. 43.

Hence those who do not have enough money to rent a space or to have their opinions printed simply have to do without the freedoms of assembly and of the press. Of course, they could always convince a millionaire to back them, as Milton Friedman has suggested. The related idea of self-ownership means very little, although, as Rothbard suggests, it is applied equally to "Neanderthal cavemen, in modern Calcutta, or in the contemporary United States." Rothbard explains that rights that can be fulfilled only in modern industrial society are not real human rights at all.

> The "right" to schooling, to a job, three meals, etc., is then not embedded in the nature of man, but requires for its fulfillment the existence of a group of exploited people who are coerced into providing such a "right."[404]

While no one knows whether the Neanderthal caveman had three meals a day, a job, or an education, we do know, however, that neither starving Indians in Calcutta have them, nor the inhabitants of American ghettos. Too bad says the libertarian.

Rothbard defines freedom and liberty as the condition in which the right to the integrity of person and property are best protected. The mugger who takes someone's wallet and the drunk who assaults someone are committing the crime of invading someone else's property, similar to the state when it levies taxes. Accordingly, safety from thieves, attackers, and tax collectors is the necessary claim of human rights and freedom in anarcho-capitalist utopia. Yet libertarian freedom goes beyond the scope of the old woman who has been mugged or the employee who has been robbed of a third of his salary by the IRS, for "the rights of personal liberty and 'freedom of enterprise' almost invariably intertwine and cannot really be separated."[405] For the retired woman on Social Security this might mean the freedom to sell her silverware if she cannot pay her rent, for the starving people of Calcutta the freedom to beg, for the American slum-dweller the freedom to deal drugs, and for the entrepreneur that unimpeded road to profit which Lord Keynes and his followers, in the libertarians' view, have been trying to dismantle.

Libertarians support specialization and division of labor, Rothbard emphasizes, for moral rather than for utilitarian reasons. In this context a look at the morality of the free market economy as expressed in a concrete, apparently non-economic example, that of parents' and children's rights, is enlightening. The insistence of most libertarians on the individual's right to shape his or her private life without interference was greeted with approval by the American left-liberal public, all the more as this included the unrestricted right to abortion. But Rothbard's argument in favor of abortion is even more bizarre than the one criticized by Sharon Presley, in which it is argued that the fetus is guilty of trespassing: he considers the unborn child to be nothing but a parasite in a woman's body.

---

404. Ibid., p. 134.
405. Ibid., p. 69.

> What the mother is doing in an abortion is causing an unwanted entity within her body to be ejected from it: If the fetus dies, this does not rebut the point that no being has a right to live, unbidden, as a parasite within or upon some person's body.[406]

Once born, the child is subject to its parents' absolute property rights, limited only by the axiom of noninvasion. To kill or maim the child would be criminal; in every other instance the child is subject to the parent's personal jurisdiction. In a libertarian world, for instance, mothers and fathers would be free to sell their offspring on a "flourishing free child market."[407] They would have this right as long as the child lived with them and could not support, that is, did not own, itself—and a child does not own itself until it leaves the parents or runs away, regardless of its age. Despite their almost unlimited authority, parents have no duties whatsoever toward their offspring. No one has the right to force parents to feed, clothe, or educate their children, because to do so would be to rob them of their freedoms and their rights, which extend to the right to let one's child starve. In order not to be misunderstood, Rothbard emphasizes that he is referring to all children, not just to deformed or unhealthy ones. The libertarians' demand for the repeal of all child labor laws, which they feel only serve to grant adults privileges over children, seems almost harmless in comparison.

The logical conclusion of Rothbard's suggestions for "revolutionary" social change is that freedom and justice in anarcho-capitalist utopia are granted only to those who are able to survive on the wages the market allots them. As for the rest—helpless children, the sick, the unemployed, old people, unrecognized artists, and others in need of support—they do not even have a right to life. Society has the right to let them starve. Rothbard's radical property morality is no different from that of social Darwinists and fascists for whom the death of the weak signifies the will of nature. Humanitarianism of any kind is cast out, replaced by the laws of the market and the rights of those able to compete. Compassion and cooperation have no base in human nature. To share, to plan collectively in solidarity, or to give something away without getting something in return is seen as suicidal. The very thought of such a compassionate outlook strikes fear into the heart of the laissez-faire advocate of freedom, who equates equality with an unnatural homogenization of humanity. Thus human rights in their real, humanitarian sense are abolished.

Inflation, Stagflation, and Deflation

For some, the autonomous cycles of nature will brook no human interference without serious retribution. For others, this is true of the market. In the minds of its most uncompromising advocates, the quasi-natural forces of the marketplace, from which laissez-faire liberals derive their concepts of law, morality, and society, take on an almost religious character.

---

406. Ibid., p. 108.
407. Murray Rothbard, *The Ethics of Liberty*. Atlantic Highlands: Humanities Press, 1982, p. 102.

> The essence and the glory of the free market is that individual firms and businesses, competing on the market, provide an ever-changing orchestration of efficient and progressive goods and services: continually improving products and markets, advancing technology, cutting costs, and meeting changing consumer demands as swiftly and as efficiently as possible . . . the free private market will supply these goods and services far more cheaply, in greater abundance, and of far higher quality than monopoly government does today. Everyone in society would benefit, and *especially* the poor.[408]

The constant rise in everyone's standard of living as a result of technological progress and bold capital investments remains the unfulfilled promise of modern free-market advocates. In their view governments impede the economy, thereby robbing humanity of the fruits of the free market's blessings. Despite their blustering promises: monetarist's policies translate, first and foremost, into cutbacks and belt-tightening, which, after an initial period of "healing" austerity, is supposed to yield unfettered prosperity. Too deep is the quagmire into which New Dealers and their successors under the tutelage of John Maynard Keynes have led us, we are told; in order to maintain full employment at all costs, they irresponsibly accumulated debts in every sector, whether in the steel industry or in the military. They consorted with big business and with the unions, fostered economic monopolies, and were even guilty of warmongering to achieve their vile collectivist ends. But in 1973 a new phenomenon occurred: stagflation, simultaneous inflation and recession. According to Rothbard, it began with the state-controlled money supply that had grown faster than production since World War II. To blame for this situation was (and still is) the state "monopoly of counterfeit money," an inflationary policy in which the currency is not backed by gold. This tendency, Rothbard explains, has continuously grown throughout the 20th century, thus enabling governments to create inflationary conditions at will. Things deteriorated progressively after 1933, when the US government abolished the gold standard.

The monetarist road out of such misery must lead through a depression, the "painful but necessary process by which the free market rids itself of the excesses and errors of the boom."[409] Rothbard recommends that the government do the exact opposite of what Keynesians suggest: it should simply abandon its policy of inflation by giving the market free reign and by reinstating the gold standard. Other than that, it should do nothing. It should neither lend money to bankrupt companies, nor support wages and prices, nor encourage consumption, nor increase expenditures. The law of the market will take care of everything.

The State, the Public Sector, and the Means to Abolish Both

Rothbard's critique of the state has impressed, if not dazzled, many an anarchist. Who doesn't enjoy seeing one's enemy attacked from another, perhaps more

---

408. Murray Rothbard, *For a New Liberty.* New York: Collier Macmillan Publishers, 1978, p. 195.
409. Ibid., p. 189.

influential vantage point? And aren't many of his arguments familiar? Take, for example, his critique of the antitrust laws, which in his view are a product of the collaboration between the state and trade unions and result in a legalized form of forced labor. Indeed, these could have been Sam Dolgoff's words—only with a reversed message: whereas the anarcho-syndicalist sees a conspiracy between the state and the unions against the labor movement, the anarcho-capitalist sees a conspiracy in favor of workers' demands at the taxpayers' expense. In the absence of state-supported "union privileges" strikes would be illegal, thus making it unnecessary to prohibit them. Inattentive leftist anarchists could also be delighted by Rothbard's definition of the state as a "criminal band"[410]— which is what social-revolutionary anarchists, themselves criminalized by the state, have always been saying: the state is the real criminal, not us. But Rothbard does not wish to be confused with his political namesakes:

> Left-wing anarchists, for example, will oppose equally government and private organizations such as corporations on the ground that each is equally "elitist" and "coercive." But the "rightist" libertarian is not opposed to inequality, and his concept of "coercion" applies only to the use of violence.[411]

This violence is always defined as violence against property. Not included therein is the violence perpetrated by the powerful and propertied classes to preserve their class privileges. The class concept to which Rothbard pays homage, which harks back to the antebellum advocate of slavery, John C. Calhoun (1782–1850), is a different one. In that ideology the state has brought forth "two unequal and inherently conflicting classes": the class of exploited "tax-payers" and the class of parasitic "tax consumers."[412] Hence not only government officials, but also the unemployed (who force taxpayers to support them) are parasites. To Rothbard's credit it must be said that he has accurately shown that in the US Social Security taxes, rather than redistributing wealth from the rich to the poor, above all bleed the middle and the working classes. Yet in the eyes of laissez-faire liberals it would be equally unjust to squeeze the rich, for it is they, Rothbard admonishes, who, with their capital investments, entrepreneurial vision, and financing of technological advances, are responsible for the high standard of living in the US. To fleece them would be to kill "the goose that lays the golden eggs."[413] What does Rothbard think should be done about the poverty and suffering of the welfare recipients? He laments that welfare expenditures have steadily increased since the 1930s, despite the purported reduction in poverty. As he sees it, the main economic reason for this is the fact that welfare benefits compete with the minimum wage. It is tragic, he says, that modern liberal morals have done away with the stigma of parasitism under

---

410.   Ibid., p. 46.
411.   Ibid., p. 47.
412.   Ibid., pp. 52–53.
413.   Ibid., p. 162.

which recipients of welfare used to suffer, and both social workers and government agencies have increasingly encouraged people to go on welfare.

The privatized welfare system which Rothbard envisions for the anarcho-capitalist future will run in accordance with the tried and true principles of 19th-century charity organizations. First and foremost is the need to put an end to the idea of welfare as a right and to return to a moral differentiation between the deserving and the undeserving poor—the malingerers, swindlers, squanderers, and other ne'er-do-wells for whom there is no hope of reintegration into productive society. This viewpoint, Rothbard tells us, has tradition and was formulated as early as 1883 by a private English charity organization. But the state welfare agencies (yes, there were some) during the heyday of Manchester capitalism were just as miserly. They made the requirements for receiving benefits as difficult and unattractive as possible. The unemployed were required to undergo an employment test, and only those living in a poorhouse qualified. Rothbard cites the practice of the Mormons, whose notorious anti-trade union stance has earned them much respect among libertarians, as another example of a sensible welfare policy. He praises them as a group which, despite poverty and persecution, managed to achieve prosperity and wealth in the 19th century through their own efforts. Their guiding principles, "independence, industriousness, thrift, and self-respect," ensured that they would never become dependent on public assistance. Mormons have "successfully internalized these admirable values,"[414] and they fear nothing more than "the curse of idleness."[415] Rothbard quotes from the private welfare program set up in 1963 by these devotees to the Puritan work ethic:

> No true Latter-Day Saint will, while physically able, voluntarily shift from himself the burden of his own support. So long as he can, under the inspiration of the Almighty and with his own labors, he will supply himself with the necessities of life.[416]

If theocratic 17th-century New England could produce true communalist localist anarchists, then who is to say that 20th-century Mormon society could not produce exemplary anarcho-capitalists?

As final evidence that everyone is capable of pulling himself up by the bootstraps if he or she only so desires, Rothbard refers us to a study by a "Prof. Banfield," who has proven that in the end moral and cultural values, not economic conditions, are responsible for success or failure. As an example Banfield cites the Albanian immigrants in the slums of New York City, who unlike their better-off African-American and Puerto Rican counterparts, do not ask for welfare, preferring a poor, yet independent life until they succeed through their own hard work.

---

414. Ibid., p. 148.
415. Ibid., p. 150.
416. Ibid., p. 149.

Following this theory, then, African-Americans and Puerto Ricans need only be cured of their culturally based laziness in order to be capable of earning as much as industrious European-Americans. Rothbard asserts that "those very parasitic values of idleness and irresponsibility"[417] need to be countered with discipline and the work ethic. He and his party propose that the government implement the following measures immediately to counter unemployment: privatization of welfare, abolition of the minimum wage and other achievements of the trade union movement, and the repeal of all licensing laws as well as all restrictions on trade and production. He would legalize the drug trade, prostitution, gambling, and peddling. Did not countless American immigrant workers, Rothbard asks, start out by peddling? Yes, one is tempted to add, and many other immigrants to America in the 19th century could not find work and simply starved to death.

In his chapter on education Rothbard examines the parallels in the arguments put forward by left and right critics of the public school system. Such conservatives as the individualist Albert Jay Nock (1872–1945) point out the futility of compulsory schooling for the "ineducable masses"[418] and the waste of neglecting educational opportunities for the gifted. Such leftists as Paul Goodman criticize upper and middle classes for forcing their cultural values onto lower class children. In Rothbard's opinion, what both of these positions are really saying is that "a whole mass of children" is "being dragooned into an institution for which they have little interest or aptitude."[419] However, this is where arguments against public education by descendents of the New Left often become conservative. They reject public education on the grounds that it is repressive, cruel, and against the will of children themselves. Then, instead of working toward a society that would create excellence in public education, they send their own children to expensive private schools. In anti-public-education positions one never fails to find that standard idea of cultural imperialism which, at first, seems to have a progressive ring.

> In fact, one of the major motivations of the legion of mid-nineteenth-century American "educational reformers" who established the modern public school system was precisely to use it to cripple the cultural and linguistic life of the waves of immigrants into America and to mould them . . . into "one people."[420]

The real issue becomes clear when Rothbard gets to the heart of the matter: he writes that most of what is taught in schools today is of no use in later working life, and whoever ignores this fact, for whatever reasons, is contributing to youth unemployment. He goes on to say that this is exactly what the unions are doing, for example, when, in order to rid themselves of potential competitors,

---

417. Ibid., p. 154.
418. Ibid., p. 121.
419. Ibid., p. 122.
420. Ibid., p. 125.

they encourage young workers to go back to school; as such they are no better than employers who force their white-collar workers to continue their education. Rothbard suggests the radical privatization of schools coupled with the abolition of compulsory schooling as an alternative to the state-run public educational system. He promises that some schools will experiment with egalitarian educational methods, while others will uphold traditional learning-by-rote and competition. There would be both secular and religious schools, capitalist and socialist teachers. He is less clear, however, with regard to the fate and the future of the "ineducable masses." In a "libertarian world" they might learn some reading and writing at home, or perhaps not at all because their parents cannot afford a private school. And, thanks to the legions of the illiterate or semiliterate, there would certainly be no lack of social diversity. Neither would there be a lack of cheap labor, which, uncontaminated by education, would not so readily meander down the wayward union path.

Their sharp criticism of the environmental pollution caused by both the public and the private sectors has earned the anarcho-capitalists a certain respect. Their diatribes against the Department of Agriculture for its irresponsible use of toxic pesticides or against the Atomic Energy Commission for its negligent and irresponsible handling of nuclear waste have gained them much public notoriety. As a leftist and environmentalist I can only support anarcho-capitalist demands that all legal means available be used to make environmental polluters accountable for their deeds. Even the definition of air pollution in terms of property rights appears to make sense because its takes capitalist society at its word. Less realistic are the libertarian promises of a clean environment thanks to privatized rivers and oceans. Of course, the owner of a clean river could sue anyone who pollutes his water and could establish profitable clubs and resorts along the waterfront. However, what if it were more profitable for the owner to rent his river as a toxic waste site to all the chemical factories and sewage plants in the area? Just as speculative is Rothbard's vision of privatized oceans as a source of food, and no less questionable is his claim that the private ownership of forests would bring about the end of the ecological devastation caused by deforestation. All this, including the promise that natural resources would be used in a responsible manner once they are privatized, is logical only to fundamentalist believers in the free market.

The chapter in *The Libertarian Manifesto* on the privatization of roads, bridges, and freeways has a truly Orwellian quality. In the world of absolute libertarian freedom no one could ever set foot anywhere without paying its owner. According to Rothbard this would end all traffic problems. Tolls on roads, bridges, and tunnels would skyrocket during rush hours, and as a result many commuters would either prefer to use public transportation or look for employment closer to home. Parking in congested city centers would become so expensive that many motorists would voluntarily give up driving altogether, which Rothbard predicts would result in fewer cars and less air pollution. The effect of privatization would be just as pleasing in residential areas, he says. For instance, in areas where houses and streets all belong to the same owner, that owner would have an interest in offering good private security. In business districts the streets would belong to the merchants, who would ensure good security in order to attract customers to the area free of charge. Rejecting the notion that the private ownership of streets could encourage class and racial discrimination, Rothbard states:

> "Discrimination" in the sense of choosing favorably or unfavorably in accordance with whatever criteria a person may employ, is an integral part of freedom of choice and hence a free society.[421]

It is not hard to picture what that freedom would entail: not only would owners of highways and "nice" neighborhoods rake in profits, but slumlords, too. If everything down to the last brick were privatized in low-income neighborhoods, for example, the residents would likely be even worse off than they are now, for the private police would help landlords collect rents and suppress resistance. Moreover, in the absence of jobs, unemployment benefits, and welfare, residents would be virtual prisoners of the ghetto, because even a trip from the Bronx to New Jersey would be too expensive. The same would apply to working class or lower-middle-class people; road and bridge tolls would be beyond their means, thus forcing them to stay at home, while the wealthy could travel anywhere they pleased. Rothbard is aware of this. In *The Ethics of Liberty* he openly states:

> The libertarian society would resolve the entire "immigration question" within the matrix of absolute property rights. For people only have the right to move to those properties and lands where the owners desire to rent or sell to them.[422]

Freedom of movement would thus be abolished world-wide. Mexicans would have to stay in Mexico, and African-Americans and other "undesirables" in their US slums, without any hope of mobility. The separation of class and race would be secured on a local and global level, and everywhere the bourgeoisie would at last be left to prosper in isolation.

Eye for an Eye, Tooth for a Tooth

When talk in left-liberal circles turns to anarcho-capitalism, one often hears words of praise for anarcho-capitalists' condemnation of vice laws, as well as for their demands to repeal laws against abortion, adultery, and homosexuality, and to legalize drugs. Amid the frenzy of the religious right, this position is refreshing:

---

421.   Ibid., p. 206.
422.   Murray Rothbard, *The Ethics of Liberty*. Atlantic Highlands: Humanities Press, 1982, p. 119.

> The libertarian holds that it is not the business of the law . . . to enforce anyone's conception of morality . . . to make anyone good or reverent or moral or clean or upright. This is for each individual to decide for himself.[423] Since sex is a uniquely private aspect of life, it is particularly intolerable that governments should presume to regulate and legislate sexual behavior.[424]

Seeing the Victorian prudery of fundamentalist fanatics and antipornography feminists, I am scarcely bothered by the stereotypical anarcho-capitalist arguments about property rights when applied to this topic. Rothbard writes that outlawing the production, trade, and sale of pornography would counter every principle of private property, free trade, and freedom of the press. The same is true of prostitution, which is just a "voluntary sale of a labor service."[425] And his argument for the legalization of drugs conforms more or less to that advanced by the left. Legal drugs, says Rothbard, would be cheaper, and addicts would not thus be automatically driven to crime. The prohibition of drugs is part of what he calls the "totalitarian cage, where people are prohibited from eating candy and are forced to eat yogurt 'for their own good.' "[426] His proposal to abolish compulsory witness and jury duty seems to be antiauthoritarian, and many would agree with his demand that police officers be punished like other people in cases of misconduct.

Things get stickier, however, when, along with the legalization of deviant sexuality, pornography, abortion, prostitution, and drugs, the demand is put forth that weapons be allowed for "self defense." Instead of prosecuting "innocent people" for possessing weapons the legal system should spend more time going after the "real criminals."[427] Rothbard argues further that, while the white middle class can afford property insurance and therefore does not need to arm itself in self-defense, an African-American store owner would be totally ruined if robbed—an idea originating less in the reality of a large contingent of African-American store owners than in the psychology of a certain segment of white middle class. Rothbard backs up his argument for vigilante self-defense by referring to the fact that in the past five years in Chicago three times as many criminals have been killed by people defending themselves as by the police.

As to the question of how far someone should be permitted to go in defense of his property, Rothbard supports the "moderate" view: in contrast to many orthodox adherents of Rand's teachings, for example, he feels that a store owner does not have the right to shoot and kill someone for stealing a pack of chewing gum. As a general rule he suggests that a criminal should be stripped of his rights in the same measure as he has infringed on the rights of another: "The punishment should fit the crime." He adds:

423. Murray Rothbard, *For a New Liberty.* New York: Collier Macmillan Publishers, 1978, p. 104.
424. Ibid., p. 105.
425. Ibid., p. 106.
426. Ibid., p. 111.
427. Ibid., p. 115.

> It should be evident that our theory of proportional punishment . . . is frankly a retributive theory of punishment, a "tooth (or two teeth) for a tooth" theory.[428]

As in the Babylon of Hammurabi, Rothbard feels that thieves should be sentenced to recompensation, ruffians to beating, and murderers to death. (The futurist in Konkin III believes that the courts should sentence criminals to the amputation or removal of replaceable organs.) For insolvent thiefs, libertarian justice would impose forced labor, which ideally "puts the criminal . . . into a state of enslavement"[429] vis-à-vis his victim. A person who commits assault and who is not beaten in self-defense at the time of the crime should be sentenced to beating, which could be carried out by the victim himself or on the latter's orders by a private police officer. The same would apply to murderers, the only general restriction being that in the case of an error the person responsible for that error should also be punished:

> Suppose, for example, that Hatfield$_1$ murders McCoy$_1$. McCoy$_2$ then decides to seek out and execute Hatfield$_1$ himself. This is fine, except that McCoy$_2$ may have to face the prospect of being charged with murder in the private courts by Hatfield$_2$. The point is that if the courts find that Hatfield was indeed the murderer, then nothing happens to McCoy$_2$ in our schema except public approbation for executing justice. But if it turns out that there was not enough evidence to convict Hatfield$_1$ for the original murder, or if indeed some other Hatfield or some stranger committed the crime, then McCoy$_1$ . . . cannot plead any sort of immunity.[430]

One might ask oneself in this context what libertarians would do with a pathologically cruel or multiple murderer. Burn him alive, draw and quarter him, and then throw him to the lions, perhaps?

In the anarcho-capitalist stateless society, justice would be meted out by competing private courts, for whose service customers would pay a premium, similar to insurance. Courts of appeal would have the final say, or the victim could pardon the criminal who would then go free. Rothbard is confident that the laws of the market ensure that the best judges are selected to provide maximum justice.

It is not hard to imagine that the anarcho-capitalist utopia would be a society bursting at the seams with thieves, robbers, murderers, ruffians, and their armed persecutors. The libertarians do not seem to question the source of the crimes they promise to fight in such an exemplary fashion, a source that seems to be human nature itself, which condemns us all to an eternal struggle with our peers. Only in the rarest of cases does free will appear to be strong enough to allow us to comply with moral (property) rules that alone could guarantee the smooth functioning of society. Hence, as there will always be murderers, thieves, and victims, justice can only mean retribution, not deterrence, let alone

---

428. Murray Rothbard, *The Ethics of Liberty.* Atlantic Highlands: Humanities Press, 1982, p. 90.
429. Ibid., p. 86.
430. Ibid., p. 89.

rehabilitation. This is the logic of an ideology in which any notion of social progress toward a compassionate, peaceful, and happy world has been lost. In light of the insistence on social inequality in a neo-barbaric world of "an eye for an eye, a tooth for a tooth," the call for equality before the law is pure cynicism. The anarcho-capitalists always serve to remind us of the intrinsic cruelty of a profit-oriented market society.

Peace, War, and the Police

Rothbard called for the abolition of the draft and the CIA, the drastic reduction of military expenditures, the destruction of bombs, missiles, and all offensive weapons, as well as for an end to the Cold War with the Soviet Union. He paraphrased the cold warriors' catchphrase "better dead than red" as "better them dead than red" and "give me liberty or give them death." Militarism, he continues, is the battle call "not of noble heroes but of mass murderers."[431] The libertarian, Rothbard stresses, is opposed to modern nuclear war between nation states, because it necessarily entails taxation and the mass murder of civilian populations. Wars, he explains, arise from competition between states, which unjustly behave as the owners of their respective territories, fictitious property that then becomes the reason for disputes. In addition, the identification of a territory and its people with the state turns "natural patriotism"[432] into statist nationalism. A dispute between rulers quickly becomes a war between peoples defending their respective rulers and suffering from the delusion that they are protected by them. In a libertarian society, however, there would be no reason for war because all land would be privately owned and governments would be abolished.

As far as US foreign policy is concerned, Rothbard suggests traditional American isolationism rooted in the principles of the laissez-faire extremists of the 18th and 19th centuries. He points to such liberals as the economist William Graham Sumner (1840-1910) and the Bostonian merchant Edward Atkinson (1827-1915), who founded the Anti-Imperialist League and opposed the Spanish-American War. Furthermore, he points out that the opposition to US participation in World War I was by no means a purely leftist position, including as it did at least an equal number of liberals and laissez-faire capitalists. The conservative camp, however, condemned the isolationists of the time as leftist, while an isolationist position during World War II raised suspicions of pro-Nazi sympathies.

In Rothbard's view 20th-century American imperialism is the antithesis of isolationism. He sounds remarkably leftist, especially when he cites William Appleman Williams, a prominent historian of the New Left. However, Rothbard

---

431. Murray Rothbard, *For a New Liberty.* New York: Collier MacMillan Publishers, 1978, p. 294.
432. Ibid., p. 58.

compares Williams's historical views with the positions of conservative and liberal isolationists such as the journalist Garet Garret. Agreeing with leftist opponents to World War I, Rothbard faults Woodrow Wilson for abandoning isolationism, thus prolonging the war and causing mass murder and terrible destruction—all of which in the end led to the victories of the Bolsheviks and the Nazis.

Rothbard's most virulent diatribes are aimed at the extreme anticommunist US foreign policy. Before the Russian revolution, he reminds us, the US had given military aid to the czarist regime. After World War II the Americans tried their best to drive the Soviets out of Eastern Europe, helped the British fight the communists in Greece, and supported Chiang Kai-shek's dictatorship in China. The US also helped the Cuban dictator Batista seize power and later used any and all means to overthrow the Castro regime, including attempts to assassinate Castro. And finally, the Vietnam War offers us "a microcosm"[433] of all the tragic mistakes of 20th-century American foreign policy.

The chapter dealing with US foreign policy reads like a pamphlet from the anti-Vietnam War movement, while the one dealing with Soviet foreign policy praises Stalin and the peace-loving Soviet Union. Rothbard begins his masterful critique of Cold War ideologists by pointing out the (alleged) Marxist theory of communism's historical inevitability. Exporting communism to foreign countries is contrary to its own idea of peaceful coexistence, he states. As a matter of fact, he tells us, after the Peace of Brest Litovsk in 1917 between Germany and Russia, the Bolsheviks proved that they valued peace at all cost. This was true in 1917, and it remained true under Stalin, who led his country back to a "conservative" brand of politics oriented toward the nation state. And he was so little intent on war that as a result the Germans almost won. After the war Stalin abandoned the revolutionary concept entirely in favor of Soviet national interests, thereby betraying the communists of other countries. Thus he succeeded in convincing the Italian and French communists, on the verge of victory in their respective countries, to enter into coalitions with noncommunist parties. He also abandoned the Greek communists at the decisive moment. Even in postwar Eastern Europe, Rothbard presumes, Stalin would have preferred neutral governments, such as the one in Finland, and only when faced with the Cold War did he install Soviet-style communism in that part of the world. Rothbard even characterizes both the suppression of the Hungarian uprising in 1956 and the invasion of Czechoslovakia in 1968 as "reprehensible."[434] This analysis is surprising in more ways than one: first, in its open identification with the Soviet-Stalinist version of the politics of peace, and second, because Rothbard's praise of Stalinism, coming as it does from a rightist, almost has the effect of a critique from the left. To expose Stalin as a

---

433. Ibid., p. 272.
434. Ibid., p. 288.

traitor of communists—isn't that Trotskyism in its purest form? Indeed, couldn't the following quote have come from an anarcho-syndicalist like Rudolf Rocker?

> Once a revolutionary movement seizes State power, it begins very quickly to take on the attributes of a ruling class with a class interest in retaining State power. The world revolution begins to pale, in their outlook, to insignificance. And since State elites can and do have conflicting interests in power and wealth, it is not surprising that inter-Communist conflicts have become endemic.[435]

Rothbard's title for the US government as the "most warlike, most interventionist, most imperialist government"[436] of the 20th century, on the other hand, is disputable. Might Germany not still deserve this distinction? The following comment about World War II smacks of revisionist history in the sense of the IHR:

> Since Germany otherwise would have been able to retain control of Europe indefinitely, it was Hitler who was led by the siren call of anticommunist ideology to throw away a rational and prudent course and launch what was to be the beginning of his ultimate defeat.[437]

According to this view Hitler was rational and smart until anticommunism clouded his senses. Isolationist Germanophilia, this time without militant anticommunism.

Rothbard's antiwar position is by no means pacifist. He is not in the least opposed to an all-volunteer army or to a professional militia organized according to free market principles and freed from the obligation to swear allegiance to the flag. His cautious sympathy for the Viet Cong corresponds to his expressed endorsement of guerrilla warfare. Statements like the following are strikingly similar to those of the radical left or of anarcho-syndicalists.

> Guerrilla warfare has proved to be an irresistible force precisely because it stems, not from a dictatorial central government, but from the people themselves, fighting for their liberty and independence against a foreign State.[438]

Only when one looks at how Rothbard distinguishes between good revolutionary wars and bad imperialist ones does the difference between his position and the leftist view become apparent. He is not at all interested in the rationale for a particular war and compares the wars of annihilation between modern nation states with the wars of medieval kings and lords that were fought with comparatively harmless weapons. Unlike the conscripted armies of today, the armies of old comprised small bands of mercenaries fighting against the enemy's mercenaries. It was a popular sport to watch such enemies' battles from the safety of the town wall, like a football match. Rothbard mentions neither the brutal looting and plundering sprees of armed medieval lords against the farmers, nor the marauding mercenaries, disastrous tribal and religious

---

435. Ibid., p. 287.
436. Ibid., p. 270.
437. Ibid., p. 285.
438. Ibid., p. 241.

wars, and crusades. The modern guerrilla war, however, he credits with the "ancient and honorable [medieval] virtue of pinpointing the enemy and sparing innocent civilians."[439] A limited war, not instigated by a state, is acceptable as long as it adheres to the libertarian principles concerning property, regardless of the war's goals. According to this ethic, Oliver North was entirely justified to obtain private financing for his Contra activities. The realization of international socialism, which would render wars superfluous, would be contrary to the libertarian credo which holds that large scale national wars will be superfluous after the state and with it any and all social functions have been abolished and laissez-faire established. In a libertarian capitalist system, however, "natural" human competition, which in present societies is but perverted into nationalism, will reign supreme in a decentralized structure: first, as economic war of each against all; second, in armed struggles between private paramilitary forces, whose service could be bought. The poor would be protected by private charities. With visible pleasure Rothbard answers the question a reader might have about the threat of a police war:

> Let us take two hypothetical countries: "Ruritania" and "Walldavia." If both Ruritania and Walldavia were dissolved into a libertarian society, with no government and innumerable private individuals, firms, and police agencies, the only clashes that *could* break out would be local and the weaponry would necessarily be strictly limited in scope and devastation. . . . At worst, they could *not* use mass bombing or nuclear destruction or germ warfare, since they themselves would be blown up in the holocaust.[440]

Thus, as in Bookchin's writings, decentralism is a localist or isolationist principle.

Rothbard, too, appears to place his hope for an end to human destructiveness on restricting social intercourse to dealings among close neighbors. But contrary to Bookchin's vision of a municipal civic guard or militia, one could imagine Rothbard's private police forces, in a future capitalist society void of all social laws and union-inspired reforms, being used against striking workers. According to Rothbard, it is just as legitimate to defend a contract by forcing compliance with it as it is to defend property rights.

The anarcho-capitalist utopia is not a peaceful place. War returns entirely to its original purpose of strengthening class rule. The new libertarian order— armed to the teeth, brimming with security guards, self-defenders, and bodyguards—is a police society. This, of course, explains Rothbard's puzzlingly tolerant view of the communist countries. As avowed enemies of socialist collectivism, mutual aid, and human cooperation, the anarcho-capitalists need no artificial foreign communist scapegoat. No, the potential altruistic opponent is not and never has been in Moscow or Warsaw, but in the domestic factories

---

439. Ibid., p. 269.
440. Ibid., p. 220.

and ghettos, and in the Third World. The radical philosophy of property is meant to be a bulwark against dangers originating there.

Critique of Marxism

Rothbard's critique of Marxism, socialism, and communism, or collectivism takes up less space and is, comparatively, less passionate than that of other libertarians. Socialism, we learn, came into existence in the 19th century as a cross between conservatism and liberalism. Rothbard refers to this so-called theoretical bastard as "quasi-conservative"[441] and defines it as follows:

> Socialism was a confused and hybrid movement because it tried to achieve the liberal goals of freedom, peace, and industrial harmony and growth . . . by imposing the old conservative means of statism, collectivism, and hierarchical privilege.[442]

For Rothbard, socialism is a technocracy in the name of the people, its government made up of scientists, labor representatives, and bureaucrats. And that, he states, is simply "absolute monarchy and feudalism with a modern face."[443]

Because it opposes private property, communism is in Rothbard's view a form of pure "parasitism." Since solidarity and sharing of material goods of any kind are unthinkable in radical-liberalist theory his anarcho-capitalist view takes him to a most peculiar interpretation of the communist critique of private property: communism means the right of every human being to own a certain share of all other humans, the exact opposite of the right to self-ownership. In the past this absurd notion, arising from the liberalist identification of property with the individual, has often been cited by other anticommunists as proof that communism was only a generalized form of prostitution. From there Rothbard deduces the universal interdependence of human beings, which only suffocates independent initiative. And if the division of labor should ever actually be abolished—this being communism's stated goal—Rothbard predicts that humankind will simply starve to death.

Rothbard also criticizes the Marxist belief in the human ability to change and its rejection of the notion of a static human nature, suspecting that behind a presumption of unlimited manipulability lurks the mistrust in a definable human nature, a notion that is in contradiction to his idea of free will. Leftist anarchists from Bakunin to Kropotkin to Chomsky have tended to believe that human nature is innately good, but that its goodness must be liberated by social change. Rothbard believes that it is human nature itself that prohibits social change in a socialist sense.

> In contrast to such utopians as Marxists or left-wing anarchists (anarcho-communists or anarcho-syndicalists), libertarians do *not* assume that the ushering in of the purely free society of their dreams will also bring with it a new, magically transformed Libertarian

---

441. Ibid., p. 14.
442. Ibid., p. 13.
443. Ibid., p. 14.

Man. We do not assume that the lion will lie down with the lamb, or that no one will have criminal or fraudulent designs upon his neighbor.[444]

Is it just a coincidence that the lion/lamb metaphor also appears in Bookchin's writings on nature? Or is this yet another piece of evidence supporting the Marxist thesis that theories on the unchangeable character of nature serve only to rehabilitate the existing state of affairs?

Rothbard, like Mises before him, considers Marxism, academic socialism, and Keynesian economics to be variants of the collectivist vice, which, we are told, began in the US (formerly a "relatively free laissez-faire economy"[445]) in the course of World War I. Collectivist mass mobilization and the top-down planning of the war economy fulfilled both big business's and progressive intellectuals' dreams of a centrally organized state and fostered the growth of the labor movement, thus elevating the latter to the corporate state's junior partner. This resulted in the monopoly of the state at home and the politics of intervention abroad. According to this view, both the capitalist state and the labor movement are collectivist and imperialist—a demagogically anticommunist image more powerful than Reagan's "warnings" of the evil empire. After World War II, Rothbard states, the pact between government, big business, and the unions was complete. The scientific jargon of (leftist) Keynesian intellectuals, Rothbard emphasizes, which serves to justify state power, matches the most obscure rantings of medieval priesthood.

Like all intellectual heirs of Ludwig von Mises, Rothbard's mistrust of intellectuals is paramount. He calls them court intellectuals and traces their key role as doctors or churchmen to the "age-old partnership between Church and state"— a thesis reminiscent of Bookchin's theory that patriarchy and instrumental reason are rooted in the ancient shaman's seizure of power. In the modern secular age, Rothbard states, the professional ideologists have been replaced by cadres of scientific experts who now try to fool the public into believing that domestic and foreign policies are issues beyond the intellectual capabilities of most people and must therefore be handled by state experts, planners, and scientists. On the traditional opportunism of intellectuals he writes:

> Put simply, the intellectual's livelihood in the free market is generally none too secure; . . . The State, on the other hand, is willing to offer the intellectuals a warm, secure and permanent berth in its apparatus, a secure income, and the panoply of prestige.[446]

This might confirm some Bakuninists' legitimate yet problematic suspicion of intellectuals and academics; however, it is to be hoped, that those Bakuninists will note that Rothbard's dislike of intellectuals is surpassed by his contempt for common people, that "majority" which he compares to a "lynch mob."[447]

---

444. Ibid., p. 234.
445. Ibid., p. 279.
446. Ibid., p. 60.
447. Ibid., p. 49.

> Most people neither originate nor disseminate ideas and concepts; on the contrary, they tend to adopt those ideas promulgated by the professional intellectual classes, the professional dealers in ideas.[448]

The attentive reader might ask: why is Rothbard railing against professionals and merchants? Don't libertarians try to successfully market their ideas? Rothbard thus joins the ranks of the philosophers criticized by Marx in *The German Ideology* for believing that it is men and ideas who move history forward. Yet Rothbard greatly admires Marxist theory, and he admonishes libertarians to come up with something just as good:

> The enormous success of Karl Marx and Marxism has been due not to the validity of his ideas—all of which indeed are fallacious—but to the fact that he dared to weave socialist theory into a mighty system.[449]

Rothbard's antipathy towards intellectuals is as great as his overestimation of their power—a fallacy encountered in other ideologists who believe in the great struggle of ideas. He belongs to those (up to and including the Leninist avant-garde) who consider the common people to be stupid, and themselves the only ones capable of thinking, and who therefore fear intellectual competition most. And woe to that competition when the likes of Rothbard come to power, for their first act is always to purge the intellectual opposition.

Patriotism and Petty Bourgeois Ideology

One would think that someone opposed to the nation state and to the identification of the ruled with their rulers would espouse an antinationalist or internationalist position. After all, Rothbard emphasizes his demand for "liberty for everyone, everywhere, not just in the United States."[450]

Nonetheless, the antinationalism of anarcho-capitalists is just as misleading as is their pacifism and their antistatism. Social-revolutionary anarchists hope that by abolishing states and nations they will create societies without borders, classes, authority, competition, armies, and police, where the peoples of this earth will live in harmony, reconcile their differences, and help each other. In contrast, what anarcho-capitalists dislike most about the state is its social function; what bothers them about nationalism is not that it foments prejudice and scapegoating in order to sustain the privileges of those in power, but that it fuels collectivist sentiments that, in Rothbard's opinion, lead straight to socialism. Thus the abolition of national governments and borders and a return to isolationist, noninterventionist policies is not intended to improve relations between peoples or to increase the international solidarity of the exploited. Rather, Rothbard aims at reviving the America of early capitalism. Like Ayn

---

448. Ibid., p. 11.
449. Ibid., p. 321.
450. Ibid., p. 239.

Rand, Rothbard extols American virtues in lofty terms, and American soil is more fertile to the seeds of libertarian ideas than any other. In his view, the spirit of the American revolution, with its distaste for taxes, trade monopolies, militarism, and executive power, was in reality just as libertarian as the Bill of Rights was antistatist. The Jeffersonian movement opposed the idea of conscription and a standing army, and an armed citizenry defending the nation against invaders is an ancient American principle. Rothbard asserts further that Americans have always been opposed to taxes, a sentiment that continuously reasserts itself in tax-cutting policies.

The last chapter of the *Libertarian Manifesto* sounds an avowedly nationalist theme:

> Libertarians are squarely in the great classical liberal tradition that built the United States and bestowed on us the American heritage of individual liberty, a peaceful foreign policy, minimal government, and a free-market economy. Libertarians are the only genuine current heirs of Jefferson, Paine, Jackson, and the abolitionists.
>
> And yet, while we are more truly traditional and more rootedly American than the conservatives, we are in some ways more radical than the radicals.[451]

Unlike future-oriented libertarians Rothbard has a weakness for the "good old days" per se, above and beyond his sympathy for the American past. In his view, the representatives of the Golden Age are the Celtic-Germanic tribes to which he ascribes "libertarian elements."[452] Unlike Mises and Rand, Rothbard never considers tribes to be a barbarian scourge.

> The basic political unit of ancient Ireland was the *tuath*. All "freemen" who owned land, all professionals, and all craftsmen, were entitled to become members of a *tuath* ... *tuatha* were voluntary associations which only comprised the landed properties of its voluntary members.[453]

Regardless of whether his description is in fact historically correct, it is undeniably one of a class society, democracy in name only of privileged men, similar to the one of ancient Greece. Rothbard goes on to tell us that in ancient Ireland the law, as handed down by a class of specialists, was administered via a system of sureties and surety relationships and that all criminals were considered debtors who owed compensation to their victims. Those who did not discharge their debt were declared "outlaws." However, Rothbard remains discretely silent about the consequences of such a refusal—whether these debtors were stoned to death or executed by some other barbaric means.

Rothbard also appears to have a weakness for the Middle Ages, as expressed by his eulogy of the Old English merchant law. His dream of a postnationalist, decentralized future certainly has a medieval ring to it—a world of bridge and

---

451. Ibid., p. 320
452. Ibid., p. 63.
453. Ibid., pp. 231-32.

road tolls, social divisions, privately organized charities, sports-like mini-wars, starving babies, revenge and retribution, and the unrestricted right to bear arms. It is his nostalgia combined with his sharp criticism of big business that sets Rothbard apart from Hayek and Mises, as well as from Rand.

Liberalism and laissez-faire liberalism are the traditional ideologies to which both the upper bourgeoisie and those who want to join it subscribe. In this context the belief in progress and technology may coalesce with religion and morality in order to win over the conservative middle classes, but it is the bait of tribalism, medieval nostalgia, and the manipulation of the relationship between small entrepreneurs and big business that wins the hearts of the "radical" petty bourgeoisie, with its class hatred of both those above and those below it. The demoralized New Left, Rothbard's former friend, was and remains a breeding ground for this mentality. However, one cannot approach it with the hysterical anticommunism advocated by Thatcher, Reagan, Friedman, et al., nor even with Hayek's thesis of totalitarianism, which blames socialism for the rise of fascism; Rothbard's charge that US intervention in foreign politics gave rise to Stalinism and fascism is much better suited to this attitude. Open racism would have most certainly been an embarrassment to the petit-bourgeois New Left, at least at the time the *Libertarian Manifesto* was written. Mises's sympathy for racial theory, Rand's anti-Semitism and Anglo-Saxon worship, or Friedman's definition of the German fascist Nuremberg Racial Laws of 1935 as a law against discrimination would be too blatant. They might be more susceptible, however, to indirect promises that immigration will be curtailed and to a moral justification for allowing the homeless to go hungry. It is indeed a stroke of perverse genius that Rothbard and Co. can convince people, who are themselves potential victims of unemployment, that they will benefit by ridding themselves of social responsibility and abolishing all social institutions.

With no hope of owning property and full of resentment Joe Blow thus becomes an anarcho-capitalist, claiming that the abolition of civil society will solve the problem of state oppression. Consequently, Rothbard need not rehabilitate the state, be it as the administrator of police and army, as suggested by Rand, or as the keeper of law and order, as advocated by Mises, or as rulemaker and umpire, as suggested by Friedman. Instead, authority and repression are to be decentralized and libertarian, that is, privatized. At the same time, Rothbard's pseudo-radicalism enables him to discard any notion of reforming capitalism. Friedman's negative income tax and his suggestion that the state dispense private school vouchers to parents are dismissed by Rothbard as reformist. Instead of paying out minimal unemployment benefits to isolate the unemployed and to defuse their grievances, he would abandon them to fend for themselves, perhaps even to die. Whereas conservative laissez-faire politicians would retain at least some token form of public education, radical libertarians are not bothered by the thought of illiterate proletarians.

Murray Rothbard

Rothbard's extremism even destroys liberalism's greatest taboo: the fear of revolution. For John Stuart Mill revolution was a deed of terror where the mob strives for power, for Mises it was synonymous with reaction and imperialism, and for Rand it was the terror of the red hordes, but for Rothbard, revolution is connected to a "war of liberation" and "libertarian" social change, enabling many a former middle-class leftist to delude himself that he is neither on the left nor the right but squarely at the forefront of events. Rothbard's message still contains a comforting message for the turncoats who, having broken with all leftist "taboos," still wish to be regarded as radical or revolutionary rather than as reformist or liberal. The most suitable ideology for this undertaking is none other than the achievement-oriented society rejected by the New Left. This is a world in which liberty means the freedom to make profits, to own property, and to use privileges to one's advantage; where ethics and reason only serve to justify social inequality; where justice is reduced to the notion of might makes right. In this world, peace means replacing atomic war with the daily war of the marketplace, and wars between guerrilla armies and private police forces; and where happiness is understood to mean the happiness of the consumer who, thanks to his army of private guards, is safe from thieves.

This fictitious supercapitalism represents a giant step backward from bourgeois society, but it is at the same time its consummation, in that Rothbard does away with all its humanitarian utopias and illusions. Liberty, equality, and fraternity—the unkept promise of the bourgeois revolution—fall victim to a deeply pessimistic and cruel view of human nature. Barely hidden behind talk of variety and diversity lies the feudal ethic of the birthright to privilege and the violence required to enforce it.

The Master's New Friends

As much as Rothbard's brave new dog-eat-dog world may be suited to certain renegades of the New Left, many of them were more attracted to the neoconservatives; and some even found their way to the conservative ecologists. Rothbard himself turned away in disappointment from the heirs of the New Left and returned from whence he had come, the isolationist "Old Right."

Since the end of the Cold War, which had united all conservatives under the common banner of anticommunism, arch-conservatives (prematurely declared dead) have been attracting attention with the revival of the anti-interventionist "America First" policy. The main targets of their criticism are the neoconservatives. This paleoconservative Old Right criticizes the neoconservatives as warmongers, social democrats, New Dealers, internationalist supporters of human rights, global-messianic idealists, pluralist civil rights workers, and feminist sympathizers. The paleoconservatives also accuse them of having seized control of almost all conservative foundations in order to use their money and prestige for their own purposes. Such polemics are laced with anti-Semitic innuendo. Early in the 1990s Rothbard retreated from the Libertarian Party and resigned his post as editor of *Liberty*, the party's publication, to forge a new coalition between libertarians or "paleolibertarians" and paleoconservatives. He founded the *Rothbard-Rockwell Report* together with Lew Rockwell, the director of the Ludwig von Mises Institute in California. This journal is fiercely critical of the neoconservatives, comparing them to leftist and moderate libertarians, who, in turn, are denounced as egalitarians, civil rights workers, New Dealers, fanatical atheists, feminists, eco-weirdos, and advocates of filth, smut, and child pornography. The alternative is defined as a " 'New Fusionism' . . . forming among paleoconservatives and paleolibertarians in which both sides speak of opposing the 'welfare-warfare state' and supporting the moral foundation on which our civilization rests."[454]

Rockwell, a zealous fusionist, writes on a number of issues popularly regarded as the traditionally favorite themes of the Old Right. For example, he has thanked Jesse Helms, the notorious censor, for his opposition to public funding of AIDS education along the lines of a poster distributed by Californian AIDS organizations. The poster depicts "two aroused young men . . . entirely naked except for a condom."[455] That Rockwell embraces the Catholic Church is not a surprise either: "Ever since the age of St. Thomas Aquinas," he writes, "the best Catholic scholars had endorsed free markets, and even *laissez-faire*, as moral and just."[456] He then goes on to praise Pope John Paul for his consistent support of profits and the free market. Rockwell was also the only one to publicly support the Los Angeles police officers whose orgy of violence against Rodney King, a defenseless African-American traffic offender, has been immortalized on videotape.

Rothbard, in turn, publicly defended Rockwell after his writings on the King affair drew heated criticism from many people, including the editor of *Liberty*. Finally, having abandoned his predecessors' anticlerical stance and antibourgeois view of morality and lifestyle, Rothbard has of late begun to praise the socially beneficial role of Catholicism; he also engages in antigay innuendo, and raises the banner of family values. Like many paleoconservatives and some libertarians, during the Gulf War in 1990–1991 Rothbard took an isolationist antiwar stance spiced with the heavy rhetoric of anti-Zionism. Only the future will show whether Rothbard has bet on the right horse. I sincerely doubt, however, that he will be able to convert the paleoconservatives to anarchism.

454. Paul Gottfried, *Rothbard-Rockwell Report*, Feb. 1991, p. 14.
455. Lew Rockwell, *Rothbard-Rockwell Report*, May 1991, p. 14.
456. Lew Rockwell, *Rothbard-Rockwell Report*, June 1991, p. 14.

EPILOGUE

Ironically, the two sides of anarchism's Janus face are most timely now, although for opposite reasons. The ruling elite everywhere is moving to eliminate hard won welfare-state reforms enacted under—or wrested from—capitalism. Anarcho-capitalism represents the most extreme variety of the rediscovered laissez-faire ideologies. If the left does not succeed in stopping this trend, we will face a worldwide social and ecological disaster. On the part of the oppressed there still remains the unfulfilled dream of a democratic socialism, an egalitarian society that provides for all without turning itself into a bureaucratic nightmare that violates individual freedom and human rights. Together with council-communist concepts, anarcho-syndicalism stands for this promise.

I have attempted to point out the differences between social revolutionary and individualist anarchism to prevent further confusion of the two, as well as to investigate their indirect similarities with regard to questions of individualism, antistatism, decentralism, the affinity to nature, and morality. Far from lumping together leftist and rightist anarchists, I hope to have shown how crucial seemingly small ideological shifts can become, as soon as the left relaxes its opposition to capitalism and becomes less vigilant in its defense of egalitarianism. Individualism, for instance, on the anarchist left stands for tolerance and humanity, but on the right, it stands for private property and is an effective weapon in the brutal competition of the marketplace. What one thinks about property—particularly about who should own the means of production—makes all the difference. The same is true for antistatism, the question whether government is to be abolished because it is an agency for, or an obstacle to, private property. Decentralization, which revolutionary anarchists consider an antidote to bureaucracy, technocracy, and power monopoly, serves conservatives to justify particularism, traditional hierarchies, isolationism, nationalism, and racism.

As far as nature is concerned, almost all leftist anarchists, past and present, share Rousseau's notion of the noble savage, inside us, irrespective of the extent to which they have abandoned early socialist utopianism. Chomsky emphasizes that it is the social nature of humans that pushes humankind toward progress and perfection, an idea reminiscent of Kropotkin's notion of mutual aid. Bookchin derives human nature from nature *per se* and equates, or at least compares, nature to society. I have tried to show how dangerously close this concept can come to a certain conservatism which, in the name of nature, vindicates social inequality and the survival of the fittest.

Left and right anarchists also share the emphasis on the effectiveness of personal ethical commitment. Social-revolutionary anarchists often play off morality and ethics against the economic determinism of self-styled Marxists. Even Chomsky, who presents cogent economic analyses of the imperialist exploitation of Third World countries, distances himself from coldly calculating economic motives for political action. Bookchin devises a theory of morality originating in a benevolent nature and regards economic thinking be it bourgeois or Marxist of any kind, as utilitarian and immoral per se. It might be surprising to find that among economists—Marxists, socialists, liberals, and conservatives—those who subscribe to laissez-faire ideology are the greatest moralists. These coldest of all utilitarians who worship the market, that is, the laws of the capitalist economic system, avidly renounce their own materialism. Their thinking and actions, they assert, are motivated by a morality inherent in nature, and because human nature is competitive, the market society is the most suitable system for it.

When anarchism was rediscovered by the European and American New Left, anarcho-syndicalism and the legacy of the Spanish Revolution got the most attention: elements of anarcho-syndicalist theory, especially the idea of workers' control, was demanded by the participants in the French revolt of May 1968. Veterans of the Spanish Revolution were invited by young New Left activists who had realized they themselves were anarchists. Daniel Guérin's book on anarchism, which favors anarcho-syndicalism (published in the US with an introduction by Noam Chomsky) became a best seller. Many tried to combine undogmatic Marxism with anarchism.

Only a few years later, the interest in anarchism began to reflect two new tendencies still effective today. There was a shift from Bakunin's ideas to those of Kropotkin, that is, from urban anarcho-syndicalism to rural communalism and eco-anarchism. European anarchists joined the so-called alternative movement in founding rural communes. In the US Bookchin moved from New York to Vermont and rediscovered the village commune as the starting point for social change. Animistic spirituality began shaping segments of the growing eco-anarchist movement. In Europe some anarchists joined urban guerrillas, although these groups were predominantly neo-Leninist, while in the US the Black Panthers were impressed with Nechaev's "Catechism of a Revolutionary." Since the 1980s putschism has been playing a role among the urban squatters in Europe and in the US. The latest developments show signs of an anarcho-syndicalist comeback, especially in Eastern Europe.

In many respects the current situation of anarchism is comparable to that at the end of the 19th century. One hundred years ago, on the left there were Kropotkinist utopianism, remnants of propaganda-of-the-deed terrorism, and anticipation of anarcho-syndicalism; and on the right Mackay's war-of-each-against-all anarchism.

Though the historical moment seems to be ripe for a leftist anarchist revival one hardly can speak of a movement, while anarcho-capitalism is gaining ground. Many contemporary anarchists think of eco-anarchism as the hope of the future. I agree with them to the extent that ecological politics must be integrated into any anarchist theory and activism, but I have the strongest reservations that ecology can unite the most diverse interests and transcend class on the basis of the old/new gospel of nature. I support what is left of the international anarcho-syndicalist organization IWA (International Workers Association), though I do not expect it to build a movement in the near future. However, some of the young militant groups in Europe, their often self-destructive nihilism notwithstanding, appear to have potential. In Germany, for instance, where they are called autonomists, these young men and women are almost the only ones to actively oppose neo-Nazi crimes against Turks and other foreigners. In the US I have seen admirable social-revolutionary, especially anarcho-syndicalist, activism. What I learned about the libertarians left me bewildered, and frightened at the same time.

Anarchism with its Janus face is still both the nightmare and the accomplice of the ruling class: it is its nightmare in the promise of a democratic, humane, and egalitarian socialism; and it is its accomplice as the champion of an unleashed capitalism and the principle of "might makes right."

SELECTED BIBLIOGRAPHY

Classical Anarchism and Anarcho-Syndicalism

Bakunin, Michael. *Statism and Anarchy.* Marshall Shatz, ed. Cambridge: Cambridge University Press, 1990.

Berkman, Alexander. *The ABC of Anarchism.* London: Freedom Press, 1992.

Chomsky, Noam, *American Power and the New Mandarins.* New York: Pantheon Books, 1969.

Chomsky, Noam, *The New World Order.* Westfield, NJ: Open Magazine, 1991.

Dolgoff, Sam. *Bakunin on Anarchism.* Montreal: Black Rose, 1980.

Dolgoff, Sam. *Fragments: A Memoir.* Cambridge: Refract Publications, 1986.

Dolgoff, Sam. *The Cuban Revolution.* Montreal: Black Rose, 1976.

Guèrin, Daniel. *Anarchism; From Theory to Practice.* New York: Monthly Review, 1970.

Kropotkin, Peter. *Memoirs of a Revolutionist.* New York: Dover Publications, 1971.

Kropotkin, Peter. *The Conquest of Bread.* New York: New York University Press, 1972.

Kropotkin, Peter. *Fields, Factories and Workshops.* New York and London: Putnam's, 1913.

Rocker, Rudolf. *Anarcho-syndicalism.* With an introduction by Noam Chomsky. London: Pluto Press, 1989.

Eco-Anarchism

Biehl, Janet. *Rethinking Eco-feminist Politics.* Boston: South End Press, 1991.

Bookchin, Murray. *Post Scarcity Anarchism.* Montreal: Black Rose, 1986.

Bookchin, Murray. *The Ecology of Freedom.* Palo Alto, CA: Cheshire Books, 1982.

Bookchin, Murray. *The Rise of Urbanization and the Decline of Citizenship.* San Francisco: Sierra Club Books, 1987.

Bookchin, Murray. *The Spanish Anarchists.* New York: Harper and Row Publishers, 1988.

Bookchin, Murray. *Remaking Society.* Montreal: Black Rose, 1989.

McLaughlin, Andrew. *Regarding Nature.* New York: State University of New York Press, 1993.

Manes, Christopher. *Green Rage,* Boston: Little, Brown and Company, 1990.

Individualist Anarchism and Anarcho-Capitalism

> Friedman, Milton. *Capitalism and Freedom.* Chicago: University of Chicago Press, 1963.

> Mackay, John Henry. *The Anarchists.* Brooklyn, New York: Revisionist Press, [1891] 1972.

> von Mises, Ludwig. *Human Action: A Treatise on Economics.* Chicago: Contemporary Books, Inc. 1966.

> Tucker, Benjamin R. *State Socialism and Anarchism.* Colorado: Ralph Myles Publishers, 1972.

> Rand, Ayn. *Capitalism: The Unknown Ideal.* Chicago: Signet, 1967.

> Rand, Ayn. *The Fountainhead.* New York: NAL/Dutton, 1952.

> Rothbard, Murray. *For a New Liberty.* New York: Collier Macmillan Publishers, 1978.

> Rothbard, Murray. *The Ethics of Liberty.* Atlantic Highlands: Humanities Press, 1982.

> Stirner, Max. *The Ego And Its Own.* London: Rebel Press, 1982.

Ulrike Heider is a freelance writer from Germany who has published books on Robert Reitzel and the Haymarket anarchists; on the West German student movement; and on sexual theory. She received her Ph.D. in political science from J.W. Goethe University in Frankfurt, where she has taught. She was a visiting scholar at Columbia University in 1988-1989, and now lives in New York City.

CITY LIGHTS PUBLICATIONS

Acosta, Juvenal, ed. LIGHT FROM A NEARBY WINDOW:
     Contemporary Mexican Poetry
Allen, Roberta. AMAZON DREAM
Angulo de, Jaime. INDIANS IN OVERALLS
Angulo de, G. & J. JAIME IN TAOS
Artaud, Antonin. ARTAUD ANTHOLOGY
Bataille, Georges. EROTISM: Death and Sensuality
Bataille, Georges. THE IMPOSSIBLE
Bataille, Georges. STORY OF THE EYE
Bataille, Georges. THE TEARS OF EROS
Baudelaire, Charles. INTIMATE JOURNALS
Baudelaire, Charles. TWENTY PROSE POEMS
Bowles, Paul. A HUNDRED CAMELS IN THE COURTYARD
Bramly, Serge. MACUMBA: The Teachings of Maria-José, Mother of the Gods
Broughton, James. COMING UNBUTTONED
Broughton, James. MAKING LIGHT OF IT
Brown, Rebecca. ANNIE OAKLEY'S GIRL
Brown, Rebecca. THE TERRIBLE GIRLS
Bukowski, Charles. THE MOST BEAUTIFUL WOMAN IN TOWN
Bukowski, Charles. NOTES OF A DIRTY OLD MAN
Bukowski, Charles. TALES OF ORDINARY MADNESS
Burroughs, William S. THE BURROUGHS FILE
Burroughs, William S. THE YAGE LETTERS
Cassady, Neal. THE FIRST THIRD
Choukri, Mohamed. FOR BREAD ALONE
CITY LIGHTS REVIEW #2: AIDS & the Arts
CITY LIGHTS REVIEW #3: Media and Propaganda
CITY LIGHTS REVIEW #4: Literature / Politics / Ecology
Cocteau, Jean. THE WHITE BOOK (LE LIVRE BLANC)
Codrescu, Andrei, ed. EXQUISITE CORPSE READER
Cornford, Adam. ANIMATIONS
Corso, Gregory. GASOLINE
Daumal, René. THE POWERS OF THE WORD
David-Neel, Alexandra. SECRET ORAL TEACHINGS IN TIBETAN
     BUDDHIST SECTS
Deleuze, Gilles. SPINOZA: Practical Philosophy
Dick, Leslie. KICKING
Dick, Leslie. WITHOUT FALLING
di Prima, Diane. PIECES OF A SONG: Selected Poems
Doolittle, Hilda (H.D.). NOTES ON THOUGHT & VISION
Ducornet, Rikki. ENTERING FIRE
Duras, Marguerite. DURAS BY DURAS
Eberhardt, Isabelle. DEPARTURES: Selected Writings
Eberhardt, Isabelle. THE OBLIVION SEEKERS
Eidus, Janice. VITO LOVES GERALDINE

Murguía, A. & B. Paschke, eds. VOLCAN: Poems from Central America
Murillo, Rosario. ANGEL IN THE DELUGE
Paschke, B. & D. Volpendesta, eds. CLAMOR OF INNOCENCE
Pasolini, Pier Paolo. ROMAN POEMS
Pessoa, Fernando. ALWAYS ASTONISHED
Peters, Nancy J., ed. WAR AFTER WAR (City Lights Review #5)
Poe, Edgar Allan. THE UNKNOWN POE
Porta, Antonio. KISSES FROM ANOTHER DREAM
Prévert, Jacques. PAROLES
Purdy, James. THE CANDLES OF YOUR EYES
Purdy, James. IN A SHALLOW GRAVE
Purdy, James. GARMENTS THE LIVING WEAR
Purdy, James. OUT WITH THE STARS
Rachlin, Nahid. MARRIED TO A STRANGER
Rachlin, Nahid. VEILS: SHORT STORIES
Reed, Jeremy. RED-HAIRED ANDROID
Rey Rosa, Rodrigo. THE BEGGAR'S KNIFE
Rey Rosa, Rodrigo. DUST ON HER TONGUE
Rigaud, Milo. SECRETS OF VOODOO
Ruy Sánchez, Alberto. MOGADOR
Saadawi, Nawal El. MEMOIRS OF A WOMAN DOCTOR
Sawyer-Lauçanno, Christopher, tr. THE DESTRUCTION OF THE JAGUAR
Scholder, Amy, ed. CRITICAL CONDITION: Women on the Edge
    of Violence
Sclauzero, Mariarosa. MARLENE
Serge, Victor. RESISTANCE
Shepard, Sam. MOTEL CHRONICLES
Shepard, Sam. FOOL FOR LOVE & THE SAD LAMENT OF PECOS BILL
Smith, Michael. IT A COME
Snyder, Gary. THE OLD WAYS
Solnit, Rebecca. SECRET EXHIBITION: Six California Artists
Sussler, Betsy, ed. BOMB: INTERVIEWS
Takahashi, Mutsuo. SLEEPING SINNING FALLING
Turyn, Anne, ed. TOP TOP STORIES
Tutuola, Amos. FEATHER WOMAN OF THE JUNGLE
Tutuola, Amos. SIMBI & THE SATYR OF THE DARK JUNGLE
Valaoritis, Nanos. MY AFTERLIFE GUARANTEED
Wilson, Colin. POETRY AND MYSTICISM
Wilson, Peter Lamborn. SACRED DRIFT
Wynne, John. THE OTHER WORLD
Zamora, Daisy. RIVERBED OF MEMORY